AMERICA'S GREAT OUTDOORS

AMERICA'S GREAT OUTDOORS

The Story of the Eternal Romance
between Man and Nature

•

*An anthology of 200 years of writing
with collected illustrations*

EDITED BY
L. James Bashline and Dan Saults

ART DIRECTOR
George H. Harrison

J. G. FERGUSON PUBLISHING COMPANY / CHICAGO

CONTRIBUTING EDITORS   Robert Bell
Homer Circle
Richard Dietz
George Feltner
Gene Hill
Willard Johns
John Madson
George Reiger
Jack Samson
Mark Sosin
Wallace Taber
Zack Taylor

CONTRIBUTING ARTISTS   Tom Rost
Ned Smith

SPECIAL ACKNOWLEDGEMENT   is due
Bob Anderson
Leonard Lee Rue III and
Jim Trefethen
for their work
and contributions
to this book.

EDITORIAL ASSISTANT   Harriet Helmer

DESIGNER   Al Josephson

PICTURE EDITOR   Holly Harrington

INDEXER   Roberta Kingan

SPECIAL PROJECTS EDITOR   Richard Dell

EXECUTIVE EDITOR   Thomas C. Jones

PREFACE

This book is like fuel added to a campfire that has glowed in America for two centuries. It is of, not about, outdoor writers, although the Outdoor Writers Association of America sponsored the wood-gathering. The resultant blaze is made up of glowing chunks of prose, fragrant bits of poetry, warmth from old paintings, gay flame of color photographs, the flare of nostalgia, backlogs from famous scribes, pieces of whimsey and branches of folklore. But it's no casual bonfire. This is a patterned campfire, lighting 200 years of Americans expressing with paint and camera and words their feelings about this land and its wildlife, mountains, streams, plains, coasts and people. It will keep an outdoorsman spiritually warm while delighting his eye.

Our book is chronological: 1776 to 1976; it is divided into four parts: Revolution to Civil War; Death of Abraham Lincoln to the presidency of Theodore Roosevelt; 1908 to that traumatic World War II; finally, the chaotic era that reaches from "Peace" to this very evening when *you* began to seek comfort at this bed of coals that came from old wood — that is, all quotations have appeared earlier.

This is not a book about hunting and fishing. It is not a history of conservation and wildlife-management. It is not a lengthy essay on outdoor recreation. And yet, all these things are in it, for it is a collection of communications over the two centuries of existence of these United States. Here writers, painters and photographers contradict each other and themselves, waxing gay and sad, sober and serious, even as you and I and Aldo Leopold.

The editors who assembled and laid the wood for this metaphorical campfire were chosen members of the OWAA. Dan Saults took primary responsibility for Sections I, II and III; Jim Bashline handled Section IV; George Harrison made the art decisions. But all of them lapped over into each other's assignments, and the three share equal responsibility for the whole spectrum.

Bashline has come full circle in 20 years of dealing with words about the outdoors. Beginning with a newspaper column for the Olean, Pennsylvania *Times-Herald,* going through a series of editorial posts at *Pennsylvania Game News. Field & Stream* and *Flyfisherman* magazines, he wrote two fishing books. A six-year interlude of free-lancing produced more than 300 articles for outdoor magazines. The circle is now completed and he is writing a thrice-weekly column for the *Philadelphia Inquirer.*

Harrison has been taking wildlife photographs and writing about the outdoors since he was in grade school. He too came out of the state fish and game ranks as associate editor of *Virginia Wildlife* and editor of *Pennsylvania Game News.* For the past ten years, Harrison has been with *National/International Wildlife* magazine as managing editor and now as field editor. He is a free-lance contributor to many magazines and is writing his own book on the dozen best places in North America to see birds.

Saults also came from a state conservation agency. Oldest of the triad, he has been a newspaperman, was for ten years information head and book-magazine editor for the Missouri Conservation Department, and for seven years more was the department's assistant director. For a decade he was an information officer in the Department of the Interior, dealing with books, art, television and motion pictures. He has been a dilettante historian all that time, and is now free-lancing in Missouri.

Many members of OWAA contributed branches for this campfire but the editors laid it. They sought advice but reserved judgment; the praise or blame is theirs. That is how OWAA's Board of Directors said it was to be, with the criteria for selection as eloquence, relevance, clarity and reader appeal.

"Outdoors" was defined as covering several fields of activity performed on the one great field called the United States — exploring, mapping, hunting, camping, fishing — all work and some play that moved writers to communicate with fellow humans by expressing their views of the landscape or bison-hunting or Indians or angling. The editors sometimes neglected famous names, by their own admission, for the unknown or little-known. They did not seek to be educational, jingoistic or even controversial, though some of these elements came in. The overall effort was to include that which was interesting, provocative and well done. A possible author who has a great name in history but a sputtering pen got little space or none.

The editors read many books, looked at hundreds of paintings and thousands of photos, then asked themselves and their colleagues (including me): Is it eloquent? Does it symbolize its period? Has it depth? And lastly, does it provide outdoor communication for readers entering the last quarter of the Twentieth Century?

No savant will be completely pleased with the answer to those questions. Every scholar will feel that a key writer has been left out, or the wrong selection was made from his works. Every historian will complain that statecraft and economics and social patterns have been neglected. Casual readers will find that some passages and pictures enthrall them while others leave them nodding by the fire.

Fine! Because that will mean these readers have thought about it. And thinking about it — of two great, fierce and troubled centuries when outdoor writers, painters and photographers tried to communicate with their fellows — is why the Outdoor Writers Association of America and J. G. Ferguson Publishing Company brought out this book — a tribute to the past, and possibly trivia to the future. Or, perhaps, a monument! History has the final vote.

F. Wallace (Wally) Taber
President-Elect 1976–77
Outdoor Writers Association of America

FOREWORD I

This is a book about outdoor writers of the United States. It is not about American scribes, for we should have had to include some great Canadians, talented Mexicans and, probably, some Central and South Americans who went out into the wild places.

This is a book circumscribed further by two dates: 1776, when the nation was born in travail, and 1976, when it is still living in travail. Outdoor writing did not begin in that year now two centuries gone; the art can claim progenitors in Homer and the author of Ecclesiastes — all is indeed vanity when humans sit down to impose their thoughts upon others. Artful Britishers like Izaak Walton were wooing men to·fishing before U. S. pundits began setting down their views; Cabeza de Vaca and Bernal Diaz were reporting upon the wild face of America long before Henry Rowe Schoolcraft set out across Missouri Territory. But we have tried to maintain our dates and our nationhood in this compendium celebrating the bicentennial of the United States with selections from our outdoor writing of the past two centuries.

I am saying "we" here because this project was birthed and nursed by the Outdoors Writers of America when I was president of that body, though I had left the post before it was published. I know well the men and women who worked on the compilation. I cherish the editors who put it into shape, and all of them were members of OWAA — that struggling, poorly-paid, contentious and deeply-devoted group of individualists who write, photograph, paint or talk about the wild animals, forests, mountains, waters and plains of our country.

So the editorial "we" hope you like this book, that you read it with pleasure, and with the profit of better understanding of our natural resources in these United States.

Bill Potter, Outdoor Editor
The Joplin (Mo.) *Globe*
Chairman of the Board, Outdoor Writers
Association of America, 1975 – 76

FOREWORD II

As president of the Outdoor Writers Association of America when this book was published, I read its galley proofs with pride that I worked in the great tradition of these authors, but with a chastening thought: did I live up to their standards?

The answer to that question had to be a personal one. But I hope that you readers ask yourselves some questions about living up to standards, too; about accepting your place in our national outdoor history; about knowing the role of rod and gun and travel during the past two centuries.

If we do not understand our outdoor history we are bound to repeat its mistakes in regard to fish, game, forests and streams. Andrew Jackson's America was not Gerald Ford's America; William Bartram had a different style for a different audience than the style and audience of Aldo Leopold. But both men wrote of the same thing: the human view of wild things and places, and their conclusions were not much different.

Our editors arbitrarily divided this book into four parts, yet their dividing lines fit our national history. The Revolutionary War (which began after the intellectual revolt) is an obvious start; our social consensus veered after the War Between the States; our history changed abruptly with Theodore Roosevelt, though not necessarily because of him; and we are just now realizing that World War II marked another profound turn in our national life.

But this is not a political history. It is not history at all, in the conventional sense, but excerpts from the writing of different people reviewing the same landscape as it was altered by time and human use.

The Outdoor Writers Association did not sponsor this book to exalt itself; not even the quotations from current authors are confined to present members. OWAA did sponsor it from pride of ancestorship — although I personally was startled to find that the more things change, the more they remain the same. This book was not compiled and written for OWAA, but for the public. We hope you find entertainment and enlightenment in these pages.

Henry S. Reynolds, Outdoor Editor
The Commercial Appeal, Memphis (Tenn.)

President, Outdoor Writers Association of America, 1975 – 76

ACKNOWLEDGMENTS

We wish to express our appreciation to the following authors, publishers, and other copyright holders who have given us permission to reprint various selections.

A. S. Barnes & Company, Inc. — *The Fisherman as Conservationist* from *The Atlantic Salmon* by Lee Wulff, published by A. S. Barnes & Company, Inc., 1958.

The Blade, Toledo — *December* from "Outdoors with Lou Klewer," December 2, 1973.

Lurton Blassingame, Agent — *Taking Tarpon on Fly* from *Salt Water Fly Fishing* by Joseph W. Brooks, Jr. Copyright by Joseph W. Brooks, Jr., 1950. Published by G. P. Putnam's Sons.

Crown Publishers, Inc. — *The Art of Fly-Fishing* taken from *A Book of Trout Flies* by Preston J. Jennings. © 1970 by Crown Publishers, Inc. Excerpt taken from *Modern Salt Water Sport Fishing* by Frank Woolner. © 1972 by Frank Woolner. Used by permission of Crown Publishers, Inc.

Detroit Free Press — *Hoodlums in Rural Areas* by Tom Opre from the Detroit *Free Press*, September 14, 1972.

Avis M. DeVoto — *The Mountain Man* from *The Year of Decision: 1846* by Bernard DeVoto. Copyright 1942, 1943, by Bernard DeVoto. Published by Little, Brown and Company, 1942.

Doubleday & Company, Inc. — *We Go Fishing* from *Under My Elm* by David Grayson, copyright 1942 by Doubleday & Company, Inc. Excerpt from *The Trout Fisherman's Bible*, copyright © 1949, 1962 by Don Holland. Reprinted by permission of the publisher.

Dover Publications, Inc. — *An Early American Art Form* from *Wild Fowl Decoys* by Joel Barber. Dover Publications, Inc., New York, 1934, 1954. Reprinted through permission of the publisher.

Field & Stream — *The Road to Tinkhamtown* by Corey Ford, from the 75th Anniversary Issue of *Field & Stream*, June 1970. *Namaycush Nightmare* by Burton Spiller, from the May 1939 issue of *Field & Stream*.

Funk & Wagnalls Publishing Company — *On Lures and Replicas* from *Salt Water Fishing Tackle* by Harlan Major, copyright © 1939, 1967 by Harlan Major.

Gary Post-Tribune — *A Boat in Distress* from Jack Parry's column "Sportsmen's Den."

Houghton Mifflin Company — *The "White Buffalo"* from *The Big Sky* by A. B. Guthrie, Jr. Copyright 1947, by A. B. Guthrie, Jr. Reprinted by permission of the publisher.

Iowa State University Press, Ames, Iowa — *A View of Nature* from *Stories From Under the Sky* by John Madson, © 1961 by Iowa State University Press.

The Izaak Walton League of America, Inc. — *While There's Life* by Nash Buckingham from *Outdoor America*, August 1937. Excerpt from *All Together, Heave* by Gene Stratton Porter from *Outdoor America*.

Victor L. Jones, Trustee of the Estate of Nancy Cooper Russell — *A Tall Western Tale* from *Trails Plowed Under* by Charles M. Russell. Published by Doubleday, Page & Company in 1927.

Journal of Forestry — *Conservation Ethic* by Aldo Leopold.

Mrs. Richard Alden Knight — *The Solunar Theory* from *Ocean Tides and Fresh Water Fish*, 1935.

Alfred A. Knopf, Inc. — *Plug Fishing for Bass* from *Just Fishing* by Ray Bergman. Copyright 1932 by The Penn Publishing Company and renewed 1960 by Ray Bergman. *Bonefish as Game* and *Big Game Fish* from *Salt Water Fishing* by Van Campen Heilner. Copyright 1937 and renewed 1965 by Van Campen Heilner. Copyright 1953 by Alfred A. Knopf, Inc. *Quetico and Far Places* from *Sigurd F. Olson's Wilderness Days* by Sigurd F. Olson. Copyright © 1956, 1958, 1961, 1963, 1969, 1972 by Sigurd F. Olson. Reprinted by permission of Alfred A. Knopf, Inc.

CONTENTS

COLOR ILLUSTRATIONS

—From a painting by William T. Ranny, Museum of Fine Arts, Boston, Mass., M. and M. Karolik Fund

Duck Hunters on the Hoboken Marshes

The Oregon Trail by Albert Bierstadt
Bierstadt painted this scene in 1869 after experiencing
life on the trail some ten years earlier.

Passenger Pigeon by John James Audubon

(*Above*) *Yellow Bream*   (*Below*) *Vulture identified by Bartram as "Carrion Crow"*

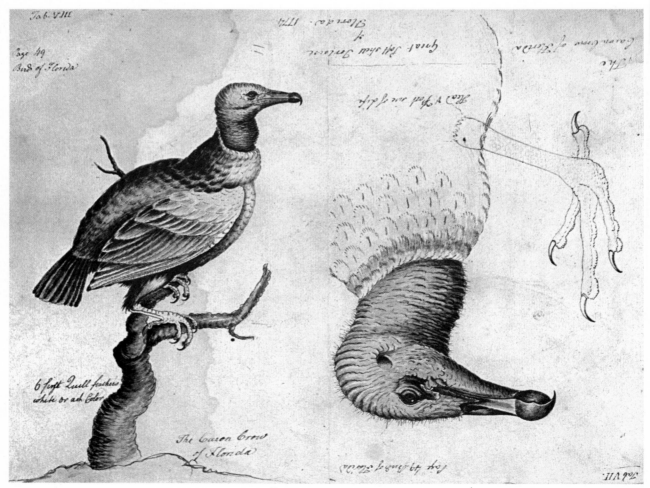

William Bartram, an 18th century American naturalist, traveled throughout the colonies observing wildlife with the eye of the trained botanist and zoologist. His drawings on these two pages give evidence of the legacy he left for generations of Americans interested in the outdoors and the treasures it provides.

*Hunting the Grizzly Bear by Carl Bodmer. Bodmer's work on the
Missouri River (1832-34) represents an invaluable pictorial documentary
of the Missouri frontier.*

Canadian Otter by John James Audubon.
Audubon earned a unique place in American art as the
first great painter of wildlife in America.

(At left)
Lewis and Clark meeting Flathead Indians by Charles Russell

(Below) Westward Ho by William Robinson Leigh.
Leigh was one of the early painters of the West.

Woodpeckers by Alexander Wilson.
Wilson painted in the late 18th and early 19th centuries.
He produced the first field guide to American birds.

(At left, top)
Buffalo Hunt, Under the White Wolf Skin
(Bottom)
Attacking the Grizzly Bear. Both paintings are by George Catlin
one of the foremost historiographers of western Indian life
in the Trans-Mississippi Wilderness. He spent eight years traveling
in the region during the 1830's.

Lake With Dead Trees by Thomas Cole

Great Dismal Swamp in Virginia and North Carolina first surveyed by George Washington —George H. Harrison photo

Arrival of the caravan at Santa Fé —Engraving from *Commerce of the Prairies, Vol. I* by Josiah Gregg

REVOLUTION TO REBELLION — 1776 to 1860   1

As every schoolchild "knows," white immigration in what is now the United States was from east to west an inexorable human tide flowing toward the sunset. The symbolism is flawed; actually the movement was highly erratic. French exploiters and explorers generally moved from north to south, with Spanish *conquistadores* reversing that direction. Even the Anglos moved in a game of leapfrog. Three generations after California became a state, the central Ozarks region had only been penetrated.

Still, the move toward the golden west is broadly valid in terms of the national culture that became dominant in the heart of a continent. English-speaking people and their immigrant allies — Irish, Germans, Scandinavians, Scots — did move westward from the Atlantic, and much of the movement was planned or at least deliberately pioneered. But much individual motion was forced by events, as in all historical migrations. Many names now venerated as "pioneers" were then fleeing their debts or vengeful law or social disapproval. Most of the rest were trying to get rich quick. A few did.

Our historical myths romanticize early migrants as people seeking a wild, free outdoor life; men and women who longed — in modern parlance — "to live off the land." (All of us everywhere live off the land, of course.) We also tend to believe these primary settlers sought and found a paradise of hunting and fishing. Actually, from Penn's German tillers to Carolina's tobacco aristocrats — and to modern agribusiness — most farmers not only saw wildlife as a nuisance and problem, but a threat. In 1629, Francis Higginson described the wild plants of Massachusetts only in terms of livestock grazing and praised the abundance of fishes only in terms of food; he never mentioned sport.

Nor did William Bradford's "History of Plymouth Plantation" mention sports. He set down of his fellows that: "They having but one boat left, they were divided into several small companies, and so wente out with a nett to take bass and such like fish. No sooner was ye boat discharged of what she brought but ye next companie took her. Neither did they returne till they had caught something, for they knew there was nothing at home, and to go home emptie would be a great discouragement to ye rest."

But St. John de Crèvecoeur had, by 1782, gotten some firm notions

3

about hunters. An early agriculturist, he preached good farming and wrote in his *Letters:*

With men as with plants

It is with men as it is with the plants and animals that grow in the forest; they are entirely different from those that live in the plains. Their actions are regulated by the wildness. Deer come to eat their grain, wolves to destroy their sheep, bears to kill their hogs, foxes to catch their poultry. This puts the gun into their hands; they kill some; and by defending their property they soon become professed hunters; once hunters, farewell to the plow. The chase renders them ferocious and unsociable; a hunter wants no neighbor, because he dreads the competition.

Success in the woods makes them neglect their tillage; . . . in order to make up the deficiency, they go oftener to the woods. That new mode of life brings with it a new set of manners . . . these being grafted on the old stock, produce a sort of lawless profligacy. Manners of Indian natives are respectable compared with this European medley. Their wives and children live in sloth . . . you may judge what education the latter receive . . . they grow up a mongrel breed. . . . Thus our bad people are those who are half cultivators and half hunters; and the worst of them are those who have degenerated altogether into the hunting state.

If manners are not refined, they are rendered inoffensive by tilling the earth. As hunters it is divided between the toil of the chase, the idleness of repose or the indulgence of inebriation. Hunting is but an idle, licentious life . . . united with bad luck it leads to want: want stimulates that propensity to rapacity . . . which is the fatal gradation.

De Crèvecoeur sounds startlingly modern in his anti-hunting fulminations, and there may be some psychological nuggets in rhetorical ore.

But most "pioneers" undertook deliberate campaigns to destroy all animals that might eat livestock or row crops, and they saw fishes chiefly as a cash crop. A few were commercial hunters trading in beaver, bear and venison, living dangerously and sometimes profitably in a style that looks like "sports" hunting only through lenses of nostalgia. It was hard, rough work, not recreation. Most frontiersmen probably shared the feeling of Andrew Jackson as related by John J. Cooney, director of the Heritage Association: "If he went hunting in his younger years, it was to get something to eat." Andrew Jr. (an adopted son) *was* an avid hunter, however, Mr. Cooney noted, and accidentally shot himself to death while hunting.

Life in western Virginia— the home of the mountaineer
—Library of Congress

4

General Andrew Jackson meets Chief Weatherford, Creek Indian. —From an engraving by W. Ridgway, Library of Congress

But there were early sportsmen if the word describes those who pursued wild places and game not for profit but for pleasure. Such people divide into two categories: aristocrats and self-outcasts. Each class had freed itself of routine, one by owning wide holdings, the other by reducing wants to bare necessities, so they had time to trail a bear, wait beside a turkey roost or seek a pass through the hills.

Where other travels ended

Henry Rowe Schoolcraft, New York-born geologist and ethnologist, wrote "I begin my tour where other travelers have ended theirs" to start his 1818 - 19 trip across Missouri Territory. He journeyed from Potosi, "last village of white inhabitants between the Mississippi river and the Pacific ocean," which had been the French mining town of Mine au Breton, to the upper White River — across the yet uncharted Ozarks. But self-exiled Anglos were there ahead of him; he described them as those who "embraced hunting from the love of ease or singularity, or who fled from society to escape the severity of laws." He did not comment upon what *he* was doing there, also self-exiled, living in a wild, rocky land by

5

his own choice among people "worse than savages." Indeed, he went in 1820 to journey in what is now Michigan and Minnesota, examined the source of the Mississippi at Lake Itasca and married an Indian girl. He saw pioneers clearly and brooded on them sullenly, as in these diary excerpts:

Thur., Dec. 3rd (1818)

While Mr. Pettibone completed preparation necessary for our journey tomorrow, I sallied into the adjoining woods with my gun, with a determination to kill something. But after spending several hours endeavoring to elude the sagacity of birds and beasts of the forests, making three unsuccessful shots, I returned to camp in a plight worse than I left it. Mr. P. took the gun and made an unsuccessful shot at a turkey. We had now but one ball left; it was near night and a flock of turkeys betook themselves to roost on a cluster of oaks at no great distance.

We resolved to try our fortune at night and to accomplish by stratagem that which we had been unable to do in any other way. I cleaned up my gun thoroughly, put in a new flint, and charged it with great care with the remaining ball,

Wild Turkey Shooting —Currier & Ives, Library of Congress

Fort Smith, Arkansas, founded as a military post in 1817
—Lithographed by T. Sinclair from a drawing by H. B. Mollhausen, Library of Congress

having cut it in 32 parts by way of shot. Taking a torch we proceeded into the midst of the flock and selecting a large one that sat low, Mr. P. fired while I held the light.

The turkey dropped. With joy we returned to camp and prepared a sumptuous feast.

Saturday, Dec. 5th

Weather being clear this morning, we got our horse packed and, fording the river, pursued a west course for Sugar-Loaf Prairie on White River. Two miles across a high ridge we struck a small tributary to the North Fork which we followed seven or eight miles up and encamped in a cane-brake. Traveling had been excessively bad owing to the hills, the roughness of the country and thickets along the streams. A proportion of canebrake and swamp had been encountered, in crossing which our horse got mired, an accident which threatened one of the most serious calamities which attended our journey. All attempts to rescue him seemed fruitless. We succeeded in getting off the pack, but after spending two hours in vain endeavors to extricate the horse, gave up. Our skins, cooking utensils, axe, some part of our food must be abandoned. Without these we could not progress with any comfort, and in resolving to renew our attempts exhibited, perhaps, less of reasonable perseverance than of desperation, for on returning to the horse he was now sunk in mud so deep that the upper part of his back and head and neck were only visible. Nevertheless we succeeded, with less than an hour's work, in drawing him out and cleaning him of mud, so that we were enabled to re-pack and travel on about three miles before encamping.

A settlement of hunters

Monday, Dec. 7th

We halted our horse by the summit of a bald mountain while we went up to survey one of those beautiful and extensive prospects the traveller frequently enjoys in this singularly wild and barren region. We had been told by the hunter to travel toward the sunset and that in going 15 miles we should reach a settlement of hunters on the banks of White river. We had now gone double that and could not, from the elevated peak on which we stood, discover any sign of river or human habitation. Returning to our horse, we turned directly south and had not proceeded more than a mile when we fell into a faintly-marked horsepath and in following this three miles, it led in another, plainer path which led us to a high bluff forming the eastern bank of White, which ran a broad and beautiful stream below. We followed down river and discovered a house on the opposite bank; fording it at a ripple where the water was only half-leg deep, we were received with hospitality by a white hunter by the name of M'Gary.

He had several acres under corn, with several horses, cows and hogs. The house was of logs; he was provided with a handmill for grinding corn, a smokehouse filled with bear and other meats, and the interior of the house, though far from being neat or even comfortable, bore evidence the occupant had once resided in civilized society. He appeared to live in great ease and comfort, surrounded by a numerous family of sons and daughters; he gave us plenty to eat and bid us welcome as long as we wanted to stay.

He represented our journey toward the head of White river as extremely hazardous on account of Osage Indians, whose hunting grounds embraced the region in which this river and its upper tributaries originate, and who never failed to rob white hunters who were so unfortunate as to fall in their way, and sometimes carried them into captivity. Numerous instances were related, all tending to prove that the Osage Indians felt hostile to white settlements along the river and that they were habitual plunderers of every person who happened to fall defenseless into their hands.

All this was new to us, as the United States have enjoyed peace with this tribe ever since the acquisition of Louisiana.

He also informed us that a deadly and deep-rooted hostility existed between the Cherokees, who had lately exchanged their lands in Tennessee for the country lying between the Arkansas and Red rivers, and the Osages, and that they were daily committing depredations upon the territories and prop-

(On opposite page, top)
A hunter and family of
Cree Indians at York Fort, 1821
—From a watercolor sketch by
Peter Rindisbacher, The Public Archieves
of Canada

(Bottom)
The Trappers, 1856
—From a painting by William Tylee Ranney,
Northern Natural Gas Company Collection,
Joslyn Art Museum, Omaha, Nebraska

9

erties of each other. Having but a short time before witnessed the treaty of peace between these two tribes, made in St. Louis under the auspices of Governor Clark, I was surprised to hear of the continuance of hostilities.

Wed., Dec. 9th

The settlement at Sugar Loaf Prairie consists of four families with the distance of eight miles, so recent that a horse path has not been worn from one cabin to another. These people subsist partly by agriculture and partly by hunting. They raise corn for bread and for feeding their horses prior to long journeys into the woods. No cabbages, beets, onions, potatoes or other garden vegetables are raised. Corn and wild meats, chiefly bear, are the staple food. In manners, morals, custom, dress, contempt for labor and hospitality, the state of society is not essentially different from that which exists among the savages.

Hunting is the principal, most honorable and most profitable employment. To excel in the chase procures fames, and a man's reputation is measured by his skill as a marksman, his agility and strength, his boldness in killing game and his endurance and contempt of the hardships of the hunter's life. They are, consequently, a hardy, brave, independent people, rude in appearance, frank and generous, travel without baggage, can subsist anywhere in the woods, and would form the most efficient military corps in frontier warfare, ready trained, inured to danger and perfect in the use of rifles.

Their habitations are not always permanent, having little which is valuable or loved to rivet their affections to any one spot; they frequently change residence, traveling where game is more abundant. Vast quantities of beaver, otter, raccoon, deer and bear are caught annually. Skins are carefully collected and preserved during summer and fall, and taken down river in canoes to the mouth of the Great North Fork or to the mouth of Black River, where traders regularly come up to the White with large boats to receive them.

They also take down some wild honey, bear's bacon and buffalo-beef, and receive in return salt, iron pots, axes, blankets, rifles, knives and such articles of first importance in their mode of life.

Gentleman of the frontier

This was not much like Tidewater planters (George Washington, for example) returning to stately manors (though these have been overglorified) after one day's pursuit of game or three months outback. These men of substance were not fleeing laws, they made them; nor shunning

George Washington, surveyor
—Ned Smith

The Squire of Mount Vernon — a fox hunt
—From a painting by John Ward Dunsmore, Sons of the Revolution, Fraunces Tavern Museum, New York

society, they created it. They were perhaps the most civilized class this nation has known, but they moved as surely to and in wilderness as the self-exiled people that Schoolcraft examined.

Mr. Washington was not just a country gentleman sitting on the terrace at Mt. Vernon; the environment that shaped him for military and revolutionary leadership was more the wild lands of the Blue Ridge, the wilderness acreage he acquired, the trails he marked to the west, his frontiersman instincts developed in the French and Indian War. For George Washington knew the forest and mountains; he knew the creatures that lived in valleys and among the trees. His private fortune — and it was great for the time — was invested in wilderness, not in coastal tobacco lands.

Yet when the American Revolution generated a new nation that had no boundaries except for the Atlantic Ocean, there was little trace of what we now call sport hunting or fishing among its people. Wildlife was so much a part of daily existence that it fitted seamless into the whole; hunting and fishing were rarely activities set apart for recreation. But those who went to the expanding frontier, for whatever rationalized reason, set down some basic truths about hills and prairies, dawns and sunsets, animals and landscapes that strike chords in the mental chimes of their spiritual and political descendants. Perhaps we still have need for freedom today.

Even 60 years later, Schoolcraft's description of Ozarkia would have been close to rural life in that country. An early M. D. on the Upper White, a Dr. Compton, said in 1872 that when he came to the region its people "kept up their old way of living by hunting and fishing" and there were "many wild beasts" which he listed as "turkey, squirrel, geese, ducks, quail, panther, bears, wildcats, catamount, gray and red foxes."

But before Schoolcraft's journey a man named William Bartram had published his "Travels" in 1791, and got it done in Philadelphia, while the geologist had to go to England for publication. William was the son of John Bartram, a distinguished botanist whose colonial garden of plant specimens is still part of a Philadelphia city park. The son's "Travels" was a favorite book for Coleridge and Wordsworth; like many another writer, these famed English poets used it for sources of their imagery. Not only Carlyle praised William Bartram's work. A modern hunting and fishing scribe, Wyatt Blassingame of Anna Maria, Fla., says he "was the finest outdoor writer ever to hook a bass (he called them trout) or shoot a turkey. . . . There were times when he was no more accurate than some of us today, but he was a lot more poetic."

He was indeed an artist; consider his description of a spring in what is now central Florida where he was wandering just two centuries ago:

The meet at the "Harp and Eagle" near Philadelphia, 1823
—Drawing by J. Wordsworth Thompson from *Some American Sporting Dogs* by William M. Tileston, *The Century Magazine*

Our camp on Indian River
—Drawing by Thomas Moran from *Bow Shooting* by Maurice Thompson, Charles Scribner's Sons

Behold an enchanting fountain

I seated myself upon a swelling green knoll at the head of the crystal basin. On the left was a projection of an entire grove of the aromatic *Illicium Floridanum;* on my right and around behind me was a fruitful orange grove with palms and magnolias interspersed; in front, just under my feet, was the enchanting crystal fountain, which incessantly threw up from dark, rocky caverns below tons of water every minute, forming a basin capacious enough for large shallops to ride in, and a creek of four or five feet depth which meanders six miles through green meadows, pouring its limpid waters into great Lake George. About twenty yards from the upper edge of the basin, opposite to the mouth of the creek, is a continual and amazing ebullition where the waters are thrown up in such abundance and force as to jet up two or three feet about the surface; while sand and small shells are thrown up with the waters, subside with the expanding flood and gently sink again, forming a large funnel round the aperture of the fountain, which is a vast perforation through a bed of rocks. . . .

Thus far I know to be real fact related as near as I could express myself. But there are yet remaining scenes inexpressibly admirable and pleasing.

Behold a vast circular expanse before you, the waters of which are so clear as to be absolutely diaphanous, transparent as the ether; the margin of the basin ornamented with fruitful and floriferous trees and shrubs, the pendent orange dancing on the surface of pellucid waters, the balmy air vibrating with the melody of birds, tenants of the encircling aromatic grove.

Great egrets
—Ned Smith

13

A hunter's paradise
—Drawing by Thomas Moran from *Bear Hunting in the South* by James Gordon, *The Century Magazine*

Innumerable bands of fish are seen, some clothed in brilliant colors; the voracious crocodile is stretched along at full length as the great trunk of a tree in size; the devouring garfish, inimical trout and all varieties of gilded, painted bream; the barbed catfish, dreaded sting-ray, skate, flounder, spotted bass, sheepshead and ominous drum; all in their separate bands, with free and unsuspicious intercourse performing their evolutions; there are no signs of enmity, no attempt to devour each other; the different bands seem peaceably to move aside, to make room for others to pass.

But behold something more admirable, see whole armies descending into an abyss, the mouth of the bubbling fountain: they disappear! Are they gone forever? I raise my eyes with astonishment; I look down again to the fountain with anxiety, when behold them emerging from the blue ether of another world, apparently at a vast distance; at first appearance no bigger than minnows; now gradually enlarging, their brilliant colors paint the fluid.

Now they come forward rapidly and instantly emerge with expanding column of crystalline waters into the circular basin; see how gently they rise, some upright, others obliquely or seem to lie on their sides, gently borne up by the expanding fluid toward the surface, floating like butterflies in the cerulean ether; then again they gently descend, diverge and move off; rally, form again, rejoin their kindred tribes.

This amazing and delightful scene appears at first but as a piece of excellent painting; there seems no medium; you imagine the picture to be within a few inches of your eyes, and that you may touch any one of the fish or put your finger in the crocodile's eye, when it really is thirty feet under the water.

And although this paradise of fish may seem to exhibit a just representation of the peaceable and happy state of nature which existed before the fall, in reality it is a representation, for the nature of the fish is the same as if they were in Lake George; but here the element in which they live and move is so clear and transparent, it places them all on an equality with regard to their ability to injure or escape from one another; (as all fish of prey, or such as feed upon each other, as well as the unwieldy crocodile, take their prey by surprise; secreting themselves in ambush until an opportunity offers, when they rush suddenly upon them); but here is no covert, no ambush; here trout freely pass by the nose of the alligator and laugh in his face, and the bream by the trout. What is really surprising is that the consciousness of each other's safety, or some other latent cause, should so absolutely alter their conduct, for here is not the least attempt made to injure or disturb one another.

The sun passing below the horizon, I arose from my seat and, proceeding on, arrived at my camp, kindled my fire, supped and reposed peaceably.

Fishing among the "Crocodiles"

Bartram's "crocodiles" were almost certainly alligators, but it's not likely anyone differentiated the giant reptiles in 1777, when the great botanist-explorer sat beside his sacred grotto and penned the description that inspired Coleridge's "Alph, the sacred river" in *Kubla Khan*. Bartram also wrote of fishing among the alligators (he alternates the names) in this piece of high adventure on the St. Johns River (here called St. Juan).

The evening was cool and calm. Crocodiles began to roar and appear in uncommon numbers along the shore. I fixed my camp near the utmost projection of the promontory, under a large live oak on the highest part of the ground. From this open situation I had a free prospect of the river, having good reason to dread the subtle attacks of the alligators, who were crowding about my harbor. Having collected a good

Bartram at the camp fire
—Ned Smith

15

quantity of wood for keeping up light and smoke during the night, I thought of supper, when I found but a scanty provision. I determined to take my bob and try for some trout.

One hundred yards above my harbor began a cove out of which opened a large lagoon. The entrance from the river was narrow but the waters soon after spread and formed a little lake extending into the marshes, verged with floating lawns of pistia and nymphae; these I knew were excellent haunts for trout. Laughing coots with wings half spread were tripping over little coves and hiding themselves in the tufts of grass; young broods of painted summer teal, skimming the still waters following a watcher parent, were frequently surprised by the voracious trout; and he, in turn, by the greedy alligator.

Behold him rushing from the reeds. His enormous body swells. His plaited tail floats upon the lake. Waters like a cataract descend from his opening jaws. The earth trembles with his thunder, when from the opposite coasts of the lagoon emerges from the deep his rival champion. They dart upon each other; the boiling surface marks their rapid course, and terrific conflict commences. They now sink to the bottom, folded together in horrible wreaths, the water thick and discolored. They rise, their jaws clap together, echoing through the surrounding forest. Again they sink when the contest ends at the muddy bottom, and the vanquished makes hazardous escape, hiding in the turbulent water. The proud victor exulting returns. Shores and forest resound his dreadful roar, together with shouts of the plaited tribe around, witnesses of the horrid combat.

My apprehensions were alarmed after being a spectator. Every delay would but tend to increase my dangers, as the sun was near setting and alligators gathered around my harbor from all quarters. I concluded to be expeditious in my trip to take some fish. Not thinking it prudent to take my fusee, lest I lose it overboard in case of battle, I furnished myself with a club, went on board, and penetrating the first line of those around my harbor, they gave way, but being pursued by several large ones, I paddled with all my might toward the entrance of the lagoon, hoping to be sheltered there. But ere I had half-way reached the place I was attacked on all sides, several endeavoring to overset the canoe. My situation became precarious; two very large ones attacked me closely, rushing up with their heads and part of their bodies above the water, roaring terribly and belching floods over me. They struck their jaws together so close to my ears as almost to stun me, and I expected every moment to be dragged from the boat and devoured.

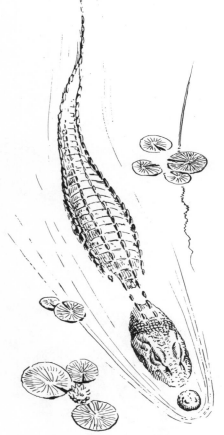

Bartram's "crocodiles" were alligators —Ned Smith

16

A successful retreat

But I applied my weapon so effectually, though at random, that I was so successful as to beat them off a little; I made for the shore as the only means left for my preservation, for by keeping close to it I should have my enemies on one side only, not surrounded by them, and if pushed to the last extremity, by jumping out of the canoe on shore, as it is easy to outwalk them on land. This last expedient fully answered my expectations, for as soon as I gained the shore they drew off. My confidence was in some degree restored. I had almost reached the entrance of the lagoon and determined to venture in to take a few fish and then return while daylight continued; for I could with caution and resolution make my way to safety along shore to the boat. I proceeded and made good my entrance into the lagoon, though not without opposition from the alligators, who formed a line across the entrance but did not pursue me into it, nor was I molested by any there, though there were some large ones in a cove at the upper end.

I soon caught more trout than I had occasion for; the air was too sultry to admit of their being kept for many hours, even though salted or barbecued. I now returned to camp with little trouble, by keeping close to the shore; yet I was pursued near to my landing (though not closely attacked), particularly by an old one about 12 feet in length. When I stepped on shore and turned to draw up my canoe, he rushed up near my feet and lay there looking me in the face, his head and shoulders out of the water. Resolved he should pay for his temerity, I ran to my camp and, returning with my fusee, found him with a foot on the gunwale of the boat in search of fish. On my coming up he withdrew sullenly but soon returned, seeming neither fearful nor disturbed. I dispatched him by lodging the contents of my gun in his head; and then took my fish out of the boat, laid them on the sand close to the water and began to scale them.

Then, raising my head, I saw before me the head and shoulders of a very large alligator moving slowly toward me. I instantly stepped back when, with a sweep of his tail, he brushed off several of my fish. It was certainly providential that I looked up at that instant as the monster probably would have seized me and dragged me into the river. This incredible boldness disturbed me greatly; supposing there would be no reasonable safety for me during the night but my keeping continually on the watch. As soon as I had prepared the fish, I proceeded to secure myself in the best manner I could.

Cutting through the canebrake
—Drawing by W. L. Sheppard from
Bear Hunting in the South by James Gordon,
The Century Magazine

I hauled my bark almost clear of the water, to prevent their sinking her; after this, every moveable was carried to my camp a few yards off; then ranging dry wood in such order as most convenient I cleared the ground around it that there might be no impediment in my way, in case of attack either from water or land, for I had discovered by this time that the small isthmus was resorted to by bears and wolves. I charged my gun and reconnoitered my camp-grounds; the peninsula and grove at the distance of 200 yards were invested by a cypress swamp which below was joined to the little lake and above to the marshes surrounding the lagoon; so that I was confined to an islet exceedingly circumscribed. There was no other retreat, in case of attack, but by ascending out of the large oaks or pushing off with my boat.

The haunt of the heron
—Drawing by Thomas Moran from *Bow Shooting*
by Maurice Thompson, Charles Scribner's Sons

A tumult in the harbor

It was by this time dusk, the alligators had nearly ceased their roar, when I was again alarmed by a tumult that seemed to be in my harbor. I found it undisturbed and continued to the point of the promontory where I saw a scene which threw my senses into such a tumult that it was some time before I could comprehend what was the matter; however, I soon accounted for the prodigious assemblage of crocodiles at this place.

How shall I convey an adequate idea of it to the reader and avoid suspicions of my veracity? Should I say that the river from shore to shore and perhaps half a mile above and below me, appeared to be one solid bank of fish of various kinds, pushing through this narrow pass of St. Juan's into the little lake on their return down the river, and that the alligators were in such incredible numbers and so close together from shore to shore that it would have been easy to walk across their heads? What can sufficiently declare the scene that for some minutes continued, whilst this mighty army of fish was forcing the pass?

During this attempt hundreds of thousands of them were caught by devouring alligators. I have seen an alligator take up several great fish at a time and squeeze them betwixt his jaws while the tails flapped about his eyes ere he swallowed them. The horrid noise of their closing jaws, their plunging amid the broken banks of fish and rising with their prey some feet above the water, the floods of water and blood rushing from their mouths, the clouds of vapor issuing from their nostrils, were truly frightful. And this continued at intervals during the night, as fish came to the pass.

After this sight, shocking and tremendous as it was, I found myself somewhat easier and more reconciled to my situation, being convinced that the extraordinary assemblage here was owing to the annual feast of fish; and that they were so well employed in their own element that I had little to fear their paying me a visit. I returned to my camp where I had left my fish broiling and my rice stewing; having with me oil, pepper and salt, and oranges hanging in abundance over my head, I sat down and regaled myself cheerfully.

William Bartram did not retreat next day; indeed he found "crocodile" nests upstream and went to visit them. He found many things that interested him, like the artificial baits devised in the swamps for angling for "trout," really largemouth bass. He was a curious man; indeed it was a curious age. Most of the early outdoor writers were setting down their observations rather than their exploits with short rod or long rifle. Perhaps the most famed individual of them all won regard in

Wild duck shooting on the Potomac
—Wood engraving from *The Illustrated London News,* Dec. 4, 1850, Library of Congress

20

many fields; agriculture, architecture, politics, statecraft, philosophy and the dream of democracy.

That was, of course, Thomas Jefferson of Virginia, the United States and the world, described by Kenneth Clark in *Civilisation* as the "universal man of the 18th century." In 1781 Jefferson stood beside that great rock now named for him above Harpers Ferry and looked long; later he recollected in tranquillity what he had viewed with emotion. His thoughts then may have determined his decision 23 years later on the Louisiana Purchase; at least his brooding foretold it. (Proper names are here spelled in accordance with modern usage; there is no other editing.)

Jefferson's Potomac passage

The passage of the Potomac through the Blue Ridge is perhaps one of the most stupendous scenes in nature. You stand on a very high point of land. On your right comes up the Shenandoah river, having ranged along the foot of the mountain a hundred miles to seek a vent. On your left approaches the Potomac, in quest of a passage also. In the moment of their junction they rush together against the mountain, rend it asunder, and pass off to the sea.

The first glance of this scene hurries our senses into the opinion, that this earth has been created in time, that the mountains were formed first, that the rivers began to flow afterwards, that in this place in particular they have been dammed up by the Blue ridge of mountains and have formed an ocean which filled the whole valley; that continuing to rise they have broken over at this spot, and torn the mountain down from its summit to its base. The piles of rock on each hand, but particularly on the Shenandoah, the evident marks of their disrupture and avulsion from their beds by the most powerful agents of nature, corroborate the impression.

But the distant finishing which nature has given to the picture is of a very different character. It is a true contrast to the foreground. It is as placid and delightful as that is wild and tremendous. For the mountain being cloven asunder, she presents to your eye through the cleft a catch of smooth blue horizon, at an infinite distance in the plain country, inviting you, as it were, from the riot and tumult roaring around, to pass through the breach and participate of the calm below. Here the eye composes itself; and that way too the road happens actually to lead.

You cross the Potomac above the junction, pass along its die through the base of the mountain for three miles, its terrible precipices hanging in fragments over you, and within about 20 miles reach Fredericktown and the fine country around that.

This scene is worth a voyage across the Atlantic. Yet here, as in the neighborhood of the natural bridge, are people who have passed their lives within half a dozen miles and have never been to survey this monument of a war between rivers and mountains, which must have shaken the earth itself to its center.

The height of our mountains has not yet been estimated with any degree of exactness. The Allegheny being the great ridge which divides the waters of the Atlantic from those of the Mississippi, its summit is doubtless more elevated above the ocean than that of any other mountain. But its relative height, compared with the base on which it stands, is not so great as that of some others, the country rising behind the successive ridges like the steps of a stair. The mountains of the Blue ridge, and of these the Peaks of Otter, are thought to be of a greater height, measured from their base, than any others in our country, and perhaps in North America.

From data which may found a tolerable conjecture, we suppose the highest peak to be about 4,000 feet perpendicular, which is not a fifth of the height of the mountains of South America, nor one-third of the height which would be necessary in our latitude to preserve ice in the open air unmelted through the year. The ridge of mountains next beyond the Blue ridge, called by us the North mountain, is of the greatest extent; for which reason they were named by Indians the Endless mountains.

A substance supposed to be pumice found floating on the Mississippi has induced a conjecture that there is a volcano on some of its waters; and as these are mostly known to their sources, except the Missouri, our expectations of verifying the conjecture would of course be led to the mountains which divide the waters of the Mexican Gulf from those of the South Seas; but no volcano having ever yet been known at such a distance from the sea, we must rather suppose that this floating substance has been erroneously deemed pumice.

Lewis and Clark, explorers

Thus in his *Notes on the State of Virginia* did Mr. Jefferson look at a landscape and speculate upon "the mountains which divide the waters of the Gulf from those of the South Seas" and to remember that the sources of the Missouri had not yet been explored. When he wrote that the mountains of the Blue ridge were thought to be higher than any others "in our country" he must have speculated that "our country," the new United States, bulked small upon the continental mass to the west.

Thus in 1802, now-President Jefferson asked the Spanish minister if

Meriwether Lewis in Indian Dress
—By St. Memin from the original

Lewis and Clark holding a council with the Indians
—Engraving from *Patrick Gass, A Journal,* 1810, Library of Congress

an expedition might explore the course of the Missouri; he was diplo-
matically turned down. But he went on planning an expedition anyway;
he acquired Louisiana Territory a year after the Spanish negation, by
purchase from the French to whom Spain had ceded it; and in 1804
began the great trip of exploration under William Clark and Meriwether Lewis.

Early literate citizens of the United States were like their English
counterparts, naturally enough, in their fondness for exploring and then
writing personal accounts. But the *Journals* of Lewis and Clark were
much more than this, if less eloquent. Captain Meriwether Lewis, who
had been President Jefferson's private secretary, and Captain William

Lewis and Clark keel boat
—Ned Smith

Female and male pronghorn antelopes
—Leonard Lee Rue III photo

Clark, a master of frontier crafts and negotiation, were 29 and 33 years old, respectively, when they started on one of the greatest feats of exploration ever performed. Bernard DeVoto credits both of them with "distinguished intelligence" which was the "principal reason for the success of the expedition. . . . They were masters of every situation and successfully handled every emergency."

Except, perhaps, that they were not "good" writers in a literary sense; the voluminous notes and diaries are crammed with information invaluable to map-makers, botanists, biologists, traders and the developers of an empire. But they weren't "literature," except as guides to a few excellent and many mediocre later essayists. Thus a nuclear quote is hard to come by, though some of the entries can spark imagination and stir the dreams of a reader. Here is an extract, complete with irregular spelling and punctuation, from Capt. Lewis's entry of September 17th, 1804, after the party struggling up the Missouri had passed the mouth of White River in what is now South Dakota:

in rear of our camp in a fine open grove of cotton wood passed a grove of plumb trees loaded with fruit, observed but little difference between this fruit and that of a similar kind common to the Atlantic States. this forrest of plumb trees garnish a plain about 20 feet more elivated than that on which were encamped; . . . it is intirely occupied by the burrows of the barking squiril heretofore described; this anamal appears in infinite numbers and the shortness and virdue of grass gave the plain the appearance of a beautifull bowling green in fine order. . . . a great number of wolves of the small kind (coyotes), halks (hawks) and some pole-cats were to be seen. I presume that those anamals feed on this squirril.

from this plane I had an extensive view of the river below, the surrounding country had been birnt about a month before and young grass had now sprung up to height of 4 Inches presenting the live green of spring . . . this senery already rich pleasing and beautiful was still farther hightened by immence herds of Buffaloe, deer Elk and Antelopes which we saw in every direction feeding on the hills and plains. I estimate the number of Buffaloe which could be compreed at one view to amount to 3000. my object was to kill a female Antelope having already procured a male; I pursued my rout on this plain to the west flanked by my two hunters. . . .

we rested ourselves about half an hour and regailed ourselves on half a bisquit each and some jirks of Elk which we had taken the precaution to put in our pouches in the morning before we set out, and drank of the water of a small pool which had collected from the rain.

Shye and watchfull antelope

we found the Antelope shye and watchfull insomuch that we had been unable to get a shot at them; . . . I had this day an opportunity of witnessing the agility and fleetness of this anamal which was really astonishing. I had pursued and twice surprised a small herd of seven . . . in the first instance they did not discover me distinctly and therefore did not turn at full speed, tho' they took care to gain an elivated

Western landscape —From a painting by Samuel Seymour, Joslyn Art Museum, Omaha, Nebraska

point where it was impossible to approach them under cover, except in one direction and that happened to be in the direction from which the wind blew towards them; bad as the chance to approach them was, I made the best of my way towards them, frequently peeping over the ridge with which I took care to conceal myself . . . the male, of which there was but one, frequently incircled the summit of the hill on which the females stood in a group, as if to look out for the approach of danger. I got within about 200 paces of them when they smelt me and fled; I gained the top of the eminence on which they stood, as soon as possible from whence I had an extensive view of the country . . . the antelopes which had disappeared in a steep reveene now appeared at the distance of about three miles on the side of a ridge . . . so soon had these antelopes gained the distance at which they had again appeared to my view I doubted at ferst that they were the same I had just surprised, but my doubts soon vanished when I beheld the rapidity of their flight along the ridge before me. it appeared rather the rappid flight of birds than the motion of quadrupeds. I think I can safely venture the assertion that the speed of this animal is equal if not superior to that of the finest blooded courser.

On the next day, William Clark wrote of the same area: "below the bend is a butifully inclined Plain, in which there is great numbers of Buffalow, Elk & Goats in view feeding & scipping on those Plains. Grouse, Larks & the Prarie bird is common in those Plains."

It sounds like a hunter's dream and a grammarian's nightmare. But what it was is a day in a journey that began at St. Louis on May 14, 1804, and ended about noon on September 23, 1806, in St. Louis. Whereupon, the next day "we rose early and commenced wrighting."

Well, Lewis and Clark may not have been journalists. But one Josiah Gregg *was* a journalist, medical student, soldier, trader, maker of maps and lover of the Great Plains. His introduction to outdoor writing began a generation later.

Twenty years after the Great Journey had begun, Congress authorized a road to be marked from Missouri to New Mexico—not yet part of the United States, of course—so wagons as well as pack animals could follow the already existing Sante Fe Trail. Wagons began moving from Independence to Sante Fe in 1824.

Six years later, desperately-ill young Josiah Gregg was in one of those wagons and "like to die." But the air of the plains somehow cured what may have been tuberculosis and he wrote later that by the time the train "reached the buffalo range, I was as eager for the chase as my companions."

Josiah got well on the prairie and was never again happy except when moving across the great plains. After nine years as a Santa Fe trader and a recorder of geographical data so detailed that even Lewis and Clark

Buffalo Bull
—From a drawing by Peale,
American Philosophical Society

26

would have envied his skill, he tried to settle down, but the established society of Independence, Missouri, was not for him. He wandered and wrote; he made a lengthy trip through Texas in 1841–42, and was in Austin when Gen. Sam Houston arrived as President elect to be sworn in as chief executive of the new nation. After hearing General Sam, Gregg wrote: "Houston was elected by a heavy majority . . . but I feel this will be found to speak badly of the judgment and morals of his constituents." Josiah was a blunt man.

He observed everything: plains, hills, trees, soil, animals, latitude and longitude. He taught himself Spanish, learned to deal honestly with Indians, became an excellent writer, a fine scientist, and kept a daily diary of objective experience when he was afield—which was most of the time.

But he could not become a social being; he wrote that a "tour of the prairies is dangerous for him who would live a contented life at home; not so dangerous to life as prejudicial to his domestic habits."

And he added: "This passion for prairie life, how paradoxical soever it may seem, will be very apt to lead me upon the plains again, to spread my bed with the mustang and the buffalo under the broad canopy of heaven—there to maintain undisturbed my confidence in men by fraternizing with prairie dogs and wild colts and the still wilder Indians—the unconquered Sabaeans of the Great American Desert."

March of the caravan across the prairies to Santa Fé —Engraving from *Commerce of the Prairies, Vol. I* by Josiah Gregg

It was not until 1842 that he wrote his fine book *Commerce of the Prairies,* which appeared in 1844. Gregg afterward studied medicine, became a doctor—and then went off with the Army to Texas and Northern Mexico in 1846.

The Army was completely unable to utilize his services properly and his diary of that period makes knife-edged comments upon generals and colonels. But he wrote more happily in the spring of 1840, upon his last return from Santa Fe; this is a condensation from his diary entries of that period, leaving out his reports of latitude and measured distances.

—Ned Smith

27 *wagons, 200 mules*

I brought from Chihuahua 21 wagons which, added to six remaining in Sante Fe, completed our caravan with upwards of 200 mules. Our company, besides myself, consists of 47 men. We left today (Feb. 25, 1840) for the U. S. with the intention of returning down the Rio Colorado, or Canadian Fork of the Arkansas. As the young grass is beginning to shoot, our stock will eat but little corn, although we have taken in upwards of 300 fanegas (rise of 600 bushels). The first appearance of spring grass sets animals crazy— they will leave all other food to seek after it.

On March 8, the grass took fire from our camp; as the wind blew back it gave us no uneasiness, but as we were catching up, the wind turned toward the east, and it was with difficulty we could get out of the burning prairies. We thought we were done with it; but this evening as we descended into the valley of a creek, the fire overtook the wagons and they were only able to keep out of its way by striking a long trot to a spot of shorter grass where the fire progressed slower. Here we set out fires and then drove wagons into the burn ground, for fire burns so slowly aback against the wind wagons can be driven through it with safety. These prairies of dry grass are dangerous; if fire gets a start in a gale, it is impossible to extinguish it, and as much so for the wagons to be kept out of its reach.

Next day we crossed El Arroyo de Monte Revuelto and struck east over a high prairie. About midday our Comanche guide came trotting and said "Over the hill are 3 buffalo bulls. Shan't we kill one?" "How do you hunt best?" said I. "With my bow and arrows," replied he. I answered, "catch my riding horse and kill us one—but don't run him much; one buffalo is a plenty." He promised and set out: but when he got in pursuit of his favorite game, he could not restrain himself and soon dispatched two, observing to some comrades later that had he not feared injuring the horse he would have killed all three.

(On opposite page, top)
Camp Comanche
—Engraving from *Commerce of the Prairies Vol. II* by Josiah Gregg

(Bottom)
Prairie Fire
—Engraving from a painting by George Winter
Courtesy The Indiana Historical Society

Charles Russell's Buffalo Hunting —Courtesy Amon Carter Museum, Fort Worth, Texas

Then we came into a region of late-burnt prairie—I fear this burn will continue for some distance. It not only deprives us of grass but the short, still grass stubs will injure the feet of the mules.

Tues., Mar. 10—Between midnight and one o'clock I was roused by the firing of guns and heard the cry of "Indians!" which was terrified by a savage yell heard around camp—mixt with the shrill of a whistle used by Pawnees and the croak clattering of Indian tongues. All hands prepared for defense. Our mules were all penned with the wagons. My two riding horses only were tethered without, one of which broke loose and fled back down the road we had come. The other was saved by a Mexican servant, Antonio Chaves, who ran out in the midst of a shower of balls and brought him in. Our sheep and goats fled in an opposite direction but we followed their trail and found them next day.

We immediately commenced firing in the direction we heard the Indians but it was quite dark; soon began a mist of rain and snow. We could not discern a single object, and could only shoot at the flash of their guns.

A careless camp site

We had been careless in pitching our camp. Head wagons were within 50 yards of a small hollow with some holes containing water. The Indians had slipped up the hollow and gained these holes, the banks of which afforded them a breastwork about a foot high behind which they kept a continual fire upon us for about two hours. I thought of driving them out by a charge but by the light of our fires, the Indians would be able to see and shoot us, while we could not see them until we were upon them. As the night was cold, our guard had built large fires of cottonwood; guards should never stand by fires—although it is too often done—for it gives an enemy every advantage. So we remained with our wagons, firing at the flashes of their guns until we worried them out of their holes.

We know not if we killed or wounded any. Of our party, a Spanish boy, Nacifor Palacio, was shot through the hand; also an Italian named Giovanni Elmini received a serious wound, a ball passing through the top of his head, deep enough to leave an inch of unbroken skin between the two holes. But he seems in a fair way for recovery. In the midst of the battle, a Spanish boy told me Giovanni was wounded; I went to the wagon and asked him. "Oh, I am shot," he said. Where? "In the head," he replied with his natural tone of voice. I could not believe it until I had lighted a match. So I bound up the wound until the battle should cease.

Our Comanche guide had hailed the attackers as soon as the attack was made, but soon found they were not Comanches but Pawnees. Also, their whistle and their being afoot convinced us that they were of that savage and marauding tribe. From the trail we saw next morning there were not more than 50 or 60 of them. Caravans are usually too care-

Attack on an Emigrant Train
—Colored lithograph by Leopold Grozelier from a painting by Charles F. Wimar, Joslyn Art Museum, Omaha, Nebraska

Pueblo of Jémez —From *Reports of the Secretary of War on the reconnaissanc*

less in encampments. They generally camp near enough the bank of some stream for it to serve as breastwork for an offending enemy; if a brave Indian force knew how to take advantage of this impudence they might much injure or even defeat large companies.

Mar. 20 — Today a couple of our company were ahead and seeing buffalo they crawled near; then they shot a cow. The herd took little notice, so our hunters crawled up behind the dead buffalo and shot two more; thus a hunter will sometimes kill half a dozen before the gang take fright. I once saw 12 lying within view of each other, killed by two hunters out of one drove. This evening I was riding ahead alone, observing half a dozen buffalo feeding in tall grass. I approached them and commenced shooting at them with Cochran's re-

peating rifle. I fired six shots at them without giving them more fright than to jump and look around at every report; but as the grass concealed me, they would commence feeding again, all except the mortally wounded, which stand sullenly as though unhurt, a peculiarity of these animals. I showed myself and they fled except one which fell dead and two others badly wounded. These would soon have died but our party approached and gave them chase; they fled and escaped. A buffalo bull, mortally wounded, if chased will run many miles, when if left quiet it would lie down and die in a few minutes. When irritated, they are extraordinarily tenacious of life. I have seen more than 20 balls (well directed) shot into an irritated bull and yet he would not die for some time afterwards; whilst with one shot only, when quiet, they will frequently fall dead.

—Ned Smith

Still wild country

Meanwhile, in the East where it all began, a Marylander named Mesach Browning had just reminded the more settled citizenry that there was still some wild country in settled land. He did this by publishing his autobiography, *Forty-four Years of the Life of a Hunter*. It covered his life in the Maryland Alleghenies where he supported himself by hunting, feeding his family on game and carrying out bear fur, deer skins and venison haunches to sell in Baltimore or Annapolis from 1795 to 1840. His account did not appear until 1859, but it seems clear he wrote every word of it himself.

Browning killed bears, panthers, thousands of deer and many wild turkeys. He slew wolves for a bounty ($8), but liked best to hunt bears. Other hunters of the area rated him best, he says, not immodestly, crediting his talents to an understanding of wild life habit and habitat. He used candles in bark reflectors to spotlight deer at night along hill streams down which he floated in a canoe; he tells how to stalk a bear; he knew mating seasons, gestation periods, browse preferences. He speculated that deer had been almost exterminated in the highlands by 1840 by the cattle that were "eating, tramping and running over every place in the glade country." He said of hunting that: "If a man undertakes a dangerous enterprise with a determination to succeed or lose his life, he will do many things with ease and unharmed which a smaller degree of energy never would have accomplished."

He suggested that the chase was more important than the kill, claimed to live by a certain ethical code toward wildlife, and insisted self-reliance was vital to him who would hunt in the wild. His contemporaries in Eastern Maryland who went out for rabbits and squirrels hardly believed his stories. They especially doubted his casual statements about killing bears with a knife; he said the rifles of that day were so inaccurate, and the powder so poor, that even at 30 yards there wasn't enough killing power. Here's how he described his pursuit of the Ursidae:

Audubon's Virginia Deer —Courtesy of The Brooklyn Museum, Gift of A. B. Baylis

Bear Hunting —Currier & Ives, Library of Congress

The extraordinary success I had in bear-hunting requires some explanation. . . . I always kept two good dogs, one of which walked before me and the other behind. The one in front would wind the bear, and lead me up to him on that side on which he could not smell me, for I would come on him unexpectedly. If he found us coming on him, and ran, the dogs would overtake him before he would be out of sight. The moment I would see one run, I would send the dogs after him; and as I could run almost as fast as any bear could, when the fight began I was close up, and a shot was certain death. In many cases, however, I killed them with my knife; but only when the fight was so close that I was afraid to shoot, lest I should kill a dog; which has often been done. I never in my life shot a dog in a fight; for I always took a knife in a close contest.

While Mesach Browning was prowling Maryland mountains, a truly professional writer, the author who invented Ichabod Crane and Rip Van Winkle, came back from Europe, and celebrated his return after 17 years abroad by heading for the country that is now Oklahoma. Washington Irving was, of course, not only a humorous writer but an artist at interpretation and a skillful observer. *A Tour on the Prairies* covers a month's trip in 1832; it is a tribute to his talents as a reporter who did not seek two-headed calves to write about but wrote about one-headed calves so his readers could see things they had not seen before.

A Tour has many hunting stories in it. The two passages joined here are extracted from Chapter XI and XV: Game Scenes and The Search for the Elk.

Herd of Elk —From a watercolor by A. J. Miller, Courtesy The Public Archives of Canada

A morning bathes the heart

It was a bright morning with a pure transparent atmosphere that seemed to bathe the heart with gladness. Our march continued parallel to the Arkansas through a varied country; sometimes we had to break our way through alluvial bottoms matted with redundant vegetation, where gigantic trees were entangled with grapevines hanging like a cordage from their branches; sometimes we coasted along sluggish brooks whose feeble current just served to link a succession of glassy pools imbedded like mirrors in the quiet bosom of the forest, reflecting its autumned foliage. Sometimes we scrambled up broken and rocky hills from which we had wide views stretching on one side over distant prairies diversified by groves, and on the other ranging along a line of blue and shadowy hills.

At one time we passed through a luxuriant bottom of meadow bordered by thickets where the tall grass was pressed down into numerous "deer beds," where those animals had couched the preceding night. Some oak trees also bore signs of having been clambered by bears in quest of acorns, the marks of their claws being visible in the bark.

As we opened a glade of this meadow we beheld several deer bounding away in wild affright until, having gained some distance, they would stop and gaze back at the strange intruders into their solitude. There was immediately a sharp report of rifles in every direction, from the young huntsmen, but they were too eager to aim surely, and the deer bounded away unharmed into the depths of the forest.

We struck the Arkansas but found ourselves still below the Red Fork and, as the river made deep bends, we again left its banks and continued through the woods until we encamped in a beautiful basin bordered by a fine stream and shaded by a clump of lofty oaks. The horses were now hobbled and then turned loose to graze.

A number of rangers, prime hunters, started off in search of game. There was no whooping or laughing about the camp as in the morning, all were either busy about the fires preparing the evening repast, or reposing upon the grass. Shots were soon heard in various directions. After a time a huntsman rode into the camp with the carcass of a fine buck hanging across his horse. Soon afterward came in a couple of stripling hunters on foot, one of whom bore on his shoulders the body of a doe. He was evidently proud of his spoil, being probably one of his first achievements; he and his companion were bantered by their comrades, as beginners who hunted in partnership.

As night set in there was great shouting, and a body of young rangers came parading around the fires bearing one of their comrades on their shoulders. He had shot an elk for the first time in his life, the first elk that had been killed on this expedition. The young huntsman was the hero of the camp for the night and "the father of the feast" into the bargain, for portions of his elk were seen roasting at every fire.

The other hunters returned without much success. The Captain had observed tracks of a buffalo, and had tracked a bear for some distance until the footprints had disappeared. He had seen an elk, which walked out on a sandbar of the river, but before he could steal round the horses to get a shot, it had re-entered the woods.

Our own hunter, Beatte, returned silent and sulky from an unsuccessful hunt. As yet he had brought us in nothing, and we had depended for our venison upon the Captain's mess.

—Ned Smith

Beatte was evidently mortified, for he looked down with contempt upon the rangers, as inexperienced woodsmen but little skilled in hunting; they, on the other hand, regarded Beatte with no very complacent eye, as one of an evil breed.

—Ned Smith

Frontier moss-troopers

Our little Frenchman, Tonish, also, by his incessant chattering and gasconading, in his balderdash dialect, had drawn upon himself the ridicule of many of the troop, who amused themselves in a kind of raillery by no means remarkable for its delicacy; but the little varlet was so fortified by self-conceit that he was invulnerable to every joke. I felt a little mortified at the sorry figures our retainers were making among these moss-troopers of the frontier. Even our equipment came in for a share of unpopularity, and I heard many sneers about the double-barreled guns with which we were provided against smaller game; the lads of the West holding "shotguns," as they call them, in great contempt, thinking grouse, partridges and even wild turkeys as beneath their serious attention, and the rifle the only firearm worthy of a hunter.

I was awakened before daylight by the mournful howling of a wolf who was skulking the camp, attracted by the smell of venison. After riding a short distance that morning we came upon a well-worn Indian track and, following it, scrambled to the summit of a hill from whence we had a wide prospect over rocky ridges and waving lines of upland, enriched by groves of trees of varied foliage. At a distance, to our great satisfaction, we beheld the Red Fork rolling its ruddy current to the Arkansas.

The soil was imprinted in many places with the tracks of deer, and the claws of bears were to be traced on various trees. Everyone was on the lookout when suddenly there was a bustle and clamor in a distant part of the line. A bear! A bear! We pressed forward to be present at the spot, when to my infinite, though whimsical chagrin, I found it to be our two worthies, Beatte and Tonish, perpetrating foul murder on a polecat! The animal had ensconced itself beneath the trunk of a fallen tree, whence it kept up a vigorous defense until the forest was in a high state of fragrance.

Gibes now broke out on all sides at the expense of the Indian hunter, and he was advised to wear the scalp of the skunk as trophy of his prowess. When they found, however, that he and Tonish were bent upon bearing off the carcass as a peculiar dainty, there was a universal expression of disgust; and they were regarded as little better than cannibals.

Mortified, I insisted upon their abandoning their prize and

resuming their march. Beatte complied with a dogged, discontented air and lagged behind, muttering to himself. Tonish, however, with his usual buoyancy, consoled himself by
eulogies on the richness and delicacy of a roasted polecat,
which he swore was considered the daintiest of dishes by
Indian gourmands. It was with difficulty I could silence his
loquacity by peremptory commands. Tonish now eased off
his spleen by bestowing volleys of oaths and blows on the
packhorses. I was likely to be no gainer in the end, by my
opposition to the humors of these varlets, for after a time

The Prize Shot —From a watercolor by Charles M. Russell, Courtesy Amon Carter Museum, Fort Worth, Texas

Thunderstorm in the Rocky Mountains —From a painting by Albert Bierstadt, Courtesy Museum of Fine Arts, Boston.

—Ned Smith

Beatte rode up to the head of the line to resume his station as a guide, and I had the vexation to see the carcass of his prize, stripped of its skin and looking like a fat suckling pig, dangling behind his saddle. I made a solemn vow, however, that our fire should not be disgraced by the cooking of that polecat.

*   *   *

With next morning's dawn the prime hunters set off in different directions to beat the country for game. Sergeant Bean was among the first, and returned before breakfast with success, having killed a fat doe almost within the purlieus of the camp.

Breakfast over, the Captain mounted in quest of the elk which he had wounded on the previous evening. I joined him in the search and we sallied forth, accompanied by the sergeant and a lieutenant. Two rangers followed on foot, to bring home a doe the sergeant had killed. We had not ridden far when we came to where it lay in a beautiful woodland scene. The rangers fell to work with hunters' skill to dismember it, while we continued on our course. We passed along sloping hillsides and scattered trees until we came to where long herbage was pressed down with numerous elk beds. Here the Captain, after looking about diligently, pointed their "trail," the footprints of which were as large as those of horned cattle. He put himself upon the tracks and went quietly forward, the rest of us following. At length he halted at the place where the elk had been when shot at. Spots of blood on the herbage showed the shot had been effective. The wounded animal had kept for some distance with the rest of the herd, as could be seen by the sprinkling of blood on shrubs and weeds bordering the trail. These suddenly disappeared. "Somewhere hereabouts," said the Captain, "the elk must have turned off from the gang. Whenever they feel themselves mortally wounded, they turn aside and seek some out-of-the-way place to die alone."

Elk track —Ned Smith

An animal of prey

There was something in this picture of the last moments of a wounded elk to touch the sympathies of someone not hardened to the gentle disports of the chase; such sympathies, however, are but transient. Man is naturally an animal of prey; and however changed by civilization, will readily relapse into his instinct for destruction. I found my ravenous and sanguinary propensities daily growing stronger upon the prairies.

After looking about, the Captain found the separate trail of the wounded elk, which turned off at right angles from that of the herd and entered an open forest. The traces of blood became more faint and at greater distances; at length they ceased altogether, and the ground was so hard, and the herbage so much withered, that the footprints could no longer be perceived.

"The elk must lie in this neighborhood," said the Captain, "as you may know by those buzzards wheeling about; they always hover that way above some carcass. However, a dead elk cannot get away, so let us follow the trail of the living ones; they may have halted at no great distance."

We accordingly resumed the trail of the elk, which led us over hill and dale. Every now and then we would catch a

—Ned Smith

glimpse of a deer bounding away, but the Captain was not to be diverted by such inferior game. A large flock of wild turkeys, too, were roused by the trampling of our horses; some scampered off as fast as their long legs could carry them; others fluttered up into trees, where they remained with outstretched necks, gazing at us. The Captain would not allow a rifle to be discharged at them, lest it should alarm the elk. At length we came to where the forest ended in a steep bank and the Red Ford wound below us. The trail descended the bank, and we could trace it with our eyes until it terminated in the river, which it was evident the elk had forded on the previous evening. "It is needless to go any further," said the Captain.

Our little party now divided, the Captain and myself taking the direction of the camp. On our way we came to a buffalo track, more than a year old. It was not wider than an ordinary footpath, and worn deep into the soil; these animals follow each other in single file. Shortly afterward we met two rangers. They had wounded an elk but he escaped; pursuing him, they had found the one shot by the Captain. They conducted us to a noble animal, as large as a yearling heifer, about a mile and a half from the place where it had been shot. The poor animal had apparently abandoned its unhurt companions and turned aside to die alone.

The Captain and the rangers forthwith fell to work to flay and cut up the carcass. It was already tainted inside but ample collops were cut from the ribs and haunches and laid on the outstreched hide. Holes were cut along the border of the hide, raw thongs were passed through them, and the whole drawn up into a sack which was swung up behind the Captain's saddle. The turkey-buzzards were soaring overhead, waiting to swoop down and banquet.

The Captain and myself mounted and jogged back to camp while the rangers resumed their hunting. Our camp presented a picture of bustle and repose. Some of the men were busy round the fires, jerking and roasting venison and bear's meat to be packed as a future supply. Some were dressing the skins of animals they had killed; others were washing their clothes in the brook and hanging them on bushes to dry; while many were lying on the grass and lazily gossiping in the shade. Now and then a hunter would return, on horseback or foot, laden with game or empty handed. Those who brought home any spoil deposited it at the Captain's fire and then filed off to their respective messes to relate their day's exploits.

The game killed at this camp consisted of six deer, one elk, two bears, and six or eight turkeys.

Out of hibernation
—Ned Smith

George Catlin painting a chief in an Indian village at the base of the Rocky Mountains
—Engraving from a painting by George Catlin from *North American Indians Vol. I*

Catlin visits Indian land

Thus the Knickerbocker chronicler wrote in his 1835 "author's introduction" to *A Tour on the Prairies* that it was "a region fruitful of wonders and adventures, and which had already been made the theme of spirit-stirring narratives from able pens; yet about which I had nothing wonderful or adventurous to offer." For two centuries, outdoor writers have secretly uttered that sentiment.

Irving also wrote *Western Journals,* an outgrowth from the trip that produced *A Tour,* and rewrote the journal of Captain B. L. E. Bonneville, titling it *The Adventures of Captain Bonneville, U.S.A.* That was an account of the officer and 110 men who spent three years in the Rocky Mountains. It was published in 1837, was popular then, but has been rather forgotten for more than a century.

About the same time that Washington Irving was wandering across Indian Territory, George Catlin was painting his great testimonials to a way of life that has disappeared from a greatly altered landscape. In 1832 he wrote this passage, somewhat condensed by deletions here:

> Nature's works are worthy of our preservation and protection; and the further we become separated . . . from pristine wilderness and beauty, the more pleasure does the mind of enlightened man feel in recurring to these scenes . . . And what a splendid contemplation, too, when one imagines them as they might in future be seen preserved in their beauty and wildness in a magnificent park, where the world could see for ages to come the native Indian in his classic attire, galloping his wild horse, with sinewy bow and shield and lance, amid the fleeing herds of elk and buffaloes . . . a nation's park containing man and beast. I would ask no other monument to my memory nor any other enrollment of my name among the famous dead, than the reputation of having been the founder of such an institution.

A great many Americans were contemplating "Nature" by the 1830s and '40s, some of them by heading west, some of them in New England or in the Southwest. Here in the old, settled lands of the original colonies was a sort of brooding introspection, set down in poetry and philosophic speculation by William Cullen Bryant, Ralph Waldo Emerson or such a minor poet and major painter as Thomas Cole, whose landscapes were as romantic as his verses but executed better. Of these men, Henry David Thoreau was the figure most close to what was called "reality;" he was less likely to see forests than a tree, and he brooded upon a specific pond rather than the abstraction of water. These people were not outdoor writers in the modern sense, although they had vastly more influence on U.S. culture than did almost-forgotten contemporaries— and they entered the schoolbooks as "required reading," which meant many quote them but few read them.

(On opposite page, top)
The juvenile members of the chief's family in front of the chief's lodge.
—Engraving from a painting by George Catlin from *North American Indians Vol. II*

(Bottom)
A view of a small portion of the village of the Comanchees showing the wigwam of the chief in the foreground and women drying meat and "graining" buffalo robes.
—Engraving from a painting by George Catlin from *North American Indians Vol. II*

But here is a brief excerpt from Thoreau's *A Week on the Concord and Merrimack Rivers* that could have been written last week by a local outdoor columnist with a penchant for old-fashioned phraseology:

> **Alewives were formerly abundant here until the dam and afterward the canal at Billerica, and the factories at Lowell, put an end to their migrations . . . It is said that those who represented the interests of the fishermen, remembering between what dates they were accustomed to take the grown shad, stipulated that the dams should be left open for that season only, and the fry which go down a month later consequently were stopped and destroyed . . . Perchance, after a few thousand years, if the fishes will be patient and pass their summers elsewhere, nature will have leveled the dam and the factories . . . Shad are still taken in the Concord River at Lowell, still patiently, with instinct not to be discouraged . . . revisiting their old haunts, and still met by the Corporation with its dam.**

American Shad
—Ned Smith

In these same years, a very proper Boston Brahmin and bright classical historian went journeying westward into a landscape that shook him out of his self-esteem at having become eminent while young.

That was Francis Parkman. He saw western Indians and wildlife with the perception of an urbanite; he looked at the great spread of mountains and plains with the eyes of a city man. And he reacted with love and passion, after the first shock, so that he did not write as a historian scribbles, with proper detachment, but set down *The Oregon Trail* as a subjective experience.

The first edition was published in 1849; there have been many editions since then. This excerpt, from "The Hunting Camp," is Parkman's account of a buffalo chase while he was living in an Oglala Sioux hunting camp, at a time when he was ill.

Breaking camp

Long before daybreak the Indians broke up their camp. The women of Mene-Seela's lodge were as usual among the first that were ready for departure, and I found the old man himself sitting by the embers of the decayed fire, over which he was warming his withered fingers, as the morning was very chill and damp. The preparations for moving were even more confused and disorderly than usual. While some families were leaving the ground, the lodges of others were still standing untouched. At this old Mene-Seela grew impatient, and walking out to the middle of the village, he harangued the people in a loud, sharp voice. Now, he said, when they were on an enemy's hunting-grounds, was not the time to behave like children; they ought to be more active and united

The Oxbow — the Connecticut River near Northampton
—From a painting by Thomas Cole, 1846, The Metropolitan Museum of Art, Gift of Mrs. Russell Sage, 1908

than ever. His speech had some effect. The delinquents took
down their lodges and loaded their pack-horses; and when
the sun rose, the last of the men, women, and children had
left the deserted camp.

This movement was made for the purpose of finding a safer
position. So we advanced only three or four miles up the
little stream, when each family assumed its relative place in
the great ring of the village, and the squaws set at work in
preparing the camp. But not a single warrior dismounted. All

the men that morning were on inferior animals, leading their best horses or confiding them to boys. In small parties they began to ride rapidly away over the plains to the westward. I had taken no food, and went to my host's lodge, which his squaws had set up with wonderful dispatch, and sat down in the centre, as a hint that I was hungry. A wooden bowl was put before me, filled with the dried meat called pemmican by the northern voyagers and wasna by the Dahcotah.

Taking a handful, I left the lodge just in time to see the last band of hunters disappear over the ridge of the neighboring hill. I mounted Pauline and galloped in pursuit, riding rather by the balance than by any muscular strength that remained to me. From the top of the hill I could overlook a wide extent of desolate prairie, over which, far and near, little parties of naked horsemen were rapidly passing. I soon came up to the nearest, and we had not ridden a mile before all were united into one large and compact body. Each hunter whipped on his horse, as if anxious to be the first to reach the game. In such movements among the Indians this is always more or less the case; but it was especially so in the present instance, because the head chief was absent, and there were but few "soldiers," a sort of Indian police, who among their other functions usually assume the direction of a buffalo hunt.

A young Indian mother fording a stream
—From a watercolor by A. J. Miller, 1867, Courtesy The Public Archives of Canada

Following the buffalo

We rode at a swift canter straight forward, up hill and down, through the stiff, obstinate growth of endless wild-sage bushes. For an hour and a half the same red shoulders, the same long black hair, rose and fell with the motion of the horses before me. Very little was said, though I observed an old man severely reproving Raymond for having left his rifle behind when there was some probability of encountering an enemy before the day was over. As we galloped across a plain thickly set with sage, the foremost riders vanished suddenly from sight, as if diving into the earth. The arid soil was cracked into a deep ravine. Down we all went in succession and galloped in a line along the bottom, until we found a point where, one by one, the horses could scramble out. Soon after, we came upon a wide shallow stream, and as we rode swiftly over the hard sand-beds and through the thin sheets of rippling water, many of the savage horsemen threw themselves to the ground, knelt on the sand, snatched a hasty draught, and leaping back again to their seats, galloped on.

Scouts kept in advance of the party; and now we began to see them on the ridges of the hills, waving their robes in token that buffalo were visible. These proved to be nothing more than old straggling bulls, feeding upon the neighboring plains, who would stare for a moment at the hostile array and then gallop clumsily off. At length we could discern several scouts making their signals at once; no longer waving their robes from the top of the hill, but standing lower down, so that they could not be seen from the plains beyond. Game worth pursuing had evidently been discovered. The Indians now urged forward their tired horses even more rapidly than before.

Pauline, who was still sick and jaded, began to groan heavily; and her yellow sides were darkened with sweat. As we were crowding together over a lower intervening hill, I heard Reynal and Raymond shouting to me from the left; and, looking in that direction, I saw them riding away behind a party of about twenty mean-looking Indians. These were the relatives of Reynal's squaw, Margot, who, not wishing to take part in the general hunt, were riding towards a distant hollow, where they saw a small band of buffalo which they meant to appropriate to themselves. I answered to the call by ordering Raymond to turn back and follow me. He reluctantly obeyed, though Reynal, who had relied on his assistance in skinning, cutting up, and carrying to camp the buffalo that he and his party should kill, loudly protested, and declared that we should see no sport if we went with the rest of the

George Catlin's Head of the Blackfoot Blood Tribe
—Courtesy National Collection of Fine Arts, Smithsonian Institution

49

Fort Union, on the Missouri River —Library of Congress

Indians. Followed by Raymond, I pursued the main body of hunters, while Reynal, in a rage, whipped his horse over the hill after his ragamuffin relatives.

The Indians, still about a hundred in number, galloped in a dense body, dust flying in the wind behind them. I could not overtake them until they stopped on the side of the hill where scouts were standing. Here each hunter sprang in haste from the tired animal he had ridden, and leaped upon the fresh horse he had brought with him. There was not a saddle or a bridle in the whole party. A piece of buffalo-robe, girthed over the horse's back, served in place of the one, and a cord of twisted hair, lashed round his lower jaw, answered for the other. Eagle feathers dangled from every mane and tail. The rider wore no other clothing than a light cincture at his waist, and a pair of moccasins. He had a heavy whip, with a handle of solid elk-horn and a lash of knotted bull-hide, fastened to his wrist by a band. His bow was in his hand, his quiver of otter or panther skin hung at his shoulder. Thus equipped, some 30 of the hunters galloped away towards the left, in order to make a circuit under cover of the hills, that the buffalo might be assailed on both sides at once. The rest impatiently waited until time enough had elapsed for their companions to reach the required position. Then riding upward in a body, we gained the ridge of the hill, and for the first time came in sight of the buffalo on the plain beyond.

They were a band of cows, four or five hundred in number, crowded near the bank of a wide stream that was soaking across the sand-beds of a large circular basin, sun-scorched and broken, scantily covered with herbage, and surrounded with barren hills, from an opening in which we could see our allies galloping out upon the plain. The wind blew from that direction. The buffalo, aware of their approach, had begun to move, though very slowly and in a compact mass.

Numerous old bulls were scattered over the plain, and, ungallantly deserting their charge at our approach, began to wade and plunge through the quicksands of the stream, and gallop away towards the hills. One old veteran was straggling behind the rest, with one of his fore-legs, which had been broken by some accident, dangling about uselessly. His appearance, as he went shambling along on three legs, was so ludicrous that I could not help pausing to look. As I came near, he would try to rush upon me, nearly throwing himself down at every awkward attempt. Looking up, I saw the whole body of Indians full an hundred yards in advance. I lashed Pauline in pursuit and reached them just in time; for at that moment, each hunter, as if by a common impulse, violently struck his horse, each horse sprang forward, and, scattering in the charge in order to assail the entire herd at once, we rushed headlong upon the buffalo.

Turmoil of the kill

We were among them in an instant. Amid the trampling and the yells, I could see their dark figures running hither and thither through clouds of dust, and the horsemen darting in pursuit. While we were charging on one side, our companions attacked the bewildered and panic-stricken herd on the other. The uproar and confusion lasted but a moment. The dust cleared away, and the buffalo could be seen scattering as from a common centre, flying over the plain singly, or in long files and small compact bodies, while behind them followed

the Indians, riding at furious speed, and yelling as they launched arrow after arrow into their sides. The carcasses were strewn thickly over the ground. Here and there stood wounded buffalo, their bleeding sides feathered with arrows; and as I rode by them their eyes would glare, they would bristle like gigantic cats, and feebly attempt to rush up and gore my horse.

I left the camp that morning with a philosophic resolution. Neither I nor my horse were at that time fit for such sport, and I had determined to remain a quiet spectator; but amid the rush of horses and buffalo, the uproar and the dust, I found it impossible to sit still; and as four or five buffalo ran past me in a line, I lashed Pauline in pursuit. We went plunging through the water and quicksands, and clambering the bank, chased them through the sage bushes that covered the rising ground beyond. But neither her native spirit nor the blows of the knotted bull-hide could supply the place of poor Pauline's exhausted strength. We could not gain an inch upon the fugitives.

At last, however, they came full upon a ravine too wide to leap over; and as this compelled them to turn abruptly to the left, I contrived to get within 10 or 12 yards of the hindmost. At this she faced about, bristled angrily, and made a show of charging. I shot at her, and hit her somewhere in the neck. Down she tumbled into the ravine, whither her companions had descended before her. I saw their dark backs appearing and disappearing as they galloped along the bottom; then, one by one, they scrambled out on the other side, and ran off as before, the wounded animal following with the rest.

Turning back, I saw Raymond coming on his black mule to meet me; we counted scores of carcasses lying on the plain, in the ravines, and on the sandy bed of the stream. Far away, horsemen and buffalo were still scouring along, with clouds of dust rising behind them; and over the sides of the hills long files of the frightened animals were ascending. The hunters began to return. Boys who had held horses behind the hill, made their appearance, and the work of flaying and cutting up began all over the field.

I noticed my host Kongra-Tonga beyond the stream, just alighting by the side of a cow which he had killed. Riding up to him, I found him in the act of drawing out an arrow, which, with the exception of the notch at the end, had entirely disappeared in the animal. I asked him to give it to me, and I still retain it as a proof, though by no means the most striking one that could be offered, of the force and dexterity with which the Indians discharge their arrows.

Herd of bison on the western pla

The hides and meat were piled upon horses, and the hunters began to leave. Raymond and I set out for the village, riding straight across the intervening desert. There was no path, and no landmarks sufficient to guide us; but Raymond seemed to have an instinctive perception of the point on the horizon towards which we ought to direct our course. Antelope were bounding on all sides, and as is always the case in the presence of buffalo, they seemed to have lost their natural shyness. Bands of them would run lightly up the rocky declivities, and stand gazing down upon us from the summit. At length we could distinguish the tall white rocks and the old pine-trees that were just above the site of the encamp-

From a painting by Charles Bodmer, Library of Congress

ment. Still we could see nothing of the camp itself until, mounting a grassy hill, we saw the circle of lodges, dingy with storms and smoke, standing on the plain at our feet.

Encroaching on the Spanish

"Americans," as they called and still call themselves, though the term properly includes Canadians and Tierra del Fuegans, spread westward rapidly, although they usually found French trappers or traders and Spanish-Mexican wanderers were there ahead of them.

Philip Freneau could write little essays in the 1780s about the Noble Savage and how westward were "savage nations almost unknown and

without a name," publishing in *The Freemen's Journal* at Philadelphia. Europeans, he said, were "wholly ignorant" of the "happy scenes, the innocent people and pastoral ages . . . in another quarter of the globe, as yet unexplored and unknown." But 40 years later, the U.S. government was surveying a trail from its newest state, Missouri, to trade with the Mexican provincial capital of Sante Fe, and Zebulon Pike had reached that justly-famed little town on March 3, 1807, with his 15-soldier expedition, to be dined by the Spanish but reprimanded for invading the New Spain that would become Mexico after its own revolution against Spain. Major Pike of Pike's Peak fame, published a book about it in 1810 — and that, of course, was 270 years after Pedro de Casteneda had set down his notes as official historian to General Francisco Vásquez de Coronado's expedition in precisely this region.

Europeans weren't quite as ignorant about the "happy scenes" as Freneau, "the poet of the Revolution," thought they were. And "the innocent people and pastoral ages" didn't quite come out like that to Spanish *conquistadores,* French *voyageurs,* or the men who penetrated from the Original Colonies into a constantly-expanding landscape stretching toward the sunset. Independence, Missouri, was the take-off point for the Oregon Trail and the Sante Fe Trail; from that town, unflatteringly described by literate travellers — an amazing number of them kept journals or diaries — the information flowed that debunked romantic Philip Freneau. And from Independence the settlers flowed: to California, to Mormon country, to Oregon Territory — and to northern Mexico.

So, despite or because of official protestations against war on both sides, armed conflict between the U.S. and Mexico became official in the summer of 1846. The war was terse and conclusive, adding California and New Mexico (which included present Arizona, Nevada and Utah) to the earlier annexed Texas.

A reporter for the New Orleans *Picayune,* one Matthew C. Field, had summered in New Mexico in 1839, and went back in 1843; his weekly columns on his adventures printed in *The Picayune* were perhaps the forerunner of contemporary newspaper outdoor columns. Matt Field did not confine himself to hunting and fishing but neither do his literary descendants.

Among the Field columns was one on the grizzly bear, published in December, 1839; it may not be accurate but it's certainly exciting:

> We heard of many "hair breadth 'scapes" which will be found full of interest, if we may judge by our own excitement in hearing them. The following anecdote we had from a wild young fellow who spent five years among the mountains. He told us the story by our campfire at night, when the winds were shrieking over our heads among the cleft mountains, and darkness hung about us like a funeral pall.
>
> With a single companion he had been five days away from his party, searching for some new stream on which to trap

beaver. As the sun was sinking on the fifth day, they stopped at a spot where wild berries were growing and a little mountain stream was trickling over the rocks. They unsaddled their horses and placed their rifles leaning against a tree. Our hero turned toward the bushes to pick some berries; being well pleased with their flavor and somewhat hungry, he did not at first notice a rustling among the bushes. When he did, however, he sprung for his rifle and had scarcely turned again before an enormous grizzly broke through the bushes and dashed directly at him.

Man and beast alone

His own rifle was a single trigger, that of his companion a double, and in his confusion he had seized it instead of his own, so that when he attempted to fire, the trigger not being properly set, his effort was useless. A deadly faintness thrilled

George Catlin's Indians and Grizzlies —Courtesy Royal Ontario Museum, Toronto

him, and an instant and terrible death stared him in the face. The furious animal was crouched to spring; his companion was too far to render any assistance, and bewildered with terror, destruction seemed inevitable.

The animal sprung and despair proved the poor trapper's salvation, for with the grizzly's movement his strength returned, the strength of desperation wrought by the last extremity of peril, and giving one wide swing he struck the beast upon the head with the heavy barrel while it was descending upon him. The bear was stunned; one of its forepaws fastened upon the shoulder of the trapper, and they came to the ground together.

The trapper described his sensations at this moment as having undergone the most wonderful change. All fear had vanished, and a savage delight seemed to have taken possession of his soul. He felt a strength equal to that of the enormous brute with which he was struggling; and as the grizzly bear opened its huge jaws to fasten its tusks upon him, uttering most appalling growls, and while he was inhaling its sickening breath, he plunged the barrel of the rifle down its throat, and springing to his feet, endeavored to force the gun completely into the animal's stomach.

His arm had been dreadfully lacerated, and his deerskin coat torn from his body by the sharp fangs of the beast, which now rose to its feet, and gripping the rifle barrel in its teeth, endeavored to wring it from the trapper's grasp. The bear, stunned and hurt, was now in a high rage. The trapper clung to his rifle and, by a furious effort of the enraged beast, he was lifted from his feet and dashed to the ground at a distance of some four yards. The fall bereft him of power to move, and here his fate had been sealed forever but for his companion who, the instant he saw the separation, discharged the other rifle and broke one of the bear's shoulder bones. The shot would have been more effectual but, he having the wrong rifle and not being aware of the mistake, had fired when he thought he was setting the hair trigger.

The bear fell, still holding the rifle fast in its teeth, close to where the first trapper was lying, who had barely strength to seize the butt end of the rifle, set the trigger, and fire down the animal's throat.

The grizzly was then soon despatched, and the unfortunate rifle is now to be seen in the museum at Chihuahua, with the heavy barrel bent and the marks of the bear's teeth plainly visible.

Matt Field also wrote of buffalo, prairie dog towns, the Bowie brothers, Comanches, how to field dress game, and señoritas. Other

—Ned Smith

(On opposite page, top)
George Catlin's party in canoe confronted by bears
—Courtesy National Collection of Fine Arts, Smithsonian Institution

(Bottom)
Hunting the grizzly bear
—From a watercolor by A. J. Miller, Courtesy The Public Archives of Canada

59

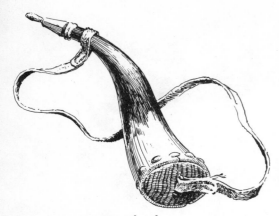

Powder horn
—Ned Smith

newspapers pirated his material, often reprinting it without credits or by-line. He helped popularize New Mexico and the war sentiment, quite unconsciously, probably, since he rarely commented upon international affairs.

To the enrichment of historic and conservation lore, the Anglos (and the Spanish) liked to set down their adventures, and while few could write even tolerable phrases, some of them commented upon their travel in surprisingly—or suspicously—good grammar. A cynic might conclude there were ghost writers even before the Civil War. Consider the *Narrative of the Adventures of Zenas Leonard,* published in 1839.

Zenas was born in Pennsylvania, drifted in his youth to St. Louis, went out to the Rockies as a trapper in 1831, went overland to California in 1833 and got back to St. Louis in the summer of 1835 with the same Captain Bonneville whom Washington Irving wrote about (and for). Then he went home to Clearfield in Penn's State, told some "tall tales" and headed west again as far as Fort Osage on the Missouri. Somehow his narratives got published in newspapers back in Pennsylvania and his book appeared in 1839, edited by a D. W. Moore who was also his publisher. It bears references to "Jack Tars" and phrases that would have fit Harvard textbooks of the period: the work just doesn't sound like "Danl. Boon kilt a bar." But it's interesting reading, if not quite up to Irving or Parkman, or as well grounded on history, geography and humanity as Josiah Gregg.

And by the 1840s and '50s, men were applying the biological sciences to wildlife. Alexander Wilson had published his *American Ornithology* in 1840; Spencer Baird's great studies *The Birds of North America* and *The Mammals of North America* came twenty years later. These were the work of naturalists, of course, rather than writers *per se.* And Newspaperman Charles Lanman was going into wilderness lakes of Michigan to fish avidly and write poetically of nature by 1846.

Lanman flatly contradicted St. John de Crèvecoeur when he wrote: "There is many a stout heart and noble soul whose dwelling place has been for many years on the border of these lakes. I have slept beneath their roofs, and partaken of their johnny-cake and fat quails. I love these men as brothers and shall always frown upon that dandy who sets down aught against them in malice or ignorance."

But a nation that had been created by a revolution and swaddled in a constitution was now moving into a rebellion that would be a War of the Brothers. The guns would fire, but at fellow-countrymen, not game. The writers would report of battles and unhappy things, not of prairies or mountains or hooved herds. And only after the Civil War would men again look upon an outdoor life with pleasure.

Hawken rifle
—Ned Smith

The Grand Tetons —Photograph by Ansel Adams

Frederic Remington's A Hard Trail
—From *Ranch Life and the Hunting Trail* by Theodore Roosevelt

FROM ABE'S DEATH TO TEDDY'S PEAK 2

—Ned Smith

When the Civil War ended, and Lincoln lay in his cool tomb, the difficulties of reconstruction and reconciliation were complicated by political and economic greed; which meant a great deal of corruption. For now the nation could turn to exploiting the Wild West that had been the province of fur trappers, great explorers, gold seekers and adventurers. Trade, expansion and agriculture became the theme, as Walt Whitman wrote:

"Our work at present is to lay the foundations of a great nation in products, in agriculture, in commerce . . . and in all that relates to the comforts of vast masses of men and families."

The wild animals of the plains tended to become a nuisance, given that pattern of the mass mood, just as deer, bears and alligators had been to the earlier settlers in the East. Socially, as Henry Steele Commager wrote a century later, the war's aftermath "brought into prominence a class of men who were eager for money and power, coarse in their tastes and unscrupulous in their acts. . . . A vulgar, brassy, greedy element was more conspicious than ever before." Basically the exploitation of natural resources was speeded up; in the public thinking it became almost patriotic to loot the land of trees, wildlife and every other object that could be turned into cash.

Given such a trend in popular thought, outdoor writing of the philosophical quality displayed by Bartram. Schoolcraft, Irving and Parkman mostly disappeared from public print. Mining, lumbering and land

A lumber sled —Drawing by Sol Eytinge
from *Deer Hunting on the Au Sable* by W. Mackay Laffan, *The Century Magazine*

speculation provided quick wealth and only a few bothered to look at future costs; isolated were the cries against extermination of the buffalo that were replaced by longhorn cattle, or the destruction of climax forests. A strange form of "sports" hunting brought a brief flare of publicity, though few took part in it. The goal of the game was numbers: how many animals could be killed in a single day, not to sell but just to pile up figures. Someone usually made profit out of it somehow, but the Plains Indians began to starve as bison were shot to rot. And everyone knows what happened to passenger pigeons.

Some of the disapproval of all this was voiced after the fact. Various Indian chiefs were reputed to have offered great oratory about the sadness of their lot but most of these interpretations became known only later. One of the most eloquent was said to have been uttered by Black Elk about 1880; the Grand Old Man of Midwestern Poetry, John G. Neihardt, said Black Elk uttered it thus:

"Once we were happy"

I learned what the fighting was about that winter. Up on the Madison Fork the Wasichu [white man] had found much of the yellow metal that makes them crazy, and they wanted to have a road up through our country to the place where the yellow metal was; but my people did not want the road. It would scare the bison and make them go away, and also it would let the other Wasichu come in like a river. They told us they only wanted to use a little land, as much as a wagon could take between its wheels; but our people knew better. When you look about you now, you can see what it was they wanted.

Once we were happy in our own country and we were seldom hungry, for the two-leggeds and the four-leggeds lived

Autumn Morning on Raquette Lake

Snowed Up— Ruffed Grouse in Winter

An Anxious Moment, Suspense: A Study from Nature

—From a painting by A. F. Tait, 1862/courtesy Adirondack Museum

Going Out: Deer Hunting in the Adirondacks

—FROM A PAINTING BY A. F. TAIT, 1872/COURTESY ADIRONDACK MUSEUM

Still Hunting on First Snow: A Second Shot

together like relatives, and there was plenty for them and for us. But the white man came, and they have made little islands for us and other little islands for the four-leggeds, and always these islands are becoming smaller, for around them surges the gnawing flood of the Wasichu; and it is dirty with lies and greed . . .

It was the summer of my twentieth year that I performed the ceremony of the elk. That fall, they say, the last of the bison herds were slaughtered by the Wasichus. I can remember when the bison were so many that they could not be counted, but more and more came to kill them until there were only heaps of bones scattered where they used to be. The Wasichus did not kill them to eat; they killed them for the metal that makes them crazy, and they took only the hides to sell. Sometimes they did not even take the hides, only the tongues; and I have heard that fire-boats came down the Missouri River loaded with dried bison tongues. Sometimes they did not even take the tongues; they just killed and killed because they liked to do that. When we hunted bison we killed only what we needed.

And when there was nothing left but heaps of bones, the Wasichus came and gathered up even the bones and sold them.

Well, it was all true. And yet there were "Wasichu," too, who saw where it all led.

Stacks of buffalo hides in Dodge City, Kansas, await shipment east on the Santa Fe Railroad during the peak of the buffalo slaughter in 1874.   —Courtesy Kansas State Historical Society

As early as 1868, a magazine called *Forest and Stream* was being published by Charles Hallock in New York. It was a well-rounded outdoor publication commenting upon ornithology, conservation, wildlife stocking, gardening and, of course, hunting and fishing. Its assistant editor in 1876 and editor-publisher two years later was George Bird Grinnell.

An early front cover of Forest and Stream *magazine*

The publication carried articles by such men as "Frank Forester," an Englishman whose real name was Henry W. Herbert, who came to the United States in 1849, and wrote prolifically about fish and fishing, and about the need for game laws. The magazine could even devote two full columns of a November 1875 issue to a critique of those fish paintings "by Gordon Trumbull Esq. of Hartford, Conn." that were being shown at Snedecor's Art Gallery in New York. *Forest and Stream* was being read by a teen-aged boy named Theodore Roosevelt; his thinking and later actions were strongly influenced by it.

The magazine gave a great deal of space to stocking fishes; it carried the results of creel censusing of salmon in Canada's Godbout River a century ago. And in its pages, someone who signed himself "Buffalo Bill" reported on a bison hunt in an article datelined November 30, 1875, at Gainesville, Texas. The author almost certainly wasn't legendary William Cody, since he admitted being afraid of Indians, was obviously literate, and had a sense of the ridiculous. Many of *Forest and Stream's* writers liked to use pseudonyms. Apart from stylistic touches, this Bill is in the direct line of descent of modern outdoor writers. Who was he? Who knows? Here, somewhat shortened, is what he wrote 100 years ago:

The rise
—From a painting by Walter M. Brackett from *Salmon Fishing* by A. G. Wilkinson, *The Century Magazine*

Four men, three blankets

On the 4th inst. your correspondent and one other mounted on mustangs and two more in a wagon took our departure for the hunting grounds—object fun and meat. Our second camp was at Squire Nichols' place, half a mile south of Cambridge. The Squire

"Lives all alone
In a little brown house he calls his own,"

and has nothing to keep him company except a half-dozen cats—enough to start a first-rate sausage factory. Through his courtesy we made a bed on his floor—mother earth's cold bosom. Blankets being scarce we tried sleeping four in a bed—but we didn't sleep. Morning found three of us the happy possessors of one blanket apiece, the fourth had been frozen out and was sitting by a fire nodding to the tune of "Hard Times."

At Henrietta we got another Nimrod whom we called our "Man Friday," making us five. The first was 50-year-old Uncle Joe; next was his son, 25; then a fat genius that played the part of Murphy's boarder, that is, never missed a meal or paid a cent and was good for nothing; then ye reporter, who of course was all right; and our man Friday, a Frenchy-looking fellow but a good man in camp. Our animals corresponded with the men—some good, some indifferent.

Wild turkey
—Ned Smith

Borrowing the Squire's horse and gun we proceeded westward. At Little Wichita river we killed a wild turkey and said "farewell to bacon." But we longed for the bacon we left behind before we got any more turkey. Recent prairie fires had devastated the country, all game was run out of that section. . . .

Frederic Remington's Buffalo Hunt —Courtesy Buffalo Bill Historical Center, Cody, Wyoming

We made next camp at a lake in the burnt region, making supper on corn dodgers and realizing that it was a poor hunter who could not kill his own meat. Then, sitting around the fire telling tales of blood and thunder, we were roused by clattering hoofs across the gully. Indians! Every man was at the wagon, gun in hand, but the noise ceased. All was quiet for several minutes while we watched our camp mule, Old Pete, working his ears like a jib sail on a nervous day. Soon we heard splashing in the lake, and started single file down the glen, this mystery to explore. Just as we thought to perform deeds of valor that would immortalize us in history and be handed down by the red man to ages yet unborn, we heard lowing cattle and by the light of a rising moon saw the brutes. We went back to camp, to dream of stampeding cattle and Indians.

We took dinner next day at a pond of red water and then drove to Harold's Ranche, a great stock raiser, on north fork of Little Wichita, where we camped and spent the evening shooting at turkeys on the roost. We scared them a good deal but took breakfast again without meat.

Early next morning, near deserted Wagefathe City, two of us came upon a large bull buffalo feeding. Crawling a half mile we found ourselves near enough to shoot. We shot. Our game looked up coolly, trotted off about 300 yards and stopped to gaze at us. I gave him a shot in the flank, when he galloped off lively over the hills. My companion went back for his horse, giving him a chase. I left him to enjoy his fun as he might and took over to a bunch of four or five that I saw feeding by themselves. I got within 100 yards, rested, took a drink out of my flask of nerve quietener, rested my gun on a large rock and fired—with the same success.

The first kill

Then my companion came up to say he had killed the first buffalo. We told our companions to go ahead to the first camp ground they could find and we would go out for more buffalo. We found plenty. We walked about ten miles and shot at several, but the monsters would go off with the bullet. We got back to camp hungry as bears and savage as Kiowas to another lunch of vegetable diet. Then we two Nimrods again went out for camp meat. My companion, whom I called Red Fox because he shot at a snag, mistaking it for a fox, rode a horse and I a mule. Red Fox cut out a fine bull and we chased him about two miles. I gave him a shot with my Burnside and he fell over dead.

After cutting out a good steak we sought the camp. It was dark and, although we had seen no Indians, we knew we were at their mercy if they were in the vicinity. However we rode to camp, tired, looked at the stars, said a verse and retired to our blankets. In my dreams I was pursued on foot by a wounded bull; he was large as an elephant. Just as he seemed to be up to me I awoke to find myself performing gymnastic feats on the wagon wheel which I had clambered thinking it a cliff of rocks.

Early next morning we took the horses and crossed the creek to the dead buffalo and skinned him. Red Fox and Friday went off; the former returned shortly saying they had killed two buffalos but Friday had lost his gun and was looking for it. So we returned to camp with the robe, got the wagon and drove to one of the bulls, cut up the meat, took

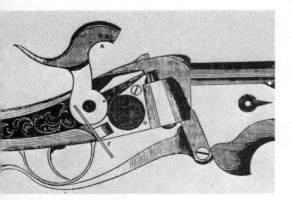

An engraving illustrating an improvement in rifles, combining Sharp's Patent Loading-Breech and Dr. Maynard's Patent Self-Priming rifles.

—From *Scientific American*, March 8, 1851

that robe and, as it was nearly night and a norther was coming, struck out for tall timber. Darkness finally stopped us, and we camped at a cave in a bluff. The night was bitter cold, but we soon had a large fire and with the two buffalo robes added to our stock of bedding, put in a very fair night, except many were the remarks of anxiety about our lost man—whether he had been thrown and lain on the prairie that long night, or whether the Indians had taken him in "out of the wet."

To our relief, when we arrived at the ford next morning, we learned he had crossed there and was safely quartered at Harold's Ranche. After searching several hours for his gun, he looked for us, not finding us he directed his attention to

the ford, failing to find it, he camped hungry. He built a large fire, lariatted his horse to a large stone, and sung himself to sleep in his saddle blanket.

At the river we salted our buffalo beef, packed away our turkeys and started for the settlements, getting home after being out from Gainesville ten days. With the exception from scarcity of water for four days, we had a good time and none regretted the trip. At the cave camp we had one pint of water between four men, and would not have had that but for one of the men who, after emptying a pint of "chill tonic" filled the bottle with water.

A buffalo hunt is a splendid place to teach a man temperance.

Charles Russell's Buffalo Hunt
—Courtesy Amon Carter Museum,
Fort Worth, Texas

71

Prairie-chicken shooting in Kansas —From a sketch by Theodore R. Davis, Library of Congress

Cross-cut saw
—Ned Smith

War against nature

But an earlier writer, with more wisdom and less humor, had bridged the chasm between post- and antebellum America with the 1864 publication of a book called *Man and Nature*. In it, author George Perkins Marsh prophesied doom if the human species continued "to wage that war against the order of nature which seems, hitherto, an almost inseparable condition precedent of high social culture, and of great progress in fine and mechanical art."

Marsh had studied the effects of land stripping in the Mediterranean basin and in Vermont, where he had been dealing in lumber. As early as 1847, he was disturbed by what was happening to New England forests and uplands; he opposed stream damming and urban pollution of rivers by 1860, bringing to his lectures against these evils a background of broad knowledge. Like Thomas Jefferson he was broadly educated in history, languages, architecture, philosophy and earth sciences. But his primary love was open spaces: streams, trees, wildlife and wild plants. He believed that humans "would find it hard to make out as good a claim to personality as a respectable oak can establish."

It would be absurd to claim that *Man and Nature* shaped much immediate thinking in the United States, except for a few naturalists and thoughtful social observers, during this period of exploitation. For George Perkins Marsh was a century ahead of public alarm about the face of our American earth. Now, of course, many a typewriter is turning out words of concern that echo his thoughts; perhaps 10 percent of us have caught up with his ideas since his death in 1882. But as Marsh wrote: "It is hard to get the floor in the world's great debating society." He had doubts about "teeming wildlife," too.

This extract from his major book is a combination of quotes from three divisions—on quadrupeds, birds, and fishes—of his broad chapter titled "Transfer, Modification, Extirpation":

> Man has too long forgotten that the earth was given to him for usufruct alone, not for consumption, still less for profligate waste. Nature has provided against the absolute destruction of her elementary matter, the raw material of her works;
>
> . . . but she has left it within the power of man irreparably to derange the combinations of inorganic matter and of organic life.
>
> There are, indeed, brute destroyers, beasts and birds and insects of prey—all animal life feeds upon and destroys other life—but this destruction is balanced by compensation. Man pursues his victims with reckless destructiveness and, while the sacrifice of life by the lower animals is limited by the cravings of appetite, he unsparingly persecutes, even to extirpation, thousands of organic forms which he cannot consume.

Passenger Pigeon
—Ned Smith

Coyote hides from an Idaho hunt —Library, State Historical Society of Colorado

73

Shooting wild pigeons in Iowa —Library of Congress

Although man never fails greatly to diminish, and is perhaps destined to exterminate, such of the larger wild quadrupeds as he cannot profitably domesticate, yet their numbers often fluctuate, and even after they seem almost extinct they sometimes suddenly increase without any intentional steps to promote such a result on his part. During the wars which followed the French Revolution, the wolf multiplied in many parts of Europe, partly because hunters were withdrawn from the woods to chase a nobler game, partly because the bodies of slain men and horses supplied this voracious quadruped with more abundant food.

So long as the fur of the beaver was extensively employed as a material for fine hats, it bore a very high price, and the chase of this quadruped was so keen that naturalists feared its speedy extinction. When a Parisian manufacturer invented the silk hat which came into almost universal use, the demand for beavers fell off, and this animal whose habits are an important agency in the formation of bogs and other modifications of forest nature, immediately began to increase. . . . Thus the convenience of Parisian fashion has unconsciously exercised an influence which may sensibly affect the physical geography of a distant continent.

—Ned Smith

"Some animals have disappeared"

But since the invention of gunpowder, some animals have completely disappeared from many European and Asiatic countries where they were formerly numerous.

The only North American quadruped sufficiently gregarious in habits, or sufficiently multiplied in numbers, to form really large herds is the bison or, as he is commonly called, the buffalo; and this animal is confined to the prairie region of the Mississippi basin and Northern Mexico. Engineers sent out to survey railroad routes to the Pacific estimated the number of a single herd on the great plains near the Upper Missouri at not less than 200,000; and yet the range occupied by this animal is now very much smaller in area than it was when the whites first established themselves on the prairies. But the buffalo is a migratory animal and at the season of his annual journeys, the whole stock of a vast extent of pasture ground is collected into a single army, which is seen at or very near any one point only for a few days during the entire season. Hence there is risk of great error in estimating the numbers of the bison in a given district from the magnitude of the herds seen at or about the same time at a single point; upon the whole, it is neither proved nor probable that the bison was ever as numerous in North America as the domestic bovine species is at present.

The elk, moose, musk ox, caribou and smaller quadrupeds popularly embraced under the general name of deer, though sufficient for the wants of a sparce savage population, were never numerically very abundant, and the carnivora which fed upon them were still less so. The Rocky Mountain sheep

A morning's work—duck hunter in Lake County, California
—Copyright 1906 by H. C. White Co., Library of Congress

Bull moose
—Ned Smith

and goat must always have been very rare. It is evident that the wild quadrupeds, even when most numerous, were few compared with their domestic successors, that they required a much less supply of vegetable food, and were far less important as geographical elements than the millions of hoofed and horned cattle now fed by civilized man on this continent.

Tame fowls play a less conspicious part in rural life than quadrupeds. The domestic turkey is probably more numerous than the wild bird of the same species ever was, and the grouse cannot have counted as many as we now number of the common hen. The dove, however, must fall short of the wild pigeon in multitude, and it is hardly probable that the flock of domestic geese and ducks are as numerous as once were those of their wild congeners. The pigeon seems to have multiplied immensely for some years after the first clearings in the woods, because the settlers warred unsparingly upon the hawk, while the crops of grain and other vegetable growths increased the supply of food. The pigeon is not described by the earliest white inhabitants as filling the air with such clouds of winged life as to astonish Audubon. At pre-

A herd of bighorn sheep —George Krakowka, U.S. Forest Service

sent, the net and gun have so reduced its abundance, that its appearance in large numbers is recorded only at long intervals, and it is never seen in the great flocks remembered by many still living observers as formerly very common.

Wild birds form a conspicuous and interesting feature of the natural landscape, and they are important elements whether we consider their immediate or incidental influence. Birds affect vegetation directly by sowing seeds and by consuming; they affect it indirectly by destroying insects injurious or, in some cases, beneficial to plant life. Hence, when we kill a seed-sowing bird, we check the dissemination of a plant; when we kill a bird which digests the seed it swallows, we promote the increase of a vegetable.

The proportional numbers of birds, their migratory habits and the ease with which they may escape most dangers, would seem to secure them from extirpation. But experience shows that when not protected by law or by popular favor, they yield rapidly to hostile influences of civilization, and though the first operations of the settler are favorable to the increase of many species, the great extension of rural and mechanical industry is destructive even to tribes not directly warred upon by man.

"Once numerous species . . ."

Nature sets bounds to the disproportionate increase of birds; man both preys upon them and wantonly destroys them. The delicious flavor of game birds, and the skill implied in the arts of the sportsman who devotes himself to fowling, makes them favorite objects of the chase, while the beauty of their plumage as a military and feminine decoration, threatens to sacrifice the last survivors of once numerous species, notably herons and egrets, for hat plumes. . . .

It does not seem probable that man will succeed in totally extirpating salt-water fish, but he has already exterminated at least one marine warm-blooded animal — Steller's sea cow — and the walrus, sea lion and other large amphibia, as well as the fishing quadrupeds, are in imminent danger of extinction.

Man has promoted multiplication of fish by making war on their brute enemies, but he has by no means compensated his own great destructiveness. The birds and beasts of prey hunt only as long as they feel the stimulus of hunger. Man angles today that he may dine tomorrow; the arrangement of his fisheries is so organized as to involve the destruction of many more fish than are secured for use.

Fish are more affected than quadrupeds by slight differences in their breeding places and feeding grounds. Every

Prairie chickens—hen with cock bird displaying
—Ned Smith

A morning catch of yellowt[a]

river, every brook stamps a special character upon its salmon, its shad, its trout which is at once recognized by those who deal in them. No skill can give the fish fattened by food prepared by man the flavor of those which are nourished at the table of nature. The superior sapidity of American trout to the European species is probably due less to specific difference than to the fact that wild nature here is not yet tamed down to the character it has assumed in the Old [World].

Almost all the processes of agriculture, and of mechanical and chemical industry, are fatally destructive to aquatic animals within reach of their influence. When, as consequence of clearing the woods, the changes produced in beds and currents of rivers are in progress, the spawning grounds of fish are exposed to mechanical disturbances, the temperature of

Catalina Island —Library of Congress

water is higher in summer, colder in winter, than when shaded and protected by wood, the smaller organisms disappear or are reduced in numbers, and new enemies are added to the foes that preyed upon them; the increased turbidness of the annual inundations chokes the fish, and the quickened velocity of its current sweeps them into larger rivers or the sea before they are yet strong enough to support a change.

Industrial operations are not less destructive to fish which live or spawn in fresh water. Milldams impede their migrations, if not absolutely prevent them; the sawdust from lumber mills clogs their gills, and the thousand deleterious mineral substances discharged into rivers from metallurgical, chemical and manufacturing establishments, poison them by shoals.

Male sockeye salmon
—Ned Smith

79

The poets speak

And the young "ecologists," middle aged "environmentalists" and old "conservationists" believe no one ever thought of it before they did!

We were all anticipated. The poets of the period had their say, too; and while it may be that few listen to the poets, they forecast what the next generation and the next century will be saying. Consider well this excerpt from "Earth Song," a portion of Ralph Waldo Emerson's *Hamatreya:*

An early view of the Fox River in Illinois about 1832
—From a painting by Charles Bodmer, Library of Congress

"Mine and yours;
Mine, not yours.
Earth endures;
Stars abide—
Shine down in the old sea . . .

The lawyer's deed
Ran sure,
In tail,
To them, and to their heirs
Who shall succeed,
Without fail,
Forevermore.

Here is the land
Shaggy with wood,
With its old valley,
Mound and flood.
But the heritors? . . .

They called me theirs,
Who so controlled me;
Yet every one
Wished to stay, and is gone,
How am I theirs
If they cannot hold me,
But I hold them?"

Walt Whitman was capturing some American yearnings a century ago, too, and these five lines from *Song of Myself* are the modern dream (and rare reality) of gunners in this last quarter of the twentieth century:

Alone far in the wilds and mountains I hunt,
Wandering amazed at my own lightness and glee,
In the late afternoon choosing a safe spot to pass the night,
Kindling a fire and broiling the fresh-killed game,
Falling asleep on gathered leaves with my dog and gun
by my side.

80

Henry Wadsworth Longfellow said his songs of Hiawatha were found "In the birds' nests of the forest/ In the lodges of the beaver/ In the hoofprints of the bison/ In the eyrie of the eagle." For even if — or perhaps because — the plow was breaking prairie sod, the ax and saw were felling the forest, and the lands that belonged to everyone were the prey of anyone, the writers who would be remembered a hundred years later were voicing a cry for preservation of open spaces and wild things. Emerson, Whitman and Longfellow were outdoor writers, too.

They wrote with a cadenced skill that Grinnell could not match, but they probably had less effect on current thinking about conservation, wildlife and wilderness than he did as publisher and editor of *Forest and Stream* magazine in 1868 and, later, owner of Forest and Stream Publishing Co., the largest publisher and distributor of outdoor books in nineteenth century America. Grinnell, like so many writers before him, went west in 1870 after his graduation from Yale to collect vertebrate fossils. The Pawnee scouts of this expedition got him involved with Indians and animals of mountain and prairie. Five years later he visited Yellowstone; he explored the Black Hills with Maj. Gen. George Custer, just a year before Custer paid the ultimate price for overestimating his tactical abilities.

Grinnell wrote 21 books on Indians, hunting, bison and conservation, but his greatest contribution was to publish the volumes that would never have seen print without him, and then to distribute these books and his magazine so they would stimulate open minds. Grinnell was also a catalyst around which gathered those of like persuasion; he helped found the Boone and Crockett Club, then helped organize its thinking; he was co-editor (with T. R.) of the club's *American Big-Game Hunting* book in 1893, with its emphasis on sportsmanship and wildlife conservation.

The Cheyennes were probably his favorite tribe among the Plains Indians, and this excerpt from *When Buffalo Ran* is about Wikis, who was probably a Northern Cheyenne lad, and how his uncle taught him to hunt. The short volume tells of Wikis growing up when "the buffalo, the deer, the wolves, and the smaller animals and birds, were the companions with which he lived and from whom he learned life's lessons." Anyone who has taught a youngster the outdoor skills will be touched by Wikis's account.

Beaver lodge
—Ned Smith

Sandhill cranes over the prairies —Photograph by George H. Harrison

Grass grown yellow

I had lived twelve winters when I did something that made my relations glad; and which first caused my name to be called aloud throughout the camp. It was fall of the year, and leaves were dropping; the grass had grown yellow and now sometimes in the morning it was white with frost. Great flocks of birds were passing, flying to the south; and many stopped in the streams, resting and feeding. There were ducks, and the larger geese, and great white birds with black tips to their wings and long yellow bills; and the cranes that fly over, far up in the sky, looking like spots but whose callings are heard plainly as they pass along. Often we saw flocks of these walking on the prairie, and sometimes they all stopped feeding, stuck up their heads and then began to dance together, almost as people dance.

We boys used to creep up to the edge of the bank, or to puddles where the different birds sat, to get close enough to kill them with our arrows. Generally the birds saw us and then, even if we had the chance to shoot, we missed and had to wade out and get our arrows.

One day I had gone with my friend up the river to a place where the point of a hill ran down close to the water, and as we rounded this point we saw three cranes on the hillside. One quite near to us was still red, by which we knew it was a young one. As soon as I saw the cranes I drew my arrow to its head and shot at the young one, which flew a few yards and then came down with its wings stretched wide, for the arrow had passed through its body. Then I was glad, for this was the largest bird I had ever killed; the crane is a wise bird and people do not often kill one. I picked up the bird and put it on my back, holding the neck in one hand and letting the legs drag on the ground behind; and so we returned to camp.

When I reached the lodge, my mother called out: "What is that great bird that is coming? I am afraid of it." Then all looked at the bird and said how big it was, and that it must be shown to my uncle. They sent word to him, and when he saw what I had killed he was glad, and told me that I had done well. "There are many grown men," said he, "who have never killed a crane. I wish to have this known."

He told my mother to cook it; and he said to her: "Save me the wing bones, that I may make from them two war whistles, which my son may carry when he has grown old enough to go to war."

I had killed the crane with a pointed arrow, of which I had three, though in hunting for little birds I still used blunt ar-

A close shot —Drawing by A. B. Frost
from *Field Sports in Minnesota* by Charles A. Zimmerman, *The Century Magazine*

rows. My uncle had made me another bow, almost as large as a man's bow, and I was practicing with it always, trying to make my right arm strong, to bend it.

Next summer, when the tribe started off to look for buffalo, I spoke to my uncle alone in his lodge and said: "Father, is it not now time for me to kill buffalo? I should like to have your opinion about this." He sat smoking and then he said: "Son, it is time you should begin to hunt. I have watched you, and I have seen that you know how to use the bow. You shall come with me and we will see what you can do. You shall ride one of my horses, you shall overtake the buffalo, and we shall see whether you are strong enough to drive the arrow far into the animal."

Not long after this, buffalo were found, and my uncle told me to ride one of his horses and keep close to him. "Today we will try to catch calves, and you shall see whether you can kill one. If you shoot an arrow into the calf and blood begins to come from its mouth, it will soon die, you need not shoot at it again, but go on to another. Remember: if you are running buffalo, do not be afraid of them. Ride your horse as close as you can and then let fly the arrow with all your force. If the buffalo turns to fight, your horse will take you away; but do not be afraid; you will not kill buffalo if you are afraid to get close."

Before the surround was made, we could see the yellow calves at one side of the herd. My uncle said: "When the herd starts, try to get among those calves, and remember all that I have told you."

Buffalo plunging and butting —Engraving from a painting by George Catlin from *North American Indians Vol. I*

Grand buffalo "surround"—Engraving from a painting by George Catlin from *North American Indians Vol. I*

Charles Russell's Roping a Wolf
—Courtesy Amon Carter Museum, Fort Worth, Texas

Men on fast horses

At length we all rushed toward the buffalo. They turned to run and a great dust rose in the air. There were many men on fast horses, but my uncle's horse was faster than all; he ran through the big buffalo and was soon close to the calves. When he ran through the buffalo I was frightened, for they seemed so big and their horns rattled as they knocked together. In a short time I was running close to a calf; it ran very fast and I could not overtake it; but then it seemed to go slower. I shot an arrow and missed it, and then another and did not miss; the arrow went deep into it, just before the short ribs, and I could see blood coming from the calf's mouth; and I ran on to get another. I did kill another, and then stopped and got down. I began to butcher the last calf and my uncle rode up to me. We put the meat and skins of both calves on my horse and returned to camp.

My uncle called a number of his friends, and older people, to come that night to his lodge, to feast with him. After all had eaten, and while the pipe was being smoked, he said: "Friends, I have called you to eat with me, because this day my son has killed two calves. He has done well. His lodge will not be poor for meat nor will his wife lack skins to tan. Today my heart is glad; I have asked you to come and hear what my son has done, that you may be pleased as I am pleased."

From that time on, I went out with companions of my own age, and we tried to kill calves, but more than once I went with my uncle. The second time I rode with him he said I must try to kill big buffalo. I remembered what he had said about riding close, but I was afraid to do this and ashamed to tell him I was afraid. When the surround was made, I was riding my uncle's fast horse. My uncle rode on my right, and when we charged and got among the buffalo we passed through the bulls and drew up on the cows and younger animals whose horns were yet straight. I thought we were going to pass through and kill calves, but suddenly my uncle, pointing to a young bull, signed to me to shoot it. My uncle kept crowding his horse more and more on me, pushing me close to the bull. I was afraid of it; I thought perhaps it would turn its head and frighten my horse, and my horse could not get away, and perhaps I would be killed. I felt I was not strong enough to kill a buffalo; but all the time my uncle was signing, "Shoot, shoot."

I drew the arrow and shot into the buffalo. The point hit between the ribs and went in deep, yet not to the feathers. My uncle sheered off and I followed him; looking back I saw blood was coming from the bull's nose and mouth. In a few minutes it fell, and I went back to it. Then truly I thought that I had done something great; I had killed a big buffalo. I forgot that I had been frightened, and had wanted to get away. I forgot that, except for my uncle, I should not have made this lucky shot. I felt as if I had done something that was very smart and great.

You see, I was only a boy.

James B. Trefethen, director of publications for the Wildlife Management Institute, says in his book *Crusade for Wildlife* that Grinnell was a small man, but in 1885, while hunting in the Land of the Walled-in Lakes in northwestern Montana, he packed out—alone—a bighorn sheep from rugged mountains. It weighed nearly 100 pounds dressed, but he carried it for three miles in which he had to climb more than 1,500 vertical feet and then descend 2,000 feet. He wrote about shooting that sheep under one of his pen-names, "Yo."

Jumping over a precipice
—Drawing by John W. Bolles from
The Wild Sheep of the Sierra by John Muir,
The Century Magazine

President Chester A. Arthur and party visit Yellowstone National Park in 1883.
—U.S. Department of the Interior, National Park Service

(At left) A Rocky Mountain bighorn
—William S. Keller, U.S. Department of the Interior, National Park Service

(Below) Crossing a canyon stream
—Drawing by George Inness, Jr., from *The Wild Sheep of the Sierra* by John Muir, The Century Magazine

88

Man and mountain sheep

I had stopped to listen and look, when suddenly saw 300 yards ahead, two tiny points rise over the ridge, and then a sheep's head. It stopped as soon as it had come in sight and we looked at each other. It tried to run by me along the upper side. Just as it started, another snow squall began, and it was difficult to follow the animal's course.

Twice it stopped to look, once at 200 yards, and once at about 100 yards, and on each occasion I tried to shoot, but the snow was flying so that I could not see the foresight of my rifle. It ran swiftly by me and stopped again; this time at about 150 yards; but directly behind a pile of rocks, over which I could just see the line of his back and between two of which its head and neck were visible. I knew it was now or never, so I drew a fine bead on the neck just below the head, and the old gun spoke out. In that wind there was no hanging of the smoke and I saw the animal give a wild bound and start at headlong speed down the mountain.

But it was hit and as I went on down the mountain side, the blood on the trail became more abundant. Further on there was a patch of low willows. Looking beyond them and down over a ledge 12 or 15 feet high I saw the game stretched on its side. It was quite dead.

The mountain on which Grinnell killed his bighorn with that one blast is still called Singleshot from his exploit. Up to that time, it had only whatever name the Blackfeet Indians and other tribes may have used. A man can have no better monument than a snowcapped mountain, and most of us have less flattering nicknames than "Singleshot."

One of Grinnell's ace reporters in outdoor affairs was Emerson Hough, later to be a famous name in fiction. The editor sent Hough out to spend the winter of 1894 in Yellowstone Park, where he worked with Jay Haynes, a wildlife photographer, to document this first National Park that was then being looted by poachers and eyed by railroad magnates and miners. The Haynes-Hough reports in words and pictures created public demands for better game law enforcement and park patrol, but nothing much happened in Congress apart from oratory.

A year or so after, Hough published *The Story of The Cowboy* and became editor of the Out-of-Doors Department of the *Saturday Evening Post*. His novels came later. *The Covered Wagon* was his most popular. Already the cowboy was passing away, but Hough, born in Iowa and an early-life wanderer in New Mexico, memorialized the breed from personal knowledge. He knew, for instance, a rancher named Pat Garrett who was elected sheriff in 1880 on his promise to kill Billy the Kid. And as every Wild West afficionado knows, Pat did just that.

The most eloquent chapter of *Cowboy* is the first one, in which Hough outlines the history of cattle drives in "The Long Trail," a passage most fitting for a study of two centuries of outdoor writing. It is notable that "E. Hough" gave special thanks in his introduction to Grinnell who inspired countless outdoor writers.

The long trail

The braiding of a hundred minor pathways, the Long Trail lay like a vast rope connecting the cattle country of the South with that of the North. It ran for more than 2,000 miles along the eastern edge of the Rocky Mountains, sometimes close in at their feet, again hundreds of miles away across hard table-lands or well-flowered prairies. It traversed the land of Texas, curled over the Indian Nations, over Kansas, Colorado, Nebraska, Wyoming and Montana, and bent as far west as Utah and Nevada, as far east as Missouri, Iowa, even Illinois; and as far north as the British possessions. . . . Its hoof marks are beyond the Musselshell, over the Bad Lands and the coulees and the prairies; and far up into the land of the long cold, you may see the shadow of that unparalleled pathway, the Long Trail of the cattle range.

The Long Trail was constructed in a century and a day. Over the Red River of the South there appeared, almost without warning, processions of strange horned kine, owned by kings who paid no tribute and guarded by men who never knew a master. Whither these were bound, what had conjured them forth, whence they came, were questions in the minds of the North and East to whom the phenomenon appeared as the product of a day. The Long Trail was begun more than a century before that day, and came forward along the appointed ways of time.

Señor José Montero, let us say, lived long ago down in the sunny land of Mexico. Mountains rose up blue beyond the *hacienda* and before it the valley lay wide. Life was calm for the *haciendado* and the peons who made a servile army about him. There was a little grain, a few fruits, and there were herds of cattle. Yes, there were the cattle, and there they had been longer than Montero or his father could remember. It might be that they had always been there, though there was talk of one Cortez. *Quien sabe?* In the splendid savagery of that land and time it made small difference when or whence they came. There they were, these cattle, lean of flank, broad of horn, muscular, active, fierce, wild animals that knew no care save the hand of force. They produced food, they produced hide and leather.

The sons of José Montero moved north in the course of years, edged into Indian country above the Rio Grande. The horses and cattle came slowly north with their owners. Thus

The kill

Skinning the beef

A cowpoke riding a cow

Dragging the carcass

Dressing it out

Cutting the herd

in the vague Southwest, in some distant portion of old, mysterious Mexico, there fell into line the hoof prints which made the first, faint beginnings of the Long Trail, the path of a half-nomadic movement along the line of least resistance.

Montero descendants spread over both sides of the Rio Grande, and their herds grew. But one day there appeared in that country men of fierce-bearded faces, many of blue eyes, and all of courage. There was a war of pillage and assassination, of theft and ambush. The strangers from the North increased, became more formidable. They even crossed the Rio Grande and drove away herds to their *ranchos,* these being little less than fortresses. In turn the sons of Montero made sallies, killed men and captured women, drove away herds. The Long Trail began to deepen and extend.

The warlike days passed, and there ensued a more pastoral time. The fierce strangers, reticent in regard to the methods by which they had obtained what they liked, now held that which they chose to call their own. It was a feudalism of the range, a barony rude enough but glorious, albeit it began like all feudalism in large-handed theft and generous murder. The flocks of these strong men multiplied amazingly. They were hardly looked upon as wealth. The people could not eat a tithe of the beef, they could not use a hundredth of the leather. Over ownerless grasslands, by the waters of mountains, by the slow streams of plains or the long, dark lagoons of the coast, the herds of tens grew into droves of hundreds and thousands and hundreds of thousands.

The trail moves north

At some time and under some condition of observation, it had been discovered that the short gray grass of the northern plains of Texas, which the buffalo loved so well, would rear cattle to a greater size than those of the coast range. It was the simplest thing in the world to gain this increase by driving cattle from the lower to the upper range. This was really the dawning of the American cattle industry. The Long Trail thus received an unmistakable extension, always to the north, and along the line of the intermingling of products of the Spanish and Anglo-Saxon civilizations.

It seemed clear that a great population in the North needed the cheap beef of Texas; and the main question was one of transportation. The Civil War stopped almost all plans to market range cattle, and the close of that war found the vast grazing lands of Texas covered with millions of cattle which had no actual value; neither they nor their increase could be converted into anything but more cattle.

An Indian Trapper
—From a painting by Frederic Remington,
Courtesy Amon Carter Museum, Fort Worth, Texas

Meantime, Indians were being driven from the plains. Railroads were pushing out into a new empire, carrying the market with them, though still some hundreds of miles north of the great herd. The Long Trail tapped no more at Missouri and Arkansas, but leaped north again across the Red River to the railroads, along well-defined channels deepened in 1866 alone by hoofs of more than a quarter of a million cattle. In 1870, over 600,000 cattle crossed Red River. Abilene, Wichita, Great Bend, Dodge, flared into a swift and sometimes evil blossoming. The coming of the markets did not make more fortunes than it lost for Southern cattle owners but a new industry was swiftly established. The men of the North came to hear of the Long Trail, though it had begun long ago.

It pushed rapidly further north, where there remained "free grass" and a new market on territorial ranges. The Government was now feeding thousands of its new red wards and these Indians needed beeves for rations. Between Government demand and that of territorial stock ranges, there was occupation for the men who made the saddle their

Life in the woods —Library of Congress

home. Cheyenne and Laramie became common words now, and drovers spoke as wisely of the dangers of the Platte as before they had mentioned those of the Arkansas.

Now the Long Trail was done. The cattle industry had spread over the entire West. Many men think of that industry as belonging only to the Southwest and consider that it was transferred to the North. Really it was extended, and the trail of the old drive marks the line of that extension. Today the Long Trail is replaced by other trails, and it remains for the most part historical only. When the last steer of the first herd was driven into the corral at the Ultima Thule of the range, it was the pony of the American cowboy which squatted and wheeled under the spur and burst down the straggling street of the little frontier town. Before that time and since that time, it has been the same pony, the same man, who have travelled the range, guarding and guiding the wild herds, from the romantic to the commonplace days of the West.

Rods, baits, and fish

So wrote Emerson Hough, outdoor writer, friend of reformers in the era of the naturalists, and a favorite author of a man moving by uncertain ways toward the presidency of the United States. But while Hough was observing longhorns and thinking the long, long thoughts of youth, *The Century Magazine* was carrying philosophical essays on fishing that owed much to English tradition.

James Henshall, Francis Endicott, Charles Ward, Alfred M. Mayer and other illustrious names in the piscatorial fraternity were writing as educated gentlemen who spent rainy evenings reading the discourses of Izaak Walton. They set down not only their rods and baits and weather; they described landscapes, geography and feeding habits. Their essays were leisured, literary and lengthy; they believed the angler gained much more than fish. They did not hesitate to write in rhymed cadences; for example, Maurice Thompson's "In the Haunts of Bream and Bass."

DREAMS come true and everything
Is fresh and lusty in the spring.

In groves, that smell like ambergris,
Wind-songs, bird-songs never cease.

Go with me down by the stream,
Haunt of bass and purple bream;

Feel the pleasure, keen and sweet,
When the cool waves lap your feet;

Catch the breath of moss and mold,
Hear the grosbeak's whistle bold;

See the heron all alone
Mid-stream on a slippery stone,

. . .

Bubble, bubble flows the stream,
Like an old tune through a dream.

Now I cast my silken line;
See the gay lure spin and shine—

While, with delicate touch, I feel
The gentle pulses of the reel.

. . .

Patiently I draw and cast
Keenly expectant, till, at last,

Comes a flash, down in the stream,
Never made by perch or bream,

Then a mighty weight I feel,
Sings the line and whirs the reel!

. . .

I follow where my victim leads,
Through tangles of rank water-weeds,

O'er stone and root and knotty log,
And faithless bits of reedy bog.

I wonder will he ever stop?
The reel hums like a humming-top!

. . .

Bubble, bubble flows the stream,
Like an old tune through a dream!

At last he tires, I reel him in;
I see the glint of scale and fin.

I raise the rod—I shorten line
And safely land him; he is mine!

The belted halcyon laughs, the wren
Comes twittering from its bushy den,

The turtle sprawls upon the log,
I hear the booming of a frog.

. . .

Glimpses of a cloudless sky
Soothe me as I resting lie.

Bubble, bubble flows the stream,
Like low music through a dream.

Like an old tune through a dream. That was the language of people who had time and opportunity to observe the world about them, perhaps because it did not occur to them there might be no tomorrow. Incidentally, poet Maurice Thompson was also an archer who wrote on bow-shooting.

Among these sport-fishing writers of a century ago was Francis Endicott, who insisted that "to the lover of rod and reel, the striped bass or rock-fish is the most important of all our sea fish." In 1882 he wrote of "a bout with the large bass which frequent the rocky shores" of the Elizabeth Islands and Martha's Vineyard; that lengthy account has been shortened here by leaving out—reluctantly—many of the Endicott asides.

There is a mysterious influence in these regions which gathers the seafrogs and holds them around the islands, shutting them in while all about the atmosphere is clear. As we approach the land we are soon lost in its dense vapors. We steam along slowly, foghorn shrieking at intervals and every eye strained for rocks or vessels which might be in the way, until we hear a distant foghorn answering us; following it we find ourselves among a fleet of sword-fishermen anchored for the night in Cuttyhook Bay. A skiff gropes its way toward us, we gather our baggage and are landed on the shingly beach, where after a short walk we find ourselves safe under the roof of the clubhouse.

We breakfast at the usual hour and, having tested lines and seen that everything is in order, we start a brisk walk over the hills led by our "chummer" bearing a basket of lobsters and menhaden for bait. Bleak as these hills appear from the water, we come unexpectedly on some little gems of beauty. We hear the abrupt notes of the upland plover as he rises and speeds his flight to far-off hills. A little later, large flocks of golden plover will stop on their way south and make it lively for the grasshoppers, which now rise before us at every step and scatter in uncertain flight.

Arrived at a large granite bowlder which stands out from shore and is connected with it by narrow planking supported by iron rods, our chummer baits hooks with lobster-tail and we cast toward rocks where the waters are swirling. The chummer is an important man; besides keeping four or five baits peeled for use, he breaks up the bodies and claws of lobsters, chops the menhaden into small bits, and throws them upon the water with an odd wood-and-tin ladle called a "chum-spoon." Without the chum you might catch an occasional straggler but . . .

Stop! That fellow takes hold as though he meant it and is laying his course straight for Newport. The line whizzes from the reel; our thumb would be blistered were it not for the

Bluefish
—Ned Smith

Fishing in style —Library of Congress

worsted thumb-stall which protects it. The rod is bent to the curve so beautiful in the eyes of an angler, and the line is strained to the utmost tension. There! He breaks on the surface. How broad his tail as he lashes the water in impotent wrath. The worst of his run is over; reel him in carefully, keeping the killing strain on him all the time. Two or three more short dashes and then you may lead him gentle as a kitten to where Perry stands with his gaff-hook. It is a pity to strike the cruel steel into his silvery sides, but it would be dangerous to attempt to land him among the rocks in-shore.

Chumming attracts less desirable fish. Your bluefish has an insatiable appetite and keen nose for a free lunch. We say this ruefully as we reel in and put on a fresh hook to replace the one just carried away. Egad! That fellow struck like a forty-pound bass and cut the line as clean as though he had carried scissors. Phew! How cold the water is! That wave struck flat against the rock, and drenched us.

There is no royal road to heavy surf-fishing; there is a certain amount of hard work to be done and exposure to be borne. Father Neptune spatters his favors lavishly on the just and unjust; unless you believe in the theory that "salt water never hurt nobody" and can take a soaking philosophically, you had better give up all thought of being a bass-fisherman. During spring tides, when wind has lashed the sea into fury, the fisherman will see white water breaking under his feet; the tide rises higher but he gives little heed, as in such perturbed waters he expects to meet with success — perhaps catch the fish which shall make him "high-hook" of the year. An exclamation causes him to look up — an enormous roller is coming on at racehorse speed. His only recourse is to hold on tight and take his ducking; when, if he be sensible, he will make for the shore, a wetter and wiser man.

Another strike! This fellow betrays himself at the start, for we see the forked tail which denotes that pirate of the deep, blue sea — the bluefish. We bring him to gaff as soon as possible, for he is seldom alone and his companions in iniquity are apt to cut him loose by striking on any bait that may run up the line, or even at the line itself. Perry opens his paunch; in it, besides many pieces of chum, are three hooks — one of them with the bait still on and a bit of line attached, our own property which he converted to his use this morning.

New England striped bass

In early accounts of New England the striped bass is frequently mentioned. "Thomas Morton of Clifford's Inn, gent." gives a glowing description of their abundance in *New English Canaan* printed by Charles Green, 1632. He writes: "The Basse is an Excellent Fish, both fresh & salt. They are so large the head of one will give a good eater a dinner, and for daintiness of diet they excell the Marybones of beef. There are such multitudes that I have seen stopped into the river with a sand at one tide, so many as well loade a ship of one hundred tonnes."

A pretty good fish story; it reads like the prospectus of a land association — as it probably was. And the famous Captain John Smith wrote in a little book entitled "Advertisements for the Inexperienced Planters of New England, or Anywhere. London, 1631":

"The seven and thirty passengers came so ill provided they only relyed upon the poore company they found, that had lived two years by their naked industry and what the country naturally afforded. It is true, at first there hath beene taken a thousand Bayses at a draught, and more than twelve hogsheads of Herrings in a night."

The Happy Moment
—From a painting by James Goodwyn Clonney
Courtesy Museum of Fine Arts, Boston,
from the M and M Karolik Collection

98

Our ancestors must have had glorious opportunities for sport, though it may be considered doubtful whether those men whose features had grown grim facing the hard realities of their pioneer life — sickness, starvation and an ever-present foe — found time to go a-angling except as a means of warding off famine from their wives and little ones.

*　　*　　*

Suddenly our line straightens out, we strike hard to fix the hook, the reel revolves with rapidity, and the line cuts through waves like a knife, as a large bass dashes away in his first mad run, rage lending him a strength beyond his weight. The strain on the fish is graduated, but the weight of line alone which he has to draw through the water would be enough to exhaust even a fifty-pounder, and he tires sufficiently to enable us to turn his head toward land. He acts like a wayward child, making for every rock in the way, and as there are many of them, it requires a little care to guide him past the danger. Presently his struggles grow weaker, his efforts become aimless, and we lead him into the undertow until a wave rolls him up, apparently dead, on shelving sand. As he lies stranded, the hook which had worked loose in his lip springs back to our feet. Our chummer rushes forward to gaff him, but we push him aside hurriedly — no steel shall mar the round and perfect beauty of the glittering sides — and rushing down regardless of the wetting, we thrust a hand into the fish's mouth and bear him safely from returning waves; then we sit on the rock, breathless, our prize gasping at our feet, our nerves quivering, but filled with such a glow of exulting pride as no one but the successful angler ever experiences, and he only in the first flush of a hard-won victory.

*　　*　　*

As I pen these lines regarding the capture of large fish with light tackle, there comes to mind a screed written long, long ago; the quaint advice given by that sainted patroness of the angle, Dame Juliana Berners, nearly four hundred years ago. Here it is, though the hand that penned it has crumbled into dust, and the generation for whose "dysporte" it was "empryntyd" have been casting their flies from the further bank of the Styx these many years:

"And yf it fortune you to smyt a gret fish with a small harnays, thenne ye must lede hym in the water and laybor hym there tyll he be drounyd and obercome; thenne take hym as well as ye maye, and ever be waar that ye holde not over the strengthe of your lyne, and as moche as ye may lete hym not come out of your lyne's ende streyghte from you; but kepe hym ever under the rodde, and evermore holde hym

A good catch
—From *Striped Bass* by Francis Endicott,
The Century Magazine

99

The partridge hunters —Currier & Ives, Library of Congress

streyghte, so that your lyne may be susteyne and berre hys lepps and plungys wyth the helpe of your cropp and of your honde."

"Hail-shot" and game birds

Endicott clearly liked to remind himself that he came of a great tradition in the gentle art of angling, and he did not intend to let the Revolution of a century earlier sever his cultural ties. It is significant that he did not cite any early American writers, but he explained that himself; men grown grim facing pioneer realities had little time for going fishing except to ward off famine. Perhaps only civilized men can afford the luxury—or is it good manners?—of sportsmanship.

Something like this appears to have developed with small game birds, too. Quail, grouse, woodcock, snipe . . . what did they yield in food so precious as the shot and powder that was used to get them? While the "hail-shot" was invented about 1550, the shotgun was not popular in early America, perhaps because flintlock fowling pieces didn't fit well into big game hunting or Indian fighting, and ammunition was a grave problem.

100

But by 1880, Alfred Mayer could write: "Of all the game birds of America, none is more endeared to the lover of country life or better appreciated by the sportsman than little Bob White. In the North and East he is called Quail; in the South and West he is Partridge; while everywhere he is known as Bob White. Let us then call him as he calls himself."

Dr. Mayer (he was a professor in the Stevens Institute of Technology) wrote often of "Bob White" and argued that it was not truly a quail, nor a partridge, but a uniquely American species, although "our distinguished ornithologist, Dr. Coues, classes Bob White among the partridges." And he said that "Bob White schools the wing-shot as severely as the wily trout tries the angler. Like the trout, he has habits which we must be acquainted with in order to find him, and when found we ourselves may be found — wanting. Am I not a convicted boaster? Was it not only yesterday when I said to myself: 'I'm a crackshot?' For 'Deeply hast sunk the lesson thou has given/ And shall not soon depart.'"

But Frank Forrester of *Forest and Stream* magazine fame, explained best how, in Oscar Wilde's phrase, each man kills the thing he loves:

Stalking rail birds
—Drawing by Joseph Pennell from
A Day with the Rails by Alfred M. Mayer,
The Century Magazine

Unlike the young broods of the woodcock, which are mute save the twitter with which they rise, the bevies of quail appear to be attached to each other by tender affection. If dispersed by accidental causes, either in pursuit of their food or being flushed by some casual intruder, so soon as their first alarm is passed over, they begin calling each other with a small, plaintive note quite different from the amorous whistling of the male bird and from the merry, daybreak cheeping, and each one running toward the sound, repeating it at intervals, they soon collect themselves together into one happy little family.

Duck Shooting
—From a painting by William Ranney, in the collection of
the Corcoran Gallery of Art, Washington, D.C.

101

Pointers of fifty years ago
—From an old print illustrating *Some American Sporting Dogs*
by William M. Tileston, *The Century Magazine*

If, however, the ruthless sportsman has been among them with his well-trained setter and unerring gun, so that death has sorely thinned their numbers, they will protract their little call for their lost comrades even into nightfall; and in such cases—I know not if it be fancy on my part—there has often seemed to me to be an unusual degree of melancholy in their wailing whistle. Once this struck me especially.

I had found a small bevy of thirteen birds in an orchard, close to the house in which I was passing a portion of the autumn, and in a very few minutes killed twelve of them, for they lay hard in the tedded clover, and it was perfectly open shooting. The thirteenth and last bird, rising with two others which I killed right and left, flew but a short distance and dropped among some sumac in the corner of a rail fence. I could have shot him certainly enough, but some undefined feeling induced me to call my dog to heel and spare his little life; yet afterward I almost regretted what I certainly intended at the time for mercy. For day after day, so long as I remained in the country, I heard his sad call from morn to dewy eve, crying for his departed friends and full, apparently, of memory, which is too often another name for sorrow.

It is singular proof how strong is the passion for the chase and the love of pursuit implanted by nature in the heart of man, that however much, when not influenced by the direct heat of sport, we deprecate the killing of these little birds and pity the individual sufferers, the moment the dog points and the bevy springs, or the propitious morning promises good sport, all the compunction is forgotten in the eagerness and emulation which are natural to our race.

Brought to bag
—Drawing by A. W. Drake from
*Bob White, the Game Bird
of America* by Alfred M. Mayer,
The Century Magazine

Duck hunting on Chesapeake

About this time, Chesapeake Bay was enjoying its well deserved reputation as a fabled area for pleasant living, a tradition that has not yet entirely faded. W. Mackay Laffan wrote that "The Chesapeake has conferred upon Baltimore the title of 'gastronomic capitol' of the country. The fish, game, reptiles of its generous waters, and the traditions of the Maryland kitchen, have made Baltimore a mecca toward which the eyes of all American *bon-vivants* are turned with a veneration that dyspepsia cannot impair."

Thus Laffan began an 1883 article on Chesapeake duck hunting where "gentlemen shoot from blinds and use decoys; market hunters use the sink-boat for the 'night reflector.'" That latter item, he explained, is "a large reflector behind a common naptha lamp mounted upon the bow of a boat." The boat was rowed in darkness to where the ducks had bedded for the night; the glow brought the birds flocking against the boat "in helpless confusion," and "from twenty to thirty ducks to each shot fired" was the result. The gunner then described his day's duck-shooting "at B.'s."

Goose-shooting from stubble
—Drawing by A. B. Frost from *Field Sports in Minnesota* by Charles A. Zimmerman, *The Century Magazine*

Results of the hunt —Currier & Ives, Library of Congress

At three o'clock our farmer called us. Breakfast—beef-steak, bacon, eggs and coffee—was crackling in the kitchen. A hasty dowse of water with an eighth-inch of ice on it, and a liberal nip of whisky—the latter for sanitary reasons of obscure origin but great weight—and we sat down. The quantity of breakfast consumed was amazing, then we were out in frosty air and bright moonlight at a quarter to four, fortified to meet the demands of the day.

We had a row of a mile and a half to the blind, getting into a steady, flat-bottomed boat in which two dogs, whom no one had called, took their place in solemn fashion. The moon hung near the tree tops, the river was dark, its outlines black

Over the decoys
—Drawing by W. Mackay Laffan
from *Canvas-Back and Terrapin*
by W. Mackay Laffan, *The Century Magazine*

An advertisement in The American Field—The Sportsman's Journal

(On opposite page, top)
Gentlemen duck hunters
—Lithographed by N. Currier,
    Library of Congress

(Bottom)
Teal shooting
—Library of Congress

and mysterious. A skim of ice had formed and as we crashed through it, odd echoes came from the gloomy shores. M. was in the bow, I in the stern and B. was rowing in the middle, when suddenly he stopped, seized his gun and loaded it. I was peering around in the gloom, seeing nothing but impenetrable shadows and the dark shore.

"Hist!" said B. "There they are." In a moment there was a most astonishing noise, and about five hundred yards to the right, a long line of bright silver broke upon the water. Thousands of ducks that had made a "bed" in the creek were taking wing simultaneously, and the noise they made by their splashing was tremendous. As the last duck lifted into the air, all was silent as before. Not a duck could be seen but my two friends had their guns cocked. Then I heard a whistling sound; it grew louder but I could see nothing. Both my companions brought up their guns and fired both barrels almost simultaneously overhead.

"Listen carefully," said B. "Mark one! Mark two! Mark three!"

I heard the splashes, the birds falling broke the water, and we could see three ducks struggling not one hundred yards off; both dogs, without an order, disappeared overboard.

"How did you know where to shoot?" I asked.

"You are not used to it," replied B. "When you are, you'll see ducks on the darkest night."

Both dogs came up to the side to be taken in. Each had a red-head in its mouth; the third bird had died and could not be detected in the darkness.

Inside the blind

A further pull of ten minutes brought us to the blind, inside of which we found Joe, the negro who had put out decoys during the night. He was asleep in the straw, though it was below freezing. We seated ourselves to wait for daybreak and ducks, and I endeavored to persuade myself that I was not cold. A southwest wind blew up the river as the moon went down, my companions spoke of it in hushed ecstacy but it struck me as the coldest wind I had ever known. A gray light stole across the eastern sky and I began to see the *canards* riding in front of our blind. I was undeniably cold, my companions had been whispering about whole days without a solitary shot, and I began to despise the whole business. The gray grew brighter, and a blue smoke seemed to creep up the river. We heard a shrill, feeble whistle, such as young puddle-ducks of the barnyard make.

Bushwhacking was productive on the Susquehanna Flats, near Havre de Grace, Maryland, where hunters sculled swan-shaped boats toward unsuspecting ducks.
—Drawing from *The Story of American Hunting and Firearms*, published by *Outdoor Life*

"Bald-pates!" said B. "Coming up the river before the wind. Quiet, everybody."

Right out of the blue haze, directly toward our blind, came not less than two hundred black-heads, straight toward the decoys. Within a hundred yards of our noses, the leader swerved and out they all went. Before I could give vent to my disappointment, B. gave his warning again: "Mark, mark! Canvas-backs!"

And from the same direction, flying within a foot of the water, came twenty ducks. They saw the decoy flock, turned in, and were hovering within a few inches of the wooden heads. We stood up, and as the ducks hung fluttering, six barrels were poured into them. Two, four, six, eight, and another—no—yes—nine ducks tumbled into the water. While it would be impossible for me to swear that I had even hit one, I had an abiding consciousness that four of the birds were mine. I was oblivious of the temperature.

"Mark again!" said the watchful B. "Single duck coming right in. Take him, he's your first choice. Now! Good, sir!" I had tumbled that single over like a professor. To say I was delighted will not do. I was wild, and I began to mark invisible ducks myself.

Shore-bird gunners on the Maryland marshes wore high hats, not for style but so that other hunters could see them over the reeds.
—Drawing from *The Story of American Hunting and Firearms*, published by *Outdoor Life*

A side shot
—Drawing by A. B. Frost from *Field Sports in Minnesota* by Charles A. Zimmerman, *The Century Magazine*

"Good sport?" asked B. "Gorgeous!" said I. "It generally drives a man crazy," said B., "and then we have to take him up in the woods and tie him to a tree till he calms down."

I did not think I was so excited, but I soothed myself. But it was sunrise and we could see ducks coming up in countless numbers. Presently a large flock left the middle of the stream and swept out into a broad bay; they turned and headed for the blind. We crouched low and hardly breathed. On they came like a whirlwind and were fluttering on the decoys as we rose and fired six barrels into the thickest part of them. Not less than twenty canvas-backs and red-heads fell.

"Mark, gemmen!" said Joe, holding the dogs. "Whir" came a flock of bald-pates, right over us from behind. B. had his gun up in an instant and fired both barrels overhead; two large birds fell wounded outside the line of decoys. Neither M. nor I had been quick enough.

Joe dived under the blind and in a moment was paddling out and picking up duck after duck with his little canoe. Here came in the dogs, whose instinct and training constitute one of the most astonishing examples of animal intelligence that one may see. They belonged to the breed known as Chesapeake duck-dogs, and they went out straight through some twenty dead birds toward the two bald-pates which, only slightly disabled, were swimming rapidly away.

Chesapeake retrievers

Each dog selected his bird and went for it. As the dog drew near, down went the duck. The dog stopped, stood up in the water, turning slowly in a circle looking for the duck to reappear. The moment it came up he went for it again. This time he got nearer. It was repeated, the dog each time waiting patiently for reappearance, and each time getting nearer. Finally, with a sudden dash and a partial dive, each dog seized his duck and, turning, swam to shore with it. They would not trouble themselves with the ducks that Joe could secure, but selected those that required their particular attention, swimming after each not less than a quarter of a mile.

When a shot is fired and a duck falls, a dog trained as these were will, unless forbidden, leave the blind immediately and secure the bird. If no duck falls the dog lies down again, using his own judgment as to the result of the shot. He will never stir without orders if he thinks the shot has been ineffectual. The breed is peculiar to these waters. It is adapted to the cold and has been cultivated for years, and is greatly prized by sportsmen of Maryland.

By nine o'clock we had ninety-six fine ducks in our blind. After that hour the birds ceased "trading," as flying from one point to another is termed, and began to form beds of countless thousands out in the open water. The middle of the stream and the broad water of the river below were covered with them. There were acres of ducks of all kinds, but "trading" was at an end, and shooting was suspended.

After a few thousand more words about "telling" ducks by throwing things in the water to attract them to the guns, and about how to cook canvasbacks, Laffan moved his narrative gracefully into terrapins, praised Baltimore cookery again, and wound up by awarding the gourmet Grand Prix to the "refined barbarism" of a "plain winter dinner in Maryland": four small oysters from Lynhaven Bay; terrapin *a la* Maryland; canvasback ducks, a small crab salad, baked potatoes, fried hominy cakes and plain celery.

Most outdoorsmen become deeply attached to a special geographical feature; a bay, river, lake, desert or mountain. While John Muir, founder of the Sierra Club, knew many a peak and massif, he seems to have been most engrossed with California's Mount Shasta and the Yosemite Valley that became a park in 1890. *Circa* 1874, the patron saint of national parks began writing about Shasta and spent a summer exploring this extinct volcano. In the fall of that year, in mid-October, with snow falling in high country, he decided to make an ascent into the storms — against all advice and with no guide willing to accompany him. But he made careful preparation and started on the afternoon of

Down charge
—Drawing by James C. Beard
from *Some American Sporting Dogs*
by William M. Tileston,
The Century Magazine

November 1, with a mountain man and pack animals accompanying him to a base camp as high as the animals could go. Before daylight on November 2, Muir set out for the summit, while his guide went home. The adventure that followed is the account of a self-sufficient man in wilderness:

Man and the mountain

After I was above the dwarf pines, it was fine practice pushing up the broad unbroken snow slopes, alone in the night. Half the sky was clouded; in the other half stars sparkled icily in the keen air; while everywhere the glorious wealth of snow fell away from the summit in flowing folds. When day dawned, clouds were crawling slowly and becoming more massive but gave no intimation of immediate danger, and I pushed on though holding myself well in hand, ready to return to the timber. The mountain rises ten thousand feet above the level of the country, in blank exposure to the deep upper currents of the sky, and no labyrinth of peaks and cañons seemed to be so dangerous as these immense slopes.

The frost was intense and drifting snowdust made breathing difficult. I frequently sank to my armpits between buried blocks of loose lava. When tired with walking, I still wallowed upward on all fours. The steepness of the slope made any kind of progress fatiguing. But the bracing air and sublime beauty of the snowy expanse made absolute exhaustion impossible. I seemed to be wallowing in a cloud; but by half-past ten o'clock I had gained the highest summit.

I held my foothold in the sky for two hours, gazing on the landscapes spread maplike around the immense horizon, tracing the outlines of ancient lava-streams and the pathways of vanished glaciers. But as I had left my coat in camp to be free in climbing, I soon was cold. The wind increased, raising snow in magnificent drifts that were drawn out in wavering banners glowing in the sun. A succession of small clouds struck against the summit like drifting icebergs, darkening the air and producing a chill as definite as if ice-water had been dashed in my face. This is the kind of cloud in which snow-flowers grow, and I turned and fled.

After I reached the end of the main ridge, descent was but little more than one continous soft, muffled slide, luxurious and rapid, though the swishing speed attained was obscured in great part by flying snow-dust—a marked contrast to the seal-wallowing upward struggle. I reached camp an hour before dusk, hollowed a strip of loose ground in the lee of a large block of red lava, rolled myself in blankets and went to sleep.

(On opposite page)
John Muir in the wilderness he loved
—Library, State Historical Society of Colorado

110

Having slept little the night before and weary with climbing, I slept late. Awakening suddenly, my eyes opened on one of the most sublime scenes I ever enjoyed. A wilderness of storm-clouds were congregated over all the lower landscape for thousands of square miles, gray and purple and pearl and deep-glowing white, amid which I seemed to be floating; while the great white cone of the mountain above was all aglow in free, blazing sunlight. It seemed a *land* of clouds—hill and dale, smooth purple plains, silvery mountains of cumuli diversified with peak and dome and hollow brought out in light and shade.

But cold gray masses, drifting like dust on a wind-swept plain, began to shut out the light, forerunners of the storm I had been watching. I made haste to gather as much wood as possible, snugging it as shelter around my bed. The storm side of my blankets was fastened down with stakes to reduce the sifting-in of drift and danger of being blown away. The

Snow House, a hotel that served travelers between Vernal and Nevada Falls from 1870 until 1890
—U.S. Department of the Interior, National Park Service

A good chance —Drawing by Henry Sandham from *Caribou Hunting* by Charles C. Ward, *The Century Magazine*

bread-sack was placed as a pillow and when the first flakes fell I was ready to welcome them. Most of my firewood was more than half rosin and would blaze in the face of the most serious drifting; winds could not demolish my bed, and my bread could be made to last indefinitely; I had the means of making snowshoes and could retreat or hold my ground as I pleased.

The storm

Presently the storm broke in full snowy bloom, and thronging crystals darkened the air. The wind swept past in

—Ned Smith

hissing floods, grinding the snow into meal, while the finer dust sifted through the sky, increasing the icy gloom. But my fire glowed bravely and, notwithstanding but little trace of my nest could be seen after the snow had buried it, I was snug and warm, and the passionate uproar produced a glad excitement.

Day after day the storm continued. There were short periods of quiet, when the sun would seem to look down eagerly through rents, as if to know how the work was progressing. During these intervals I replenished my fire or busied myself with my notebook, watching the gestures of the trees in taking the snow, examining crystals under a lens, and learning the methods of their deposition as an enduring fountain for the streams. Several times a Douglas squirrel came frisking from a clump of dwarf pines, moving in sudden interrupted

Returning from the hunt —Drawing by Henry Sandham from *Moose Hunting* by Charles C. Ward, *The Century Magazine*

spurts over the bossy snow. The mountain sheep, quite a large flock of them, came to my camp and took shelter beside a clump of matted pines a little above my nest.

The storm lasted about a week, but before it ended Sisson became alarmed and sent up the guide with animals to recover the camp outfit. The news spread that "there was a man on the mountain and he must have perished;" while I was as safe as anybody in the lowlands, lying like a squirrel in a warm, fluffy nest, busied about my own affairs and wishing only to be let alone.

Probably the most literary and certainly most prolific of the "nature writers" of this era was that charming essayist named John Burroughs, whose collections of "papers" appeared in magazines, pamphlets and 10-volume sets of books. He wrote of birds, bees and poets, of strawberries and porcupines, of trout and camp rhymes. A sample of that latter genre, credited to C. D. Shanly, is in these six of thirteen verses Burroughs originally quoted in 1879:

Not far into the valley had I dipped upon my way,
When a dusky figure joined me in a capuchin of gray,

Bending upon the snow-shoes with a long and limber stride;
And I hailed the dusky stranger as we traveled side by side.

No token of communion gave he by word or look,
And the fear-chill fell upon me at the crossing of the brook.

For I saw by sickly moonlight as I followed, bending low,
That the walking of the stranger left no foot-marks on the snow.

Then the fear-chill gathered o'er me like a shroud around me cast
As I sank upon the snow drift where the shadow hunter passed.

The otter-trappers found me before the break of day,
With my dark hair bleached and whitened as the snow
   in which I lay.

—Ned Smith

—Ned Smith

The poem was quoted by "Om John," as Teddy Roosevelt called him, in the essay "A Bed of Boughs," an account of camping in the Catskills "to eat locusts and wild honey."

About this same time, John Burroughs wrote an article titled "Speckled Trout" in which he said "we shall get at the meaning of those dark water-lines and . . . the significance of the glancing iridescent hues." That essay, condensed by deletions of many delightful paragraphs, is more about fishermen than fish; no angler can read it without self-recognition.

Caught on the fly—From a drawing by Thomas Worth, Currier & Ives, Library of Congress

A seeker of trout

I have been a seeker of trout from boyhood, and on all expeditions in which this fish has been the ostensible purpose I have brought home more than my creel showed. I find I got more of nature into me, more of the woods, the wild, nearer to bird and beast, while threading streams for trout than in any other way. It furnished a good excuse to go forth; it pitched one in the right key; it sent one through the fat and marrowy places of field and wood. Then the fisherman has a harmless, preoccupied look; he is a vagrant that nothing fears. His approaches are gentle. He times himself to the meandering, soliloquizing stream. The birds know he has no designs upon them, and the animals see his mind is in the creek.

Then what acquaintance he makes with the stream! He woos it till he knows its most hidden secrets. It runs through his thoughts no less than through its banks; he feels the fret and thrust of every bar and bowlder. Where it deepens, his purpose deepens; he knows how to interpret its every glance and dimple; its beauty haunts him for days.

I run no risk of overpraising a well-fed trout stream; every drop of water in it as bright and pure as if nymphs had brought it in crystal goblets. When the heated, soiled and jaded refugee from the city first sees one, he would like to turn it into his bosom and let it flow through him a few hours, it suggests such healing freshness. How his roily thoughts would run clear; how the sediment would go downstream! The next best thing he can do is to tramp along its banks and surrender to its influence. If he reads it intently, he will be taking it into his mind and heart, and experiencing its ministrations.

Trout streams coursed through every valley my boyhood knew. We bathed in them during long summer noons, and felt for the fish under their banks. A holiday was a holiday indeed that brought permission to go over to Rose's Brook or up Hardscrabble; all-day trips through meadows and pastures and woods, wherever the stream led. What an appetite it developed! a hunger that was fierce and aboriginal, and that wild strawberries teased rather than allayed. Alert and wide-eyed, one picked his way along, startled now and then by the bursting-up of a partridge or by the whistling of the dropping snipe, pressing through brush and briers, carefully

Rising to the fly —Currier & Ives, Library of Congress

Marsh marigold
—Ned Smith

letting his hook through some tangle into a still pool or standing in some high avenue watching his line float in and out amid moss-covered bowlders.

But a meadow brook was always a favorite. Trout like meadows; doubtless their food is more abundant there, and the good hiding-places more numerous. As soon as you strike a meadow the character of the creek changes; it goes slower and lies deeper; it loves the willows, or rather the willows love it and shelter it from the sun; its spring runs are kept cool by overhanging grass. Then there are the bobolinks and starlings and meadowlarks, always interested spectators; there are the marsh marigolds, the buttercups, or the spotted lilies, and the good angler is always an interested spectator of them. The patches of meadow that lie in an angler's course are like the happy experiences in his own life, or like fine passages in the poem he is reading.

Landing a double
—Drawing by J. H. Cocks from *Black Bass Fishing* by James A. Henshall, *The Century Magazine*

The pasture oftener contains shallow and monotonous places; the cattle scare the fish, soil their element and break down their retreats. Woodland alternates the best with meadow; the creek burrows under the roots of a great tree to scoop out a pool after leaping over the prostrate trunk, to pause at the foot of a ledge of moss-covered rock; the current strikes and glances off, but accumulates, deepens with well-defined eddies; on the edge of these the trout lurk and spring upon their prey.

The angler learns that it is some obstacle that makes a deep place in the creek, as in a brave life; and his ideal brook lies in well-defined banks yet makes many a shift, meets with rebuffs and adventures, waylaid by snags and trees, tripped up by precipices, but sooner or later reposing under meadow banks, eddying beneath bridges, prosperous in some level stretch of cultivated land with great elms shading it.

I early learned that from almost any stream the true angler could take fish, and that the great secret was that whatever bait you used, worm, grasshopper, grub or fly, there was one thing you must always put upon your hook, namely, your heart.

When you bait your hook with your heart the fish always bite; they will jump from the water after it; it is a morsel they love above everything else. With such bait I have seen the born angler take a noble string from the most unpromising waters on the most unpromising day,—surely his heart was upon his hook, and it was a tender, unctuous heart, as that of every angler is.

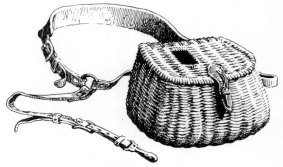

Willow creel
—Ned Smith

If your heart is a stone, or an empty husk, there is no use to put it upon your hook; the bait must be quick and fresh. A certain quality of youth is indispensable to the successful angler, a certain unworldliness and readiness to invest yourself in an enterprise that doesn't pay in current coin. Not only is the angler born and not made, as Walton says, but there is a deal of the poet in him, and he is to be judged no more harshly; he is the victim of his genius: those streams haunt him; he will play truant to dull care and flee to them.

My grandfather when he was eighty years old would take down his pole as eagerly as any boy and step off toward the beloved stream; it used to try my young legs to follow him. And no poet was more innocent of wordly ambition. He laid up treasures but they were not in this world. Though the kindest of husbands he was not a "good provider" except in providing trout in their season, though it is doubtful if there was always fat in the house to fry them. But he would tell you they were worse off than those at Valley Forge, and that any fish were good roasted in ashes under the coals.

Biting lively! —From a drawing by Thomas Worth, Currier & Ives, Library of Congress

He had the Walton requisite of loving quietness and contemplation, and was devout withal. In many ways he was akin to those Galilee fishermen who were called to be fishers of men. How he read the Book, even at times nodding over it, and laying it down to take up his rod — over which, unless the trout were very dilatory or the journey very fatiguing, he never nodded!

*   *   *

I have run over some of the features of ordinary trouting. People inexperienced in such matters, sitting in their rooms and thinking of these things, of all poets have sung and romancers have written, are apt to get sadly taken in when they attempt to realize their dreams. They expect a sylvan paradise of trout, laughing brooks, picturesque views and balsamic couches; instead they find hunger, rain, smoke, gnats, dirt, vulgar guides and salt pork; and they are very apt not to see where the fun comes in. But he who goes in a right spirit will find the taste of this kind of life better, though bitterer, than the writers have described.

Fly fishing in the Adirondacks

Thus John Burroughs, who said trout streams gurgled about the roots of his family tree. But a literary New Englander, Charles Dudley Warner, had a different view of this species, somewhat more sardonic.

Warner was once editor and rural columnist of the Hartford, Connecticut, *Courant;* he had a style akin to Washington Irving and a friendship with Mark Twain, with whom he collaborated on *The Gilded Age,* a poorer book than either man ever wrote alone. His *Being a Boy* followed Twain's *Tom Sawyer* and was written by a better craftsman. The difference lay in the fact Twain was a genius.

Warner also wrote well about the Adirondacks with a volume called *In the Wilderness,* did a series of travel books, wandered widely and spent some time as a lawyer in Chicago and even as a surveyor in Missouri. But his heart was in the Northeast. His satiric strain was showing when he wrote "A Fight With a Trout." It is very much a putdown of angling purists 95 years after he wrote it.

Trout-fishing in the Adirondacks would be a more attractive pastime than it is, but for the popular notion of its danger. The trout is a retiring and harmless animal, except when he is aroused and forced into a combat; and then his agility, fierceness, and vindictiveness become apparent. No one who has studied the excellent pictures representing men in an open boat, exposed to the assaults of long, enraged trout flying at them through the open air with open mouth, ever ventures with his rod upon the lonely lakes without terror, or

The last fish of the season —From an engraving in *Harper's Magazine*

ever reads of daring fishermen without admiration for their heroism. Most of their adventures are thrilling, and all of them are, in narration, more or less unjust to the trout; in fact, the object of them seems to be to exhibit the shrewdness, skill, and power of the sportsman. My own simple story has few of these recommendations.

Day's end in an old-time fishing camp

We had built our bark camp one summer on one of the popular lakes of the Saranac region. It would be a very pretty region, if it were not so flat, if the margins of the lakes had not been flooded by dams at the outlets,—which have killed the trees, and left a rim of ghastly dead-wood, like the swamps of the under-world pictured by Doré's bizarre pencil,—and if the pianos at the hotels were in tune. It would be an excellent sporting region also (for there is water enough), if the fish commissioners would stock the waters, and if previous hunters had not pulled all the hair and skin off from the deers' tails. Formerly, sportsmen had a habit of catching the deer by the tails, and of being dragged in mere wantonness round and round the shores. It is well known that if you seize a deer by this "holt," the skin will slip off like the peel from a banana.

We had been hearing of a small lake in the heart of the virgin forest, some ten miles from our camp, which was alive with unsophisticated, hungry trout; the inlet was described as stiff with them. In imagination, I saw them lying there in ranks, each a foot long, three tiers deep, a solid mass. The lake had never been visited, except by winter sable-hunters and was known as the Unknown Pond. I determined to explore it, fully expecting that it would prove to be a delusion. Confiding my purpose to Luke, we stole away from the shanty one morning at day-break. Each of us carried a boat, a pair of blankets, a sack of bread, pork, and maple sugar; while I had my rods, creel, and book of flies, and Luke had an axe and the kitchen utensils. We think nothing of loads of this sort in the woods.

Salmon fly
—James Bashline

Tamarack swamp and rapids

Five miles through a tamarack swamp brought us to the inlet of Unknown Pond, upon which we embarked our fleet, and paddled down its vagrant waters. They were at first sluggish, winding among triste fir-trees, but gradually developed a strong current. At the end of three miles, a loud roar ahead warned us that we were approaching rapids, falls, and cascades. We paused. The danger was unknown. We had our choice of shouldering our loads and making a detour through the woods, or of "shooting the rapids." Naturally, we chose the more dangerous course. Shooting the rapids has often been described, and I will not repeat the description here. It

—Ned Smith

123

is needless to say that I drove my frail bark through the boiling rapids, over the successive water-falls, amid rocks and vicious eddies, and landed half a mile below, with whitened hair and a boat half full of water; and that the guide was upset, and boat, contents, and man were strewn along the shore.

After this common experience we went quickly on our journey, and, a couple of hours before sundown, reached the lake. If I live to my dying day I never shall forget its appearance. The lake is almost an exact circle, about a quarter of a mile in diameter. The forest about it was untouched by axe and unkilled by artificial flooding. The azure water had a perfect setting of evergreens, in which all the shades of the fir, the balsam, the pine, and the spruce were perfectly blended; and at intervals, on the shore in the emerald rim, blazed the ruby of the cardinal-flower. It was at once evident that the unruffled waters had never been vexed by the keel of a boat. But what chiefly attracted my attention was the boiling of the water, bubbling as if the lake were a vast kettle, with a

Shoving off after completing a portage in northern Minnesota.

fire underneath. A tyro would have been astonished at this common phenomenon; but sportsmen will at once understand me when I say that the water boiled with the breaking trout. I studied the surface for some time to see upon what sort of flies they were feeding, in order to suit my cast to their appetites; but they seemed to be at play rather than feeding, leaping high in the air in graceful curves, and tumbling about each other as we see them in Adirondack pictures.

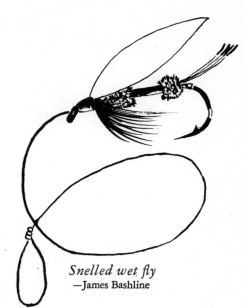

Snelled wet fly
—James Bashline

A reputation at stake

It is well known that no person who regards his reputation will ever kill a trout with anything but a fly. It requires some training on the part of the trout to take to this method. The uncultivated, unsophisticated trout in unfrequented waters prefers the bait; and the rural people, whose sole object in going a-fishing appears to be to catch fish, indulge them in their primitive taste for the worm. No sportsman, however, will use anything but a fly, except he happens to be alone.

While Luke arranged his seat in the stern, I prepared my rod and line. The rod is a bamboo, weighing seven ounces, which has to be spliced with a winding of silk thread every time it is used. This is a tedious process; but by fastening the joints in this way, a uniform spring is secured in the rod. No one devoted to high art would think of using a socket-joint. My line was forty yards of untwisted silk upon a multiplying reel. The "leader" (I am very particular about my leaders) had been made to order from a domestic animal with which I had been acquainted. The fisherman requires as good a cat-gut as the violinist. On six feet of this superior article I fixed three artificial flies, — a simple brown hackle, a gray body, with scarlet wings, and one of my own invention. The trout-fly does not resemble any known species of insect. It is a "conventionalized" creation, as we say of ornamentation. The theory is that, fly-fishing being a high art, the fly must not be a tame imitation of nature, but an artistic suggestion of it. It requires an artist to construct one, and not every bungler can take a bit of red flannel, a peacock's feather, a flash of tinsel thread, a cock's plume, a section of a hen's wing, and fabricate a tiny object that will not look like any fly, but still will suggest the universal conventional fly.

I took my stand in the center of the tipsy boat; and Luke shoved off, and slowly paddled toward some lily-pads, while I began casting. The fish had all disappeared. I got out fifty feet of line and gradually increased it to one hundred. It is not difficult to learn to cast; but it is difficult to learn not to snap off the flies at every throw. I continued casting for some moments, until I became satisfied that there had been a miscalculation. Either the trout were too green to know what I was at, or they were dissatisfied with my offers. I reeled in and changed the flies. After studying the color of the sky, of the water, and of the foliage, and the moderated light of the afternoon, I put on a series of beguilers, all of a subdued brilliancy, in harmony with the approach of evening. At the second cast, which was a short one, I saw a splash where the leader fell, and gave an excited jerk. The next instant I perceived the game, and did not need the unfeigned "damn" of Luke to convince me that I had snatched his felt hat from his head and deposited it among the lilies.

Discouraged by this, we paddled over to the inlet, where a little ripple was visible. At the very first cast I saw that the hour had come. Three trout leaped into the air. The danger of this maneuver all fishermen understand. It is one of the commonest in the woods; three heavy trout taking hold at once, rushing in different directions, smash the tackle into flinders. I evaded this catch and threw again. I recall the moment. A hermit-thrush, on the tip of a balsam, uttered his liquid evening note. Happening to look over my shoulder, I saw the peak of Marcy gleam rosy in the sky (I can't help it that Marcy is fifty miles off, and cannot be seen from this region; these incidental touches are always used). The hundred feet of silk swished through the air, and the tail-fly fell as lightly on the water as a three-cent piece (which no slamming will give the weight of a ten) drops upon the contribution-plate. Instantly there was a rush, a swirl. I struck, and "Got him, by _____!" never mind what Luke said I got him by. "Out on a fly," continued that irreverent guide; but I told him to back water and make for the center of the lake.

A smoking line

The trout, as soon as he felt the hook, was off like a shot, and took out the line with a rapidity that made it smoke. "Give him the butt!" shouted Luke, the usual remark in such an emergency. I gave him the butt; and recognizing my spirit, the trout sank to the bottom and sulked. It is the most dangerous mood of a trout; for you cannot tell what he will do next. We reeled up a little, and waited five minutes for him to reflect. A tightening of the line enraged him, and he soon developed his tactics. Coming to the surface, he made straight for the boat faster than I could reel in, and evidently with hostile intentions. "Look out for him!" cried Luke, as he came flying in the air. I evaded him by dropping flat in the

—Ned Smith

bottom of the boat; and when I picked my traps up, he was spinning across the lake as if he had a new idea; but the line was still fast. He did not run far. I gave him the butt again; a thing he seemed to hate, even as a gift. In a moment, the evil-minded fish, lashing the water in his rage, was coming back again, making straight for the boat as before. Luke, who was used to these encounters, having read of them in the writings of travelers he had accompanied, raised his paddle in self-defense. The trout left the water about ten feet from the boat, and came directly at me with fiery eyes, his speckled sides flashing like a meteor. I dodged as he whisked by with a vicious slap of his bifurcated tail, and nearly upset the boat. The line was of course slack; and the danger was that he would entangle it about me and carry away a leg. This was evidently his game, but I entangled it, and only lost a breast-button or two by the swiftly-moving string.

The trout plunged into the water with a hissing sound, and went away again with all the line on the reel. More butt; more indignation on the part of the captive.

The contest had now been going on for half an hour, and I was getting exhausted. What I feared was that the trout would start up the inlet and wreck us in the bushes. But he began the execution of a maneuver which I had never read of. Instead of coming straight toward me, he took a large circle, swimming rapidly, and gradually contracting his orbit. I reeled in, and kept my eye on him. Round and round he went, narrowing his circle. I began to suspect the game, which was to twist my head off. When he had reduced the radius of his circle to about twenty-five feet, he struck a tremendous pace through the water. It would be false modesty in a sportsman to say that I was not equal to the occasion. Instead of turning round with him, as he expected, I stepped to the bow, braced myself, and let the boat swing. Round went the fish, and round we went like a top. I saw a line of Mount Marcys all round the horizon; the rosy tint in the west made a broad band of pink along the sky above the treetops; the evening-star was a perfect circle of light, a hoop of gold in the heavens. We whirled and reeled, and reeled and whirled. I was willing to give the malicious beast butt and line and all, if he would only go the other way for a change.

When I came to myself Luke was gaffing the trout at the boatside. After we had got him in and dressed him he weighed three-quarters of a pound. Fish always lose by being "got in and dressed." It is best to weigh them while they are in the water. The only really large one I ever caught got away with my leader when I first struck him. He weighed ten pounds.

Theodore Roosevelt on a cow pony —Library of Congress

*Fishing on the Mississippi
by George Caleb Bingham
Bingham grew up on the
Mississippi and his paintings
captured scenes of the era
before the Civil War.*
—Courtesy Nelson Gallery
Atkins Museum, Kansas City

(At right)
Breaking Off by Belmore Brown
—Courtesy Glenbow-Alberta Institute

Renaissance of an American art form . . .

DECOYS

STORY AND ILLUSTRATIONS BY NED SMITH

PROBABLY NOWHERE ELSE in the world did waterfowl and shorebird hunting ever assume the proportions it did in the United States from the middle of the nineteenth century to the early 1900s. There were no closed seasons or bag limits then, and the nation's burgeoning cities needed meat. Consequently, the bayman and the river rat responded in the way they knew best — by shooting for the market. And to lure birds into shooting range, they fashioned incredible numbers of wooden decoys: replicas of the ducks, geese and shorebirds they hunted.

Today, more than a half century after the heyday of those unique American artifacts, decoys have become prized antiques with almost universal appeal. Craftsmen admire the skillful handling of wood and paint. Bird students are fascinated by just what it took to fool a mallard, a black duck or a plover. Hunters compare the pulling power of homemade decoys to their own modern factory-made equipment. To all, the old decoys tell volumes about the men who made them, the way they were used and the birds they attracted.

Commonly called "blocks" or "stools," the original decoys ran the gamut from crude to flawless. Under average conditions, finely detailed and elegantly formed decoys were unnecessary. For a Chesapeake Bay market hunter, just staying out of sight in a nearly submerged battery, surrounded by up to six hundred decoys, was enough. Even with mediocre blocks, he could bag hundreds of canvasbacks on a good day for the restaurants of New York, Baltimore, or Washington. And before they were outlawed, a few live decoys could attract geese and ducks to the poorest stools.

But in areas where these deadly methods were not practical, more convincing decoys were needed, and thus the golden age of decoy making began. On many tidal rivers, for instance, only the most lifelike decoys could attract skittish black ducks and keep them from taking wing before a grass-covered boat could be sculled into range. With increasing gunning pressure, many species became progressively harder to fool, and hunters learned that decoy quality really did make a difference. It's no accident that some of the later decoy craftsmen of that era — "Shang" Wheeler, Charlie Perdew, John Dawson, Charles Walker, and the Ward Brothers, who still live in Crisfield, Maryland — turned out the most realistic models of all.

In some cases, however, it was found that some birds required less realism. On Pamlico Sound, in North Carolina, for instance, silhouette decoys cut out boards, and later of plywood, have largely replaced the burdensome, full bodied stakeouts once thought necessary for bringing Canada geese within shotgun range.

In the old days, design and construction were dictated largely by local tradition and hunting methods. The most common decoy type had a solid body carved out of white cedar or white pine, with a white pine head. Battery stools were of this type because picking up several hundred decoys in the face of an approaching storm, and stacking them like cordwood in a bouncing dinghy, called for sturdy construction. On the other hand, decoys used on much of Barnegat Bay in New Jersey were usually transported to the shooting grounds in smaller numbers on the deck of a little boat called a "sneakbox," which served as a one-man blind when covered with dead grass. To save space, the Barnegat decoys were a bit on the small side, and to save weight they were made with hollowed-out bodies. Duck decoys used on the Connecticut River had high, overhanging breasts to ride

Originally, profile decoys — also called silhouettes or shadows — were cut out of tin or thin wood. Most represented shorebirds, like the dowitcher or "robin snipe" at left. Nesting shadow decoys at right imitate white-winged scoters.

Some of the finest goose decoys known were the hollow models made in New Jersey by old-time Barnegat Baymen. Here, gunners are crouching out of sight in a pit blind. Their grassed-up sneakbox, pulled up on the point, is barely distinguishable.

over floating ice. Those used on open, rough water were usually larger than life, for greater visibility among the waves. The earliest decoys were usually round-bottomed like their living models; later makers learned that flat bottoms prevented pitching and rolling unnaturally when the water got choppy. One very different type of decoy was made of cast iron by local foundries.

Most silhouette, or profile, decoys gained rather late and limited acceptance in waterfowl hunting, and were largely limited to goose shooting. In shorebird hunting, however, such "flatties" were early favorites. They were usually made from thin wood or tin, and mounted on slender stakes or wire legs. Full-bodied shorebird stakeouts were used, too.

Many species were represented among the profiles. Golden plover (often lured by blackbellied plover decoys), Eskimo curlews (nearly wiped out by market hunters), and yellowlegs were in great demand. Dunlins, godwits, small plovers and even diminutive least sandpipers were considered fair game for city sports, if not by professional hunters.

Many shorebird stools are hard to identify, for they were painted to resemble the birds in autumn plumage, which in many shorebirds is a nondescript gray. However, the presence of "robin-snipe" (dowitchers in spring plumage), golden plovers with black bellies, and knots and godwits in reddish nuptial plumage are evidence of spring shooting.

Most shorebirds responded to decoys readily, and few early decoys would win prizes for realism. But as with ducks, some shorebirds eventually became warier, leading to more lifelike designs. Late rigs often included running, feeding, preening and sleeping models.

Not all antique decoys represented waterfowl or shorebirds. Swan decoys are mute testimony that baymen were not averse to dining on these great birds. Other decoys resembled the great blue heron, an unconventional table bird that apparently tasted far

better than its fish diet would indicate. Some beautifully carved gulls have been discovered, also. These were not used to lure gulls to the gun, but were "confidence decoys," displayed near other stools to allay the fears of suspicious waterfowl.

For all their short-sightedness in matters of conservation, the old-time waterfowl hunters were superb students of bird behavior, at least as it applied to hunting. While not always exact replicas, their blocks nevertheless showed the attitude and general appearance of each species. Their brant rested buoyantly on the water with sterns elevated; their diving ducks rode the waves with tails awash.

They knew which decoys would bring in other species as well as their own. The tides, weather, wind direction and season told them where

Young whistling swans (center), acceptable table-fare for old-timers and their families, were attracted by decoys. This one was used at Havre de Grace, Maryland.

The Eskimo curlew — a gourmet's choice that was all but exterminated by market hunting — was often attracted by stick-up decoys.

to set out their stools. They knew where to leave openings in their spread of decoys, gaps that would beckon invitingly to passing flocks.

We'll probably never know the sight of so many canvasbacks, redheads, black ducks, curlews or godwits as the old-timers saw. Those species were beaten back too hard, and the marshy world they knew is surrendering too rapidly now to development. But we still have a huntable population of most species of waterfowl and protection for the others. With luck and good management, there should be a place for decoys — albeit plastic ones — in the American sporting scene for years to come.

Meanwhile, the current revival of interest in handmade decoys shows no signs of slackening. Coveted by collectors, some antique blocks fetch more at auctions than their makers earned in years of carving and painting. Modern sportsmen, too, are learning how much fun it is to convert a chunk of cedar, pine, or basswood into a mallard or pintail that seems ready to fly. Few of the new decoys will ever see a duck marsh; most are not working decoys at all, but decorative creations for mantlepiece or den. But the spirit behind those elegant carvings is still the desire to recreate the living bird — and that's where it all began.

Ned Smith is a nature photographer, writer and artist from Millersburg, Pennsylvania.

Decoy painting was the true test of the maker's artistic skill. The brant (upper) is nicely painted in simplified version of natural plumage, whereas the two mergansers are highly stylized. The American merganser (right) probably began as a female, hence the crest.

Outlawed more than fifty years ago, the battery was the deadliest device used by market hunters. Basically, it was a box in which one or two hunters reclined below water level. Canvas "wings" helped break up the waves and a sheet lead coaming kept out the "slop." Here, a gunner rises to meet an incoming flock of canvasbacks.

In spite of the lifelike decoys, these wary mallards flushed prematurely at the stealthy approach of a "turn-over" Susquehanna sneak boat. Professional gunners tipped this unique craft on its side by sitting off-center, the hull itself shielding the paddler and the shooter from view. When in range, the boat is "opened" by turning it sharply to the left.

Black-bellied plover

Ruddy turnstone

Greater yellowlegs

A real, live black-bellied plover in spring plumage looks over some counterfeits.

Most wooden battery decoys were crudely made with solid bodies.

These cast iron decoys were placed on battery decks to sink them to water level.

On the Road by Thomas Otter. This canvas, painted in 1860, symbolizes the end of one era and the beginning of another.

After the Hunt by William Michael Harnett

TR: sportsman, conservationist, leader

Still, it was a period when America was described by Thomas Hart Benton (the artist, not his great-uncle the Senator) as an era when: "Our land has been gutted, the people have been tricked into mortgaging their lives. The potentialities for good lying in our resources have been sacrificed to . . . financial skullduggery . . . our forests have been stripped for short-range profit. Out of this our great cities have risen. Meccas for cunning and merciless schemers, packed with self-seeking, but possessed as well of a dark and strange beauty."

Out of this age of exploitation rose conservation education's foremost early proponent: Teddy Roosevelt. Intellectually nurtured by the 19th-century naturalists, Teddy applied their precepts so well that the first five words on his monument in New York's American Museum of Natural History are not "statesman" but *Ranchman, Explorer, Scientist, Conservationist* and *Naturalist.* The seventh is *Author.*

In these fields, his contributions may have been more considerable than his roles of politician and soldier, though he demonstrated that a President of the United States can do great things if he really believes in forests, parks and wildlife. Roosevelt was a true believer.

His rhetoric was considerable; he wrote about everything: ants and elephants, war and peace, hunting and camping, birds, Indians, foreign affairs, conservation, and how to win elections. He would interrupt Cabinet meetings to report an early warbler in the White House grounds, where he took part throughout his Presidency in the Audubon Society's Christmas bird count. John Burroughs said he probably "knew tenfold more natural history than all the presidents who preceded him." And Henry Fairfield Osborn wrote "he was not one man but many . . . combined and harmonized into one." Gifford Pinchot added that "he was loved by those who should love him and hated by those who should hate him."

The flow of history has eroded some fame, but he was indeed a complex man, who seems more so to those who look back over three generations of increasing specialization. But he fit his time. The great naturalists and conservationists who reached maturity toward the close of the nineteenth century were "generalists" in the classical example of Thomas Jefferson, with wide interests and historic and aesthetic values. Thus Theodore Roosevelt could check off another specimen on his bird list, shoot a mule deer to feed the camp, set down geological and biological observations about the campfire, then ponder the course of a nation in his pallet before next morning's hunt for pumas.

Some of his bully exhortations are dated now, when he seems to have been a better observer of wild animals than of humans. But his conservation philosophy holds true today: "The nation behaves well if it treats natural resources as assets which it must turn over to the next generation—and not impaired in value." . . . "There are no words that can tell the hidden spirit of the wilderness, that can reveal its mystery, melancholy and charm." Or "Conservation means development as much as it does protection."

No one ghosted these sentiments; Theodore Roosevelt believed them, and tried to practice them. He wrote to Audubon Society's then-President Frank Chapman that "The destruction of the wild pigeon and the Carolina parakeet has meant a loss as sad as if the Catskills or Palisades were taken away. When I hear of the destruction of a species I feel as if all the works of some great writer had perished." President a decade later, he established, with dubious legality but undoubted authority, the first national wildlife refuges.

He did not originally understand the agricultural revolution that began about the time he was living on a North Dakota ranch, a revolution that damaged more species of wildlife (through loss of habitat) than the gun did. But he came to that realization, too: "Where natural conditions have been restored for a few years, vegetation has again carpeted the ground, and birds and deer are coming back."

Apart from his other achievements, he was a practitioner of outdoor writing as it is presented by its better journalists today. He knew his subject or he did not write; he was perfectly willing to contradict earlier statements if evidence justified the change; he never stopped learning; he could assert the joy of hunting while denouncing the greed of some hunters; he poured out words in support of conservation while attacking nature-fakers.

He wrote hundreds of articles on the outdoors: books, essays, editorials and letters. None was a masterpiece; all were vigorous, informed journalism (which describes the genre in 1976, too). Perhaps typical of his work are the 1893 sketches on "Old Ephraim, the Grisly Bear" and "Hunting the Grisly," a spelling of "grizzly" that he chose. This account is considerably condensed by deletion.

Hunting the "Grisly"

The king of the game beasts of temperate North America, because the most dangerous to hunters, is the grisly bear; known to the few remaining trappers of the Rockies and Great Plains as "Old Ephraim." Bears vary greatly. Old hunters speak much of them over campfires and in snowbound winter huts. They insist on many species; not merely the black and the grisly, but the brown, cinnamon, gray, silvertip. But most old hunters are untrustworthy in dealing with points of natural history. They usually know only so much about any given animal as will enable them to kill it.

Among the grislies the fur varies much in color and texture even among bears of the same locality; it is richest in the deep forest, while bears of the dry plains and mountains are of a lighter hue. A full grown grisly will weigh from five to seven hundred pounds; but exceptional individu-

Silver tip grizzly —Leonard Lee Rue III photo

als reach more than twelve hundredweight. Alaskan bears are even bigger beasts; the skin of one which I saw was a good deal larger than the average polar bear skin; and the animal could hardly have weighed less than 1,400 pounds. Both this huge Alaskan bear and the distinct bear of the barren grounds differ widely from the true grisly.

131

Colt .45 and Winchester carbine
—Ned Smith

When there was no rifle-bearing hunter in the land, to harass him and make him afraid, the grisly roved hither and thither at will, in burly self-confidence. If the humor seized him he would roam for days over the prairie, searching for roots, digging up gophers, or perhaps following the great buffalo herds to prey on some unwary straggler or to feast on the carcasses of those which died by accident. Old hunters, survivors of the long-vanished age when the vast herds thronged the high plains, followed by wild red tribes and by bands of whites scarcely less savage, have told me that they often met bears under such circumstances. These bears sleep in rank sage brush, the niche of a washout or under the lee of a bowlder, seeking their food abroad even in full daylight.

However, the grisly has in most places become a cover-haunting animal, sly, wary and clinging to the shelter of the deepest mountain forests and of the tangled thickets in the plains. Hence he has held his own better than such game as the bison and elk. He is much less common than formerly, but is still to be found throughout most of his former range.

The length of time a grisly hibernates in its den depends upon the severity of the season, and the latitude and altitude of the country. In the coldest regions all the bears hole up, and spend half the year in a state of lethargy; in the south only shes with young and fat he-bears retire for the sleep, and these but for a few weeks.

When the bear first leaves its den the fur is in fine order but becomes thin and poor. Sometimes it does not betray any great hunger for a few days after its appearance; but in a short while it becomes ravenous. When the woods are still barren and lifeless, while snow yet lies in deep drifts, the lean, hungry brute, maddened and weakened by long fasting, is more of a flesh eater than at any other time, most apt to show its prowess at the expense of wild game, or of herds of the ranchman. Bears are capricious in this respect, however. Some are confirmed game and cattle killers; others are not; yet others either are or are not accordingly as the freak seizes them.

In the early summer of 1888, bears killed no cattle near my ranch; but in the early fall of that year a big bear which we well knew by its tracks suddenly took to cattle-killing. It

Many a hunter was forced to climb a tree, thankful to be able to take advantage of the grizzly bear's inability to climb.
—Drawing from *The Story of American Firearms and Hunting,* published by *Outdoor Life*

The front page of The American Field—
The Sportsman's Journal, *July 27, 1895*

A full-page advertisement for guns in
The American Field—The Sportsman's Journal

began just before berry time but continued its destruction
long after wild plums and buffalo berries had ripened. It
seemed to attack the animals regardless of their size and
strength; victims included a large bull and a beef steer as
well as cows, yearlings and gaunt "doughgies" brought in
very late by a Texas cow-outfit.

The crafty old grisly usually lay in wait for cattle when
they came down to water, choosing some thicket of dense
underbrush and twisted cottonwoods through which they
had to pass before reaching sandbanks on the river. Some-

133

times he pounced on them as they fed through the thick cover of the bottoms. When within a few feet, a quick rush carried fairly on the terrified quarry; and though a clumsy animal compared to the great cats, the grisly is far quicker than one would imagine. In one or two instances the bear had grappled with his victim by seizing it near the loins and striking a disabling blow on the small of the back; in one instance he had jumped on the animal's head while his fangs tore open the throat.

Several of the ranchmen, angered at their losses, hunted their foe eagerly, but always with ill success; until one of them put poison in a carcass, and thus at last, in ignoble fashion, slew the cattle-killer.

When a grisly can get at domestic animals it rarely seeks to molest game. Its heaviness and clumsiness do not fit it well for a life of rapine against woodland creatures. When a grisly does take to game-killing it is likely to attack bison, moose and elk; it is rarely able to catch deer, still less sheep or antelope. In the old days, the grisly did not hesitate to attack the mighty bison bulls themselves; perhaps the grandest sight which it was ever the good fortune of the early hunters to witness was one of these rare battles between a hungry grisly and a powerful buffalo bull.

Mr. Roosevelt went on describing "grislies" at length; what they ate (mostly berries and roots), how they mated, how they were trapped or poisoned or hunted. He reported observations and details told him by people he trusted, along with matters of personal study. Then he reported on his own hunts for the grizzly, including one where "the beauty of the trophy and the circumstances under which I procured it, made me value it perhaps more highly than any other in my house."

A lonely, dangerous kill

I spent much of the fall of 1889 hunting on the headwaters of the Salmon and Snake in Idaho, and along the Montana boundary from Big Hole Basin to Red Rock Pass. During the last fortnight my companion was an old mountain man, a crabbedly honest fellow and skillful hunter, but much worn out with age and rheumatism, and his temper had failed even faster than his bodily strength. Finally, during my absence from camp one day, he found my whiskey-flask, which I kept purely for emergencies, and drank all the contents. After some high words I left him, and struck off homewards on my own account. I took a gentle little bronco mare which possessed the trait of staying near camp, even when not hobbled.

I was not hampered with much of an outfit, only my buffalo sleeping-bag, a fur coat and my washing kit, with a couple of pairs of socks. A frying pan, salt, flour, baking powder, a small chunk of salt pork and a hatchet made up a light pack which, with the bedding, I fastened across the stock saddle. My cartridges and knife were in my belt, compass and matches as always in my pocket. I walked, while the little mare followed almost like a dog.

The country was fairly open, as I kept near the foothills where glades broke the pine forest. There was no trail but the course was easy to keep; I had no trouble save on the second day. That afternoon I was following a stream that "canyoned up," that is, sank to the bottom of a ravine impassable for a horse. I started up a side valley, got enmeshed in the tangle at the foot of steep mountains, and as dusk was coming on halted and camped by the side of a small, noisy brook.

The place was carpeted with wet, green moss, dotted red with kinnikinnic berries, and under trees where the ground was dry I threw down the buffalo bed on a mat of sweet-smelling pine needles. I opened my pack, knee-haltered the little mare, dragged up a few dry logs, and strolled off, rifle on shoulder through the gloaming to see if I could pick up a grouse for supper.

I walked quickly over the pine needles, across a succession of slight ridges separated by narrow, shallow valleys; the forest was lodge-pole pine. The sun was behind the mountains; there was plenty of light by which to shoot, but it was fading rapidly.

As I was thinking of turning toward camp, I stole up one of the ridges and looked into the valley sixty yards off. Immediately I caught the loom of some large, dark object; another glance showed a big grisly walking slowly off, his head down. He was quartering me and I fired into his flank, the bullet I afterward found ranging forward and piercing one lung. He uttered a loud, moaning grunt and plunged forward at a heavy gallop, while I raced obliquely downhill to cut him off. After going a few hundred feet he reached a laurel thicket, which he did not leave. I ran to the edge and halted, not liking to venture into the mass of close-growing stems and glossy foliage. Moreover, I heard him utter a savage kind of whine from the brush. Accordingly I skirted the edge, standing on tiptoe to see if I could not catch a glimpse of his hide. When I was at the narrowest part of the thicket he suddenly left it directly opposite, then wheeled and stood broadside me on the hillside a little above. He turned his head toward me; scarlet strings of froth hung from his lips; his eyes burned like embers in the gloom.

Theodore Roosevelt in 1885
—Photograph by Bain, Library of Congress

135

I held true, aiming behind the shoulder, and my bullet shattered the point of his heart, taking out a big nick. Instantly the great bear turned with a roar of fury, blowing the bloody foam from his mouth; I saw the gleam of his white fangs, and then he charged straight at me, crashing through the laurel so that it was hard to aim.

I waited till he came to a fallen tree, raking him with a ball which entered his chest and went through the cavity of his body, but he neither swerved nor flinched and at the moment I did not know that I had struck him. He came steadily on and was almost upon me. I fired for his forehead but my bullet went low, smashing his lower jaw and going into the neck. I leaped to one side almost as I pulled the trigger; and through the hanging smoke the first thing I saw was his paw as he made a vicious side blow at me.

The rush of his charge carried him past. He lurched forward, leaving a pool of bright blood where his muzzle hit the ground; but he recovered and made two or three jumps onward, while I jammed a couple of cartridges into the magazine, my rifle holding only four. Then he tried to pull up, but as he did his muscles gave way, his head dropped, and he rolled over and over. Each of my first three bullets had inflicted a mortal wound!

This is the only instance in which I have been regularly charged by a grisly. On the whole, the danger of hunting these great bears has been much exaggerated.

—Ned Smith

The Golden Gate before the Bridge —Photograph by Ansel Adams

THE TWENTIETH CENTURY BEGINS 3

As the United States traded off a vigorous outdoorsman-president, Theodore Roosevelt, for a portly chief executive, William Howard Taft, it seemed that one of the Emersonian dictates was being proven on a national scale. Ralph Waldo had written:

"You shall have joy, or you shall have power," said God. "You shall not have both."

Teddy had had both. But the nation's consensus seemed to be for power. Black clouds were piling up over Europe, though few citizens yet recognized the gathering storm there. The United States was filling up, not just with people living on the land but with people utilizing landscapes for mining, railroads, factories and a rapidly expanding tech-

Jay N. (Ding) Darling's tribute to Theodore Roosevelt
—Courtesy Ding Foundation

Cartoonist Ding Darling of the **Des Moines Register** *was a leading spokesman for conservation and ecology in the 1930s and '40s.* —Courtesy Ding Foundation

(On opposite page)
First known photograph of Old Faithful Geyser, taken by William Henry Jackson in 1872.

139

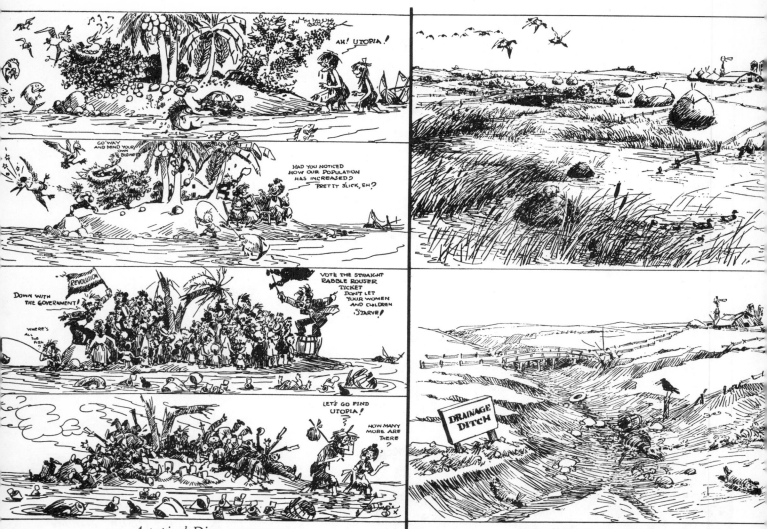

A typical Ding comment
—Courtesy Ding Foundation

*One of Darling's chief concerns
was waterfowl management.* —Courtesy Ding Foundation

nology, as expressed in such matters as the Panama Canal that Teddy Roosevelt had politically engineered.

The frontier had passed, the transcontinental railroads were completed, the Civil War generation was dead now. And Mark Twain's half-savage laughter had faded into silence. The Twentieth Century really did make a change: the "new" writers had to take Marx and Darwin into account. Educators became important on the national scale, so that a professor and Princeton University head could become President before and during World War I.

There was a revolution of social thought, of basic ideas; in the search for new formulas and patterns of thought, the leading communicators of outdoor experiences changed, too. The leisurely, gentlemanly essays upon hunting or fishing, the eloquent dissertations of visitors to plains and mountains that became literary expositions read by people who relished the well-turned phrase more than the terrestrial information—

140

these faded away to be replaced generally by angry polemicists or by historians looking backward at pioneers. A few Southern writers, like Nash Buckingham or Archibald Rutledge, kept the patrician convention alive, but already they were writing nostalgia.

In the period between the Theodore and Franklin Roosevelt presidencies — about a quarter-century — it became clear that the United States was one of the greatest world powers. But it also became clear that much of the joy had gone out of the national soul. Zane Grey, James Oliver Curwood, Gene Stratton Porter and other novelists became wildlife crusaders. Men with scientific training began to suggest patterns of management for fish and game, not simply to call for reform but to outline techniques of sustained yield in forests and wild things, the renewable resources.

A lot of the earlier exuberance seemed to have gone from the citizenry; willy-nilly, the United States had plumped for power and given up simple joy. In 1872, a mining engineer and organizer of the U. S. Geological Survey named Clarence King could write a joyful and beautifully-composed book on *Mountaineering in the Sierra Nevada* that was a graceful and optimistic classic, hailed as a literary gem. He delighted in "typical mountaineers — outcasts from society, discontented with the world, comforting themselves in the solitude of nature by the occasional excitement of a bearfight." King was wry, humorous, poetic and gay. But then the nation chose power — and grimness. So the scribes of the wild responded in kind. For example:

In the second decade of the Twentieth Century, Henry Fairfield Osborn was president of the New York Zoological Society and William T. Hornaday headed New York's Zoological Park. The two men agreed on at least one subject, phrased by Osborn as: "Nowhere is Nature being destroyed so rapidly as in the United States." He went on to write that "it is not savages . . . who are doing this, but men and women who boast of their civilization. Air and water are polluted, rivers serve as sewers and dumping grounds, forests are swept away and fish are driven from the streams. . . . Vulgar advertisements hide the landscape and in all that disfigures the beauty of Nature today, we Americans are in the lead." Sound familiar — and true?

A man who loves Nature

Dr. Osborn wrote that in his foreword to Hornaday's 1913 book called *Our Vanishing Wild Life.* Hornaday was a curmudgeon, and not a lovable one; he is remembered too often as an antihunting fanatic which is not fair. For instance, he defined sportsmen more than sixty years ago as well as anyone does today:

"A sportsman is a man who loves Nature, and who in the enjoyment of outdoor life and exploration takes a reasonable toll of Nature's wild animals, but not for commercial profit, and only so long as his hunting does not promote the extermination of species."

Buffalo were trucked to the Wichita National Wildlife Refuge in the early 1900s to provide breeding stock. After they were sprayed with crude oil to protect against ticks, they were released in special pens and later turned into the refuge. The project was highly successful and helped save the American buffalo from extinction.
—U.S. Fish and Wildlife Service

142

In his early years, William Hornaday was a collector of specimens for taxidermy, then first superintendent of the National Zoological Park in Washington; he shot alligators, elephants and tigers over the world, and became a founder of the American Bison Society that provided pure stock for Wichita National Wildlife Refuge in Oklahoma where buffaloes could be bred back in quantity. The killing of fur seals in the Pribilofs and indiscriminate shooting of song birds started him on the crusade of invective that earned his reputation as a violent protectionist. For he certainly did overstate his case in many paragraphs: equally, he did get laws passed and, more importantly, enforced. Thus he disproved some of his own predictions: that the pronghorn would become extinct by 1932 (he was almost right); that the bighorn sheep would disappear shortly thereafter; that elk were improbable survivors and mule deer likely candidates for extermination; that the whooping crane and trumpeter swan were inevitably doomed. He believed that "the white-tailed deer will be the last species of our big game to be exterminated," which was certainly good judgment. He didn't miss the others by much, either, at the time.

A Colorado deer hunting party of the 1890s —Denver Public Library photo

Hornaday's vitriolic strain has been exaggerated a bit, but his statements still bite. Here is a sampling of them from that 1913 edition of *Our Vanishing Wild Life:*

I am appalled by the mass of evidence proving that throughout the United States the existing legal system for the

143

Before 1900, egrets and other plumed birds were slaughtered to adorn milady's fashions.
—Courtesy National Audubon Society

preservation of wildlife is fatally defective. There is not a single state from which the killable game is not being persistently shot to death, legally or illegally, much more rapidly than it is breeding, with extermination for most of it close in sight. This statement is not open to argument; for millions of men know that it is literally true. We are living in a fool's paradise.

The rage for wildlife slaughter is far more prevalent today than it was in 1872, when buffalo butchers paved the prairies of Texas and Colorado with festering carcasses. From one end of our continent to the other, there is a restless, resistless desire to "kill, kill!" . . . Fully nine-tenths of our protective laws have practically been dictated by the killers of game, and in all but a few instances hunters have been exceedingly careful to provide "open seasons" for slaughter as long as any game remains to kill!

I am now going to ask the true sportsmen and the people who do not kill wild things to awake and do their duty in protecting and preserving the game and other wild life which belongs partly to us, but chiefly to those who come after us. . . . We have reached the point where the alternatives are long closed seasons or a gameless continent; and we must choose one or the other speedily. A continent without wild-life is like a forest without leaves.

. . . Song-bird slaughter is growing and spreading, with the decrease of game birds! It is a matter that requires instant attention and stern repression. At present it seems that the only remedy lies in federal protection for all migratory birds—because so many states will not do their duty.

We are weary of the greed, selfishness and cruelty of "civilized" man toward the wild creatures of the earth. We are sick of slaughter and carnage. It is time for a sweeping Reformation; and that is precisely what we now demand. . . .

The fatalistic idea that bag-limit laws can save the game is the curse of all our game birds, mammals and fish. It is a fraud, a delusion and a snare. That miserable fetish has been worshipped much too long. Our game is being exterminated by blind insistence upon "open seasons" and solemn reliance upon "legal bag limits." . . .

The only thing that will save the game is by stopping the killing of it! In establishing and promulgating this principle, the cause of wildlife protection greatly needs three things; money, labor and publicity. With the first, we can secure the second and third. But can we get it—and get it in time to save? . . .

Sportsmen and gunners, for God's sake elevate your viewpoint to the game of the world. There is something in a game

A 1910 Pennsylvania rabbit hunt
—*Pennsylvania Game News* photo

The bag of a 1913 rabbit hunt in Colorado
—Denver Public Library photo

(At right) Ladies joined in this 1917 rabbit hunt.
—*Pennsylvania Game News* photo

A great egret
—George H. Harrison photo

bird over and above its pound of flesh. You don't need the meat any longer; for you don't know what hunger is, save by reading of it. Birds and mammals are literally dying for your help in the making of long closed seasons, and in the real stoppage of slaughter.

[Ed. note: And this just from his personal preface, before he really got into the book itself. Further along, he quoted an aging Emerson Hough, an extract from an article printed in *Outdoor World* for April, 1912.]

I have read the views of a veteran sportsman, Mr. Emerson Hough, on the wildlife situation as it seems to him today. It is a strong utterance, even though it reaches a pessimistic and gloomy conclusion which I do not share. . . . I believe most sincerely—in fact, I know, that it is possible to make a few new laws which, in addition to the many good laws we already have, will bring back the game just as fast and far as man's towns, railroads, mines and schemes in general ever can permit it to come back. However its breadth of view, its general accuracy, entitle it to a hearing:

Emerson Hough's view

There is no well posted sportsman, no manufacturer of sporting goods, no man versed in American outdoor manners, who does not know that we are at the evening of the day of open sport in America. Our old ways have failed. Our sportsmanship has failed. Our game laws have failed, and we know they have failed. Our game is almost gone and we know it is almost gone. The old America is done and it is gone, and we know that to be the truth.

The old order passeth, and we know that the new order must come soon if it is to work any salvation for our wild game and our life in the open pursuit of it.

There are many reasons. Perhaps the greatest lies in the advance of civilization into the wilderness, the usurpation of many of the ancient breeding and feeding places of the wild game.

I have seen the whole story of American sportsmanship, so called. It has been class legislation and organized selfishness. I have no more reverence for a sportsman than for anyone else, and no reverence for him at all because he calls himself a sportsman. He has got to be a man; he has got to be a citizen.

I have seen millions of acres of breeding grounds pass under the drain and the plow, so that the passing whisper of the wild fowl's wing has been forgotten there now for many years. I have seen a half dozen species of fine game birds become extinct in my own time.

You and I have seen one protective society after another, languidly organized, paying in a languid dollar per capita each year, and so swiftly passing, also to be forgotten. We have seen one code and the other of conflicting and selfish game laws passed, and seen them mocked and forgotten, seen them all fail.

We have seen both selfish and unselfish sportsmen's journals attempt to solve this problem, and fail. Their record has not been one of disgrace, although it has been one of defeat; for some of them really desired success more than they desired dividends. These bore their share of a great experiment in a new land under a new theory of government, which says a man should be able to restrain and govern himself. . . . It was to fail in one of its most vitally interesting and important phases.

A pair of canvasbacks
—Ned Smith

—Drawing by Bob Hines from *Crusade for Wildlife*

147

Zane Grey, outdoorsman

George Reiger of *National Wildlife* magazine wrote his book *Zane Grey: Outdoorsman* in 1972, and this evaluation of the prolific novelist-outdoorsman in 1975 for this volume:

Zane Grey lived more lives than most cats dream of: he was the star hitter of an undefeated University of Pennsylvania baseball team that beat the New York Giants in an exhibition game at the Polo Grounds. He was a Manhattan-based and mighty-bored dentist who solaced himself with weekends of canoeing on the Delaware. He was a California entrepreneur who joined film producer Jesse Lasky to start a movie studio called Paramount. He was literary history's most successful western writer who earned better than half a million dollars a year in royalties from 1922 until long after his death in 1939.

Yet these were sidelines to the real triumphs of Zane Grey's life: he mapped wild rivers in Mexico, roped mountain lions in the Grand Canyon, was the first person to catch a broadbill swordfish in New Zealand. In 1924 he announced he was off to Nova Scotia to catch a world record bluefin tuna—and did so. He pioneered steelhead fishing with fly on Oregon's Umpqua River, and bonefishing in the Florida Keys. He was the first man in history to catch a thousand-pound fish on rod and reel. He was the explorer of what he called America's vanishing wilderness, and he captured the wonder of these experiences in ten books and 100 articles.

Grey was one of the first white men to see Utah's Rainbow Bridge—Nonnezoshe, the Navajos call it. In the spring of 1913, he joined guide John Wetherill, first white to see the monument, Nas ta Bega (also spelled Nasja Begay), the Paiute who took Wetherill to this Navajo shrine, and a couple of Arizona cowboys for the long journey into the desert country where Nonnezoshe is found. (Today, after a leisurely boat cruise on the dammed waters of the Colorado, tourists visit this same marvel with a minimum of effort. Shouts and laughter reverberate from canyon walls that once knew only silence and the sigh of wind.)

Nonnezoshe

"Nonnezoshe" was first published in *Recreation Magazine* in February, 1915:

I had been tired for a long time and now I began to limp and lag. . . . Finally all I could do was to drag myself onward with eyes down on the rough ground. In this way I kept on until I heard Wetherill call me. He had stopped—was waiting for me. The dark and silent Indian stood beside him, looking down the canyon.

I saw past the vast jutting wall that had obstructed my view. A mile beyond, all was bright with the colors of sunset,

Zane Grey views Nonnezoshe. —Romer Grey photo, courtesy B. P. Singer Features, Inc.

and spanning the canyon in the graceful shape and beautiful hues of the rainbow was a magnificent natural bridge.

"Nonnezoshe," said Wetherill, simply.

This rainbow bridge was the one great natural phenomenon which I had ever seen that did not at first give vague disappointment, a disenchantment of contrast with what the mind had conceived.

But this thing was glorious. It absolutely silenced me. My body and brain, weary and dull from the toil of travel, received a singular and revivifying freshness. I had a mystic perception that this rosy-hued, tremendous arch of stone was a goal I had failed to reach in some former life, but had now found. Here was a rainbow not transparent and ethereal, but solidified, a work of ages, sweeping up majestically from the red walls, its iris-hued arch against the blue sky.

Then we plodded on to circle the huge amphitheater. The way was a steep slant, rough and loose. The rocks were as hard and jagged as lava, and cactus hindered progress. Soon the rosy lights had faded, the walls turned steely and the bridge loomed dark.

149

We were to camp under it. Just before we reached it, Nas ta Bega halted with one of his singular motions. He was saying his prayer to this great stone god. Then he began to climb straight up the steep slope. Wetherill told me the Indian would not pass under the arch.

When we got to the bridge and unpacked the lame mustangs, twilight had fallen. When our simple meal had been eaten there was gloom in the canyon and stars had begun to blink in the pale strip of blue above the lofty walls.

Strange, dark shadow

Presently I moved into the strange dark shadow cast by the bridge, a weird black belt, where I imagined I was invisible, but out of which I could see. There was a slab of rock upon which I composed myself to watch, to feel.

A stiffening of my neck made me aware that I had been continually looking up at the looming arch. Near at hand it was too vast for immediate comprehension. I wanted to pon-

der on what had formed it—to reflect upon its meaning. White stars hung along the dark curved line. The rim of the arch appeared to shine. The far side of the canyon was now a black wall. Over its towering rim a pale glow brightened. The shades in the canyon lightened; then a white disk of moon peeped over the dark line. The bridge turned to silver.

I became aware of the presence of Nas ta Bega. Dark, silent, statuesque, with inscrutable face uplifted, with all that was spiritual of the Indian suggested by a somber and tranquil knowledge of his place there, he represented to me that which a solitary figure of human life represents in a great painting. Nonnezoshe needed life, wild life, life of its millions of years—and here stood the dark and silent Indian.

Afterward I walked alone under the bridge. The moon had long since crossed the streak of star-fired blue above, and the canyon was black. At times a current of wind, with all the strangeness of that strange country in its moan, rushed through the great stone arch. At other times there was silence such as might have dwelt deep in the center of the

Zane Grey exploring the Arizona desert
—Photo courtesy George Reiger

151

Mountain lion treed by dogs
—Courtesy B. P. Singer Features, Inc.

earth. An owl hooted, and the sound was nameless. An echo of night, gloom, melancholy, death, age, eternity!

There was something nameless in that canyon, and whether or not it was what the Indians embodied in the great Nonnezoshe, or the death of the ages, or the nature magnificently manifested in those silent, waiting walls—the truth was that there was a spirit.

I did sleep a few hours under Nonnezoshe, and when I awoke the tip of the arch was losing its cold darkness and beginning to shine. The sun had just risen over some break in the wall to reach the bridge. Slowly, in wondrous transformation, the gold and blue and rose and pink and purple blended their hues, softly, mistily, until once more the arch was a rainbow.

Long before life had envolved upon the earth this bridge had spread its grand arch from wall to wall, black and mystic at night, transparent and rosy in the sunrise, at sunset a flaming curve against the heavens. When the race of man had passed it would, perhaps, stand there still. It was not for many eyes to see. The tourist, the leisurely traveler, the comfort-loving motorist would never behold it. Only by toil, sweat, endurance, and pain could any man ever look at Nonnezoshe. It seemed well to realize that the great things of life had to be earned. Nonnezoshe would always be alone, grand, silent, beautiful, unintelligible.

Don

The best dog stories are about working animals, not pets that chase balls and roll over, but dogs that serve as sheep herders, retrievers, pointers or tracking hounds. Zane Grey knew and loved many fine hunting dogs, but his favorite was a part-bloodhound from Mexico named Don, the leader of a pack of lion dogs owned by "Buffalo" Charles Jesse Jones, whose favorite entertainment was roping cougars in the Grand Canyon and then selling the cats to zoos. (Grey described him in *The Last of the Plainsmen,* and once wrote, "No doubt something of Buffalo Jones crept unconsciously into all the great fiction characters I have created.")

Since the mountain lions took a regular toll of his pack, Jones picked up new dogs wherever they could be found and trained them through the simple expedient of shooting them with bird shot every time they took off after something that was not a mountain lion. Don had been so trained and never forgave Jones the injury and insult. Zane Grey admired the dog's spirit and befriended the hound by nursing it back to health after a cougar had torn its throat.

Here is the conclusion of one of the great dog stories of American literature. "Don" first appeared in *Harper's* in 1925:

One day Jones and I treed three lions. The largest leaped and ran down into the canyon. The hounds followed. Jones strode after them, leaving me alone with nothing but a camera to keep those two lions up that tree. I had left my horse and gun far up the slope. I yelled after him, "What'll I do if they start down?"

He turned to gaze up at me. His grim face flashed in the sunlight. "Grab a club an' chase them back," he replied.

Then I was alone with two ferocious-looking lions in a piñon tree scarcely thirty feet high. While they heard the baying of the hounds they paid no attention to me, but after that ceased they got ugly. Then I hid behind a bush and barked like a dog. The lions grew quiet. I barked and yelped until I lost my voice. Then they got ugly again! They started down. With stones and clubs I kept them up there, while all the time I was wearing to collapse. When I was about to give up in terror and despair I heard Don's bay, far away. The lions had heard it before I had. I could see the beating of their hearts through their lean sides. My own heart leaped. Don's bay floated up, wild and mournful. He was coming. Jones had put him on the back trail of the lion that had leaped from the tree.

Deeper and clearer came the bays. How strange that Don should vary from his habit of seldom baying! Soon I saw him far down the rocky slope, climbing fast, ringing out that wild bay. It must have curdled the blood of those lions, the herald of that bawling pack of hounds.

Don saw me before he reached the piñon in which were the lions. He bounded right past it and to me, leaped up and placed his forepaws on my breast. He licked my face. Then he whirled back to the tree, where he fiercely bayed the lions. While I sank down to rest the chorus of the hounds floated up. As usual they were far behind the fleet Don, but they were coming.

Another day I was heading for camp, with Don trotting behind. When we reached the notch of a huge cove that opened down into the main canyon the hound let out his deep bay and bounded down a break in the low wall. Don had scented a lion or crossed one's trail. Suddenly several sharp yelps came from below, a crashing of brush, a rattling of stones. Don had jumped a lion.

Tracks of a lion

I threw off coat and chaps. Then, with camera over my shoulder and revolver in my belt, I plunged down the break in the crag. Reaching a dry stream bed, I saw in the sand the

A cornered mountain lion
—Leonard Lee Rue III photo

Dogs and the prey —A. G. Wallihan photo, Denver Public Library

tracks of a big lion, and beside them smaller tracks that were Don's. And as I ran I yelled, hoping to help tree the lion. I was afraid that the beast might wait for Don and kill him.

Finally I came to an open place near the main jump-off into the canyon, and here I saw a tawny shape in a cedar tree. It belonged to a big tom cat. He swayed the branch and leaped to a ledge, and from that down to another, and then vanished round a corner of wall.

Don could not follow those high steps. Neither could I. We worked along the ledge, over huge slabs of rock toward the corner where our quarry had disappeared. We were close to the great abyss.

At last I worked out from the shade of rocks and trees and, turning the abrupt jut of wall, I found a few feet of stone ledge between me and the appalling chasm. How blue, how fathomless! I was shocked into awe and fear.

Then Don returned. The hair of his neck was bristling. He had come from the right, from round the corner of wall where the ledge ran, and where surely the lion had gone.

I meant to track that beast to his lair and photograph him if possible. So I strode to the ledge and round the point of wall. Soon I espied huge cat tracks in the dust. And ahead I saw the ledge—widening somewhat and far from level— stretch before me to another corner.

Don followed close at my heels. He whined. He growled. I did not stop to think then what he wanted to do. But it must have been that he wanted to go back. The heat of youth and the wildness of adventure had gripped me, fear and caution were not in me. Nevertheless, my sensibilities were acute. When Don got in front of me there was something that compelled me to go slowly. The ledge narrowed. Then it widened again to a large bench with cavernous walls overhanging it. I passed this safe zone to turn on to a narrowing edge of rock that disappeared round another corner. When I came to this point I flattened myself against the wall and worked round it.

Again the way appeared easier. But what made Don go so cautiously? At the next turn I halted short, quivering. The ledge ended—and there lay the lion, licking a bloody paw.

On that instant I did not seem conscious of fear. Jones had told me never, in close quarters, to take my eyes off a lion. In the wild excitement of a chance for an incomparable picture, I forgot. A few seconds were wasted over the attempt to focus my camera.

Then I heard quick thuds. Don growled. I jerked up to see the lion had leaped half the distance. He was coming. His eyes blazed purple fire. They seemed to paralyze me, yet I began to back along the ledge. Whipping out my revolver I tried to aim. But my nerves had undergone such a shock that the gun wobbled. I dared not risk shooting. If I wounded the lion it was certain he would knock me off the narrow ledge.

So I kept on backing, step by step. Don did likewise. He stayed between me and the lion. Therein lay the greatness of that hound. How easily he could have dodged by me to escape the ledge!

A mountain lion watches his pursuers. —Leonard Lee Rue III photo

Moment of terror

A precious opportunity presented itself when I reached the widest part of the bench. Here I had a chance. Then, when the overhanging wall bumped my shoulder, I realized I had come to the narrowing part of the ledge. Not reason but fright kept me from turning to run. I backed along the strip of stone that was only a foot wide. My nerve was gone. Collapse seemed inevitable. I had a camera in one hand and a revolver in the other.

That purple-eyed beast did not halt. My imagination gave him a thousand shapes and actions. Bitter, despairing thoughts flashed through my mind. Jones had said mountain lions were cowards, but not when cornered—never when there was no avenue of escape!

Then Don's haunches backed into my knees. I dared not look down, but I felt the hound against me. He was shaking, yet he snarled fiercely. The feel of Don there, the sense of his courage, caused my cold blood to flow. In another second he would be pawed off the ledge or he would grapple with this hissing lion. That meant destruction for both, for they would roll off the ledge.

The quarry on the edge of Grand Canyon —Courtesy B. P. Singer Features, Inc.

Zane Grey on Tonto Rim
—Romer Grey photo,
courtesy B. P. Singer Features, Inc.

156

I had to save Don. That thought was my salvation. Physically, he could not have saved me or himself, but his grand spirit pierced to my manhood. Leaning against the wall, I lifted the revolver and steadied my arm with my left hand, which still held the camera. I aimed between the purple eyes. That second was eternity. The gun crashed. The blaze of one of those terrible eyes went out.

Up leaped the lion, beating the wall with heavy thudding paws. Then he seemed to propel himself outward, off the ledge into space—a tawny figure that careened majestically over and over, down to vanish in the blue depths.

Don whined. I stared at the abyss, slowly becoming unlocked from the grip of terror. I staggered forward to a wider part of the ledge and there I sank down. Don crept to me, put his head in my lap.

I listened. How endlessly long seemed that lion in falling! But all was magnified. At last puffed up a sliding roar, swelling and dying until again the silence of the canyon enfolded me.

Don sat up and gazed into the depths. Then he turned his sleek dark head to look at me. He whined and licked my hand. It seemed to me Don and I were more than man and dog. He moved away then round the narrow ledge and I had to summon energy to follow. I turned my back on that awful chasm and held my breath while I slipped round the perilous place. Don waited there for me, then trotted on. Not until I had gotten off that ledge did I draw a full breath. Then I toiled up the steep rough slope to the rim. Don was waiting beside my horse. Between us we drank the water in my canteen, and when we reached camp night had fallen. A bright fire and a good supper broke the gloom of my mind. My story held those rugged Westerners spellbound. Don stayed close to me, followed me of his own accord, and slept beside me in my tent.

Grey was not afraid to write about fear or defeat. He saw no conflict in the fact that mountain lions and bears both frightened him and fascinated him; that he loved to pursue them, yet prayed for the end of each hunt. So the famous saltwater angler of the 1920s and 30s was comfortable with the thought that big ones often do get away.

Zane could be vain; he lied about his age to *Who's Who* so that biographical dictionaries list his birth year as 1875 when it was actually 1872. He was occasionally arrogant; when Arizona enacted game restrictions for the first time in 1930, ZG demanded a permanent free hunting license because, he argued, he had done so much to put Arizona on the map. However, he approached the great fishes of the sea with humility. And if among his many world records were still greater records that might have been, so be it.

Zane Grey with one of his lion-hunting dogs
—Photo courtesy George Reiger

Zane Grey hunting in the wilderness —Courtesy B. P. Singer Features, Inc.

A me-and-Joe story

The me-and-Joe story that Zane Grey typified was the bread-and-butter style for outdoor magazines and books for the first half of the Twentieth Century. The formula is a fairly simple one—"me and Joe went fishing (or hunting or whatever) and we overcame (or didn't overcome) a heap of obstacles and we finally caught (or shot) a pile of something." The story has an alternate ending which involves not-catching but, invariably, the author ends up by saying, "next time, things will be different."

Editors and writers proclaim that the "me-and-Joe story is dead!" It isn't. It never will be. The readers will not allow this to happen. The specialist writer who dwells on tackle, firearms, camping gear or the latest gee whiz invention has to put some of this gear to the test now and then. He probably won't do it alone, but he will do it successfully, in another episode of "me-and-Joe."

Here is a classic example. One of the characters is actually named Joe and the guide (of course!) is John. Burton Spiller (of "Grouse Feathers" fame) provides "Namaycush Nightmare" from the May, 1939, issue of *Field & Stream* magazine.

Sleep still had its hold upon me, but something within told me that the tent was moving. Eyes still closed, I listened. Presently it moved again. The flap fluttered, and the fly screen billowed down until it touched my face. I dug my elbow into Ernie's ribs with a force that brought a startled groan and caused him to sit upright.

"What is it?"

"Grab the tent," I cried, "and hang on! The mosquitoes are flying off with it!"

Ernie listened for a moment, then lay back and drew the blanket up.

"That's wind," he said. "Right from the north pole."

It was wind, and a lot of it. The tent fluttered and trembled, trees moaned, and out there in darkness I could hear the roar of the lake on the sandy shore. It was cold, too, unbelievably cold, for the two previous days had been like summer.

"No fishing today." I lay back, tucked the woolly blanket around my neck and inhaled great draughts of crisp air.

Ernie sat erect once more.

"What did you say!" he asked. "No fishing?"

"Yes. And I'm going to sleep until dinner-time."

It was the seventeenth day of June, and for eight days we had fished from crack of dawn until it had grown too dark to see the fly. Eight days, and some of them had furnished the finest landlock fishing I had ever known. I lay there thinking about them, aware that Ernie was talking, but paying no heed until he asked what I thought of the plan.

"What plan?"

"About going up there after some of those big lake trout."

"Huh? What big lake trout?"

"Haven't you been listening?"

"No," I told him; "and I don't intend to. I came up here to catch salmon, not those lazy underwater babies."

"Lazy! Do you mean to say that big lake trout are lazy? Look!" he said, "Joe was telling me yesterday. There's a lake somewhere—he knows where—that has some big ones in it. Look! It's going to be too rough to fish this lake today but we can go up there. We only have to portage two or three miles, and it's small enough so that it won't be rough."

"No!" I said flatly.

"Look!" He was growing argumentative. "We came up here to fish, didn't we? What are we going to do? Sit around camp all day?"

"Not me," I replied firmly. "I'm going to sleep."

"Look!" he reiterated. "Joe was telling me about—"

He was still talking when, a half hour later, his face began to grow visible, and by that token I knew another morning was breaking.

"All right," I agreed wearily. "I'll go."

When we had acquainted Joe with the plan, it developed that the beginning of the portage lay some two miles up the lake. "Too rough for that," he said, practically echoing my

A trout takes a fly
—Pennsylvania Fish Commission photo

159

thought. "We go around, though. Take one canoe. Easier for carry. One fish and one stay on shore."

Presently we were on our way. Ahead of us went John, a young Montagnais just returned from his first winter on the trap-line. His shoulders were almost as broad as the canoe which rested upon them, but he tapered down, wedgelike, to thin, narrow hips and legs which propelled him about nine feet to a stride. Joe carried the tackle box, fish net, bread, bacon and fry-pan. Ernie and I brought up the rear, weighted down with a rod and puffing already with the steepness of the trail.

An hour later I wiped sweat from my eyes, and looked about. The lake lay before me, encircled on three sides by high, spruce-clad shores which deflected the wind and left but a dancing ripple on the surface. There was a primitive newness about it which was suggestive of something different in the way of lake trout. Joe pointed to where, unmindful of our presence, a moose grazed along the marshy shore.

I began assembling the rod. "Come on," I said. "Let's go."

A few yards out from shore, at the edge of the weeds, we found a school of minnows—chunky, silvery fellows, unexcelled for live bait. With tiny hooks and bits of bacon we

Sliding a canoe over a beaver dam —Leonard Lee Rue III photo

took a dozen and went ashore to determine by drawing straws which of us should be the first to lower one of them into the depths.

The lot fell to Ernie—he has a way of snapping straws between his fingers which I could never master. I watched them strike off toward the farther shore where the deep water lay. Then I turned to John.

"It's a cold morning," I ventured.

"O.K." he answered.

I tried again. "Some pretty big fish here, eh?"

"O.K."

"How big?" I asked.

"O.K." he said again.

"Look," I said, borrowing Ernie's ejaculation. "You don't understand a word, but what's the difference? Let's whittle out whistles and play the 'Sextette from Lucia'."

"O.K."

I proceeded to carve whistles. A thin, piping one seemed to attract his fancy, and he blew it repeatedly. Suddenly the air was filled with cliff swallows hovering above us, darting down until they all but flicked our hat brims. John grinned delightedly, and when they would have departed he called them back with the quavering, reedy note.

Thus an hour passed, and then Ernie was back, holding up a fat 5-pounder, his face glowing.

"Look!" he cried. "There are fish out there that could swallow this one. Get out there and try it."

Presently John and I were circling the farther shore. With a shiner sewn on and an ounce of lead weighting it down, I was running line out from the fly reel. Down, down it went, until but a few yards of backing remained on the spool. John slowed the canoe to a crawl, and presently I felt the sinker touch bottom.

Or was it bottom? The lead seemed to bump over some obstruction, caught, came free, and then anchored into something solid. The old fly rod took on a new arc, and I shot a frightened glance at the scant coils of line on the reel.

"Whoa! I called to John. "Back up. I'm hung up on the bottom."

He said, "O.K." and dug his paddle in a backward surge.

In that moment when our forward progress ceased I felt the thing to which I was fast rise up and turn over, then settle back. "It's a strike!" Before the half-moon of the old bamboo could straighten, something went into action there in the depths. The tactics were those of a lake trout, for I could feel the well-remembered rollings and bulldog shakings, but there was a power behind them which was new.

—Drawing by Betty R. Thomas
from *A Conservation Saga*

The fight begins

The fish had merely been indulging in a few warming-up exercises; all at once it started off with a speed and determination which set John to digging with the paddle. Straightaway it went, with every last inch of line out, and then, just as I felt that something must part, it stopped, shook itself vigorously — and the line went limp.

I sat there lifeless, the line forgotten in the catastrophe of losing such a fish. SMASH! Without an instant's warning, the rod bent as the tip and half of the second joint shot under the canoe. I swung it free around the bow and brought it up just as the line twanged tight. Doubling back, the fish had passed beneath us and at breakneck speed was headed for the lower end of the lake. There was no line left to give him, not even the spring of the rod, for it was pointed directly at him. I sat there dumbly, hanging on. I could feel the line stretch and then it came back to me with a recoil which rocked the canoe. There was no question about it this time.

The hook, when I reeled in, had parted company with the leader, but the line was intact, and I was soon paying it out once more, with a wabbling, darting minnow plowing its way down to the bottom.

It was the sort of fishing of which a sportsman sometimes dreams. Fifty miles northwest of Lake Saint John, and miles beyond the last road, the lake was practically virgin so far as being fished. Deep and crystal-clear, the shores and hills bore evidence that it was spring-fed, and schools of fry in the shallow waters were proof that there was no food shortage.

With a caution born of my previous experience, I kept a bit more reserve line on the spool, but I had scarcely made up my mind that I had enough out when once more the rod sagged steadily back in that characteristic strike of the big laker on live bait. No snappy, electrifying tug such as the brook trout gives, nor the smashing strike of the landlock, but just a remorseless closing of those serrated jaws upon the bait.

Once more I struck, wishing that I might exchange the warped old fly rod and single-action reel for something which would leave us a bit more evenly matched. As on the previous occasion my action touched off fireworks, but this time I was fast to a smaller fish. For a few minutes it had things pretty much its way, but John was able to follow its rushes, and after a time I could check them myself. When I had drawn the fish alongside, John shipped his paddle, picked up the net and lifted it in.

It was another five-pounder, the emblematic gray color of its kind, but so dark that it appeared almost black, while its pale rounded spots glowed as from an inner light.

"That's a nice trout," I declared, and John nodded agreement.

"O.K." he said.

The memory of those trolling rods and reels which I should have had sense enough to take along arose to haunt me. Our rods were wholly inadequate, and neither of us had nearly line enough to stop one of the big fellows when it decided to run. It was a pretty problem, and I wrestled with it while John paddled to the head of the lake.

"Get in here," I said to Ernie when we came to where they were sitting. "Let's splice our lines together, go out there and take a big one."

"That," he scoffed, "is a brain-storm. The reel won't hold it."

"Mine will hold some of it," I insisted. "We'll let the rest drag, and after we've tired him out we'll tow him ashore."

He laughed, but it did not require much persuasion to get him into the canoe. The reels would each hold a hundred yards of backing, which left approximately thirty-five yards of fly line protruding. Ernie expressed his opinion of such an outfit, but he accepted it, eagerly.

Another big one

Never have I seen lake-trout fishing to equal what we found that day. It was impossible to get a line to the bottom without having a fish strike. Ernie brought in a two-pounder, stripping the line in by hand at the last. No sooner did he bait up and get it down once more than a mate to the two we had previously taken nailed it. We alternated, releasing the fish as soon as they were netted, but the big ones failed to strike.

Then, after I had passed the rod back to him for perhaps the tenth time, I saw it settle back as it had done with me in the morning. With self-control such as I could never attain, he waited for the fish to turn the shiner in its mouth and then struck with a sweeping pull to compensate for the stretch in the long line.

I wonder what enables us to picture a fish accurately long before we have seen it. There was I, sitting in the bow with nothing but the play of the flimsy rod on which to base my opinion, yet knowing that the trout cutting circles and figure eights beneath us was something worth writing home about. The wind was chill, but I found myself growing warm, and

A fine lake trout —Courtesy *Field and Stream*

envied the poise that was Ernie's as he sat there unperturbed, knowing that the chances were all against him, yet grinning delightedly as the rod arched until tip and butt were separated by only a few feet. John followed the fish; once we were out in the center, again we were close in by the rocky shore. Occasionally Ernie sighed and changed hands on the rod, but the smile never left his face.

At last he began to retrieve line, a little at a time, losing it and recovering again. We were out toward the center of the lake once more when I caught a glimpse of the fly line. Ernie gave the reel a few more turns and then began stripping the line carefully through the guides. Presently I saw the fish coming reluctantly up from the depths, looking unbelievably huge in that limpid water.

He was within six feet of the canoe before he saw us. For a moment he lay there motionless, and then, with a mighty sweep of his tail, he turned and started off. From the bottom of the canoe loose coils of line leaped as they shot out through the guides, and then I saw one coil twist about another, draw it up and loop it neatly around the reel; in that infinitesimal moment before the leader parted I thought how accurate was Ernie's definition of such an outfit as that.

Two days later, at the lower end of the big lake, we grounded the canoes before a small Indian encampment and watched John go ashore and greet his people. When it came my turn to say good-by, I held his hand for a moment.

"Next year," I promised him, "we're coming up here with tarpon tackle and see what can be done about landing some of those baby whales. We'd like to have you with us."

He gave me that winning smile, his teeth shining in their copper setting.

"O.K." he said.

Camping first class in 1919 —Denver Public Library photo

"Youth communes" of the late 1960s and early '70s tended to frighten conservative businessmen and crabgrass-conscious suburbanites who felt anyone wanting to live outside a consumer society was un-American. But the dream of an existence freed of daily duties and monthly bills is as old as the nation. From the early explorers to Leonard Hall writing of Possum Trot farm for the St. Louis *Globe-Democrat,* American people have longed for an uncomplicated life amid birds and flowering wild plants. Only a few wrote at length of such rural idylls, but millions read what those few wrote.

One of the few was David Grayson, a pseudonym for Ray Stannard Baker, who lived for 30 years on an Amherst hillside where he "gave up something of the world in order to know something more of the earth." He wrote ten books, plus many essays for *Saturday Evening Post* and other magazines. *Adventures in Contentment* and *Adventures in Understanding* were probably most read (or at least bought) by pre-World War II citizens who were busily wiping out the traces of their own rural heritage while reading the words of a man who praised that same pastoral simplicity.

"We Go Fishing"

Grayson's little tale about a quiet outing "We Go Fishing" is from *Under My Elm,* published by Doubleday, Doran, and here somewhat deleted.

It was in the morning that my friend Waugh called me up. "How about going trout fishing tomorrow?"

Many a year, near the beginning of apple blossoms, when New England hillsides are at their best, Waugh and I have been going fishing. But my first impulse was to say no. Had I not promised five pages of copy? Did not my garden demand immediate attention; might not my bees go off in swarms?

"The hills will never be better," commented Waugh beguilingly. "The shadbush is in bloom."

"But—" said I.

"Barrus says the trout are really rising."

"But—" said I.

"We can take along the old frying pan."

I think it was the old frying pan that was my undoing.

"I'm your man," said I. "What's work anyhow?"

A man and a Colorado stream —Bureau of Reclamation photo

A 1917 gentleman fisherman shows his catch. —Denver Public Library photo

All that day I heard something singing in the dusky places of the mind. When I read in the papers of the woes of a turbulent world, I said to myself, "Never mind, we're going fishing." When I thought of the dire confusion of Europe, my mind slipped aside to remembered glimpses of swift-running water, and I flecking the pools with a choice Montreal or a Parmachene Belle. That afternoon I went up to the attic, got out my best rod and fitted it together, making sure it was in perfect condition. I looked over my flies. Were three leaders enough? Where was my small canvas creel? And my old fishing coat with the roomy pockets?

If you are not a fisherman, you do not know the thrill of wetting up felt pads in a leader box and putting half a dozen leaders to soak, the joy of choosing flies for an early May trip to the Goshen Hills.

I took a superior delight in replying to anybody who wanted me to do anything on Friday: "Can't do it; going fishing." Every time I said it I felt somehow freer. Among our hills it is a thoroughly accepted excuse, as though one said, "Sorry. Can't. Getting married." If I had argued, I should have been regarded with suspicion and subjected to pressure. But fishing. . . .

Sunshine and soft breezes

Friday morning proved perfect: all sunshine, soft breezes from the south. Here was I in soiled fishing coat, shapeless old hat; here was Waugh, his rucksack on his shoulder, rods and boots in his hands. It was going to happen. We were off for a day in the hills.

In our country, fishing is one of the permitted joys. I think it evaded the dour old puritan suspicion of joy or pleasure. For when spring steals in after the long winter, who can resist it? There is an earlier joy: the maple sugar season; but that is an aimed and labored joy, with a reward to satisfy the conscience of a seasoned Yankee. Something that can be sold afterward. But fishing? Two strong men toiling among logs, sloshing through ice-cold water, coming in at night with a few ounces of little fish. No, there is no excuse for fishing except joy.

On the hills we were among the glories of spring woods. Shadbush was a white mist upon the hillsides. The fragrant sassafras on the southern slopes was at its best. In old fields we saw the ruddy glow of high-bush huckleberries, and along the hedges the pin cherries with their rounded blossom clusters were beginning to come out. No moment of the year is so disturbingly beautiful.

We crossed an opening where there had been a sawmill — a dune of sawdust marked the spot — and came to the brook near the end of a broken-down loggers' bridge. The stream has been partially dammed by the obstructions, and a little pond reflected the morning sky, a fleecy cloud, and trees. Water rushed visibly among boulders just below. One's eye chose where to cast the first fly — just above the timbers, where it would drift to dark waters where the mythical big one was lurking. So we sat on the brookside to join our rods, thread through the line, choose the little dark fly suited to the earliness of the season. Then we strapped up our boots and were ready for the fray.

The perfections of a New England trout brook! Hills clad with birches and great old hemlocks, ferns crowding near the water, the stream full of round boulders, and pools, and eddies, and delightful little gravel bars. The music of it all, and the sunshine of a morning in May. . . .

Climbing slippery boulders, straddling fallen logs, wading with swift water sucking at one's boots, this exertion was considerable. I sat down on a mossy bank to rest alone — as a man ought to be when he approaches the momentous events of life — for Waugh chose to fish up the stream and I down it. Among the undergrowth are clumps of mountain laurel not yet in bloom, and dogwood. As I sat there listening to the calming music of the stream rushing over shining stones, I heard off in deep woods the reedy trill of a hermit thrush. Nothing in all the wild places has so much of the mystery, the spirit of the place, as the note of the hermit thrush.

A nice brook trout
—Leonard Lee Rue III photo

An assist for the angler —Denver Public Library photo

(When I left home I had put aside several knotty problems in warm deep places of the mind. While I was not looking, the sunshine somehow got into them, and clear air, the music of the water, and the birds—and next morning I had my problems out again; there they were, quite clear and simple, no more perplexities.)

Being thirsty, I found a rivulet flowing down the hillside among ferns and wintergreen. Just before it made its long leap into the brook, it paused in an adolescent pool. Standing there in the brook, I leaned over and drank from the edge, clear water fresh from the earth itself.

At nearly every likely pool I had a strike at first cast, though the fish, too well fed by high water, were not so voracious as one would wish. Unlike streams I knew as a boy, this one was stocked by a benevolent state and then fished out before the poor fingerlings had a chance at maturity. (A comment on the times! A state pouring its lavish beneficences, and individuals unwilling to restrain themselves.) Nevertheless, I was lured onward; there was a more inviting pool below. And the joy of fishing does not consist merely in the number taken.

Near a branch there is an old sugar-house. In March the maple syrup is boiled down, but for the remainder of the year the place is the home of chipmunk, wild bees and wasps, possibly a porcupine. Here we built our little fire with as few sticks as possible, here Waugh squats with the frying pan to cook a few of the fish. This is one of the high moments — the baiting of the fish themselves.

So we sit there in still woods, declaring no fish has a finer flavor than brook trout. We drink from tin cups dipped in the spring. We discuss the events of the forenoon and plan in detail for what is yet to come. We discuss also the wild things, which Waugh knows by their intimate names. He thinks that human beings are shrinking in significance (though not from modesty) and that they travel too fast to know quiet beauty.

"At forty miles an hour," he says, "one cannot see violets. About all he can recognize is an apple tree in bloom. And when we change to airplanes, only a whole orchard will catch the eye. Perhaps if man shrinks enough, he will again find the violets."

Of all the sensations of the day, none is more delightful than well-earned weariness at the end of it. Not nervous, not mental, but that sense of physical fatigue which steals over a man's body, soothing and relaxing. The ride through the woods in the cool of evening, supper at home with an appetite one has not had for weeks, and early afterward to bed. . . .

This is to go fishing.

Big game

Although much has been written about big game, such writing sometimes reveals more about the writer than about the subject, says John Madson, an eloquent writer-biologist and author who offers here comments on, and excerpts from, four major figures of the period.

There is often something wrong with stories of big game seen only through rifle sights — and something wrong with some accounts of big game that *weren't* seen through rifle sights. The first are often self-consciously intrepid, and the second are often done in a precious style that imbues animals with human qualities that do no credit to honest beasts. Each style has its own distortions, and good nature writing does not distort. It must be true writing, whether fiction or non-fiction.

This is probably the best measure of good animal writing — is it truth? Not just in the literal sense of unadorned fact, but in the inherent truth of mood and spirit as well. It is possible for a frontiersman's tall tale to be true, in the sense of understanding the spirit of the animal and its place, and it is possible for the cool account of a trained naturalist to be untrue if it misses the flavor and spirit of the subject. The best writing, of course, is a skillful blend of both elements — objective fact and subjective spirit.

The examples offered here were chosen for certain literary qualities. Part of that involves skill of expression and vigor of style, but the greater part is the quality of truth that pervades these tellings of animals on their home grounds.

One of America's most remarkable hunter-naturalists was Charles Sheldon, born in Rutland, Vermont in 1867. By 1903, he had proven so successful in business that he retired at the age of 36 and devoted the rest of his life to the study of wild animals and wild places. A man of great physical endurance and courage, he often spent long periods alone in the remaining wilderness regions of North America. One of these was the Mount McKinley district of Alaska which, in 1906, was about as wild as they come. His two expeditions there resulted in "The Wil-

Majestic Mount McKinley —Photo by N. J. Reid, National Park Service

derness of Denali", published by Charles Scribner's Sons in 1930, from which the following account of the mountain, and its Dall sheep, is taken:

December 6–7, 1907. The 6th was a clear day and at dawn I was off to secure a good ram for a trophy. In addition to a few fall and winter specimens for the Biological Survey, I wanted four trophies in winter and spring pelage for myself, each illustrating a different type of horn. Several sheep were on Intermediate Mountain, and from opposite Bear Draw eight or nine ewes were seen on the summit of Cabin Peak, with a ram of fair size standing near but outside the band. At times it would trot about and look off as if something were approaching. When near the summit of the Draw I saw, up on the slopes of the south side, two good rams and two ewes, all feeding close together. Not far away a ewe appeared, running, followed by a ram with splendid large horns; he soon caught up and served her. Then another big ram came around a slope and going up to the same ewe smelled her, while the other stood close by without showing any objections. Two or three other rams and a few ewes were feeding near but only this ewe received special attention. Two of the rams I recognized by their horns as having belonged to the band I had observed during the fall, and it was certain that all were members of the same band.

I decided to stalk them and if possible kill the largest. Rapidly snow-shoeing in a diagonal course up through the spruces and climbing around the slope, I crept forward but found all the sheep in places where it was not possible to approach them. Therefore I waited in the hope that they might move to some point where a stalk might be possible. Before I had been there long the wind increased, squalls suc-

A Dall ram —Leonard Lee Rue III photo

cessively whirled around picking up the snow in clouds that filled the air. Except at intervals between squalls, I could see nothing, but presently caught a glimpse of all the sheep ascending, led by the big ram. The ewes were next behind and were followed by the other rams. I knew they were going up to shelter and that soon they could look down and see me, so I returned to the cabin.

At this period the sun, or probably its reflection, like the dim globe of a setting sun, came only just above the horizon of the mountain crests for an hour each day, giving five hours of daylight, which most of the time was sufficient to admit of taking successful photographs. Before daylight next morning I was well up the bar and soon saw three or four sheep near the spot where they had been observed the day before. One was a ram, but there was not enough light to enable me to see the size of his horns.

In passing through the woods I saw seven or eight beautiful white ptarmigan, not fifteen feet away, hide behind a spruce tree; they flushed while I was maneuvering to photograph them. Emerging from the trees I scanned the west slopes of the mountain leading to the forks. High up near the crest was a ram with splendid horns, slowly walking along the upper sheep trail toward Bear Draw. He continually stopped to feed. The rugged and craggy west slopes of this mountain, furrowed by deep canyons and gorges, were twice divided by long and wide canyons extending up to amphitheaters near the crests, which were extremely jagged and bordered by many precipices. I planned a climb to the foot of a cliff near the trail, where I could watch the face of the mountain and at the same time intercept the ram should he continue, as seemed likely, to Bear Draw.

White-winged ptarmigan
—Leonard Lee Rue III photo

The last hundred yards

After ascending the slope, I took off my snowshoes, stuck them in the snow, put on my creepers and zigzagged slowly upward the last hundred yards, where the incline was very steep and icy, with deep snowbanks that might slide. Using my rifle as a staff, at times jamming the butt into the crust to make footholes for my steps, I finally reached the last snowbank below the icy cliff. Here I hesitated, fearing the snow would slide under my weight, but finally made the attempt and crossed upward to the rocks that had been selected as a waiting place. The surface was windswept and the footing secure. Putting on my squirrel-skin parka to insure warmth I took position and waited.

Red fox—Leonard Lee Rue III photo

From this point the view was free along the west face of the mountain and around the slopes of Bear Draw. Directly ahead, in the direction of the big ram, were steep slopes with rough out-jutting spurs and canyons filled with snow or with walls bared by slides. To the left were the north slopes, equally rough, leading to the amphitheater of mountains surrounding Bear Draw, some windswept, others white, the rolling area of the basin contrasting with the severe surroundings. Below were wide ice-capped bars, while above, the crests of Old Camp Mountain were touched with sunlight. Beyond, a sea of summits, the domed bulk of Denali, fringed with gold, loomed in the heavens. Behind were the outside mountains, their crests shining white in the sun's rays, while the cabin woods seemed like a dark island set in a sea of snow. In the pastures leading to the cabin woods, a fox was careening in a hunt for mice, the grace of his movements pleasing my senses during the hour he was in view. On Cabin Peak were a few ewes and lambs peacefully feeding about the summit, while not far to my left were all the ewes seen there the day before. But the largest rams were absent, leaving only two very small ones and an old one. The old ram carried a type of horns that I coveted, for they were short, compact, and closely curled. He paid exclusive attention to the same ewe, often chasing her for long distances and following wherever she went. Finally he moved away a little and began to feed quietly. Later, a few of the ewes separated from the others and traveled up the slopes to the east, apparently forming an independent little band.

All this time I had kept an eye on the approaching big ram, as he gradually came toward me along the sheep trail. He would appear over the crest of a spur, then disappear, only to reappear still nearer. Often he remained a long time feeding in a small canyon; at other times he loitered in plain sight on open spaces. A slight wind was gently blowing from me in his direction, but I did not feel that this would necessarily alarm him, for the slopes were rough and the currents of air uncertain.

A two-hour wait

During the two hours that I remained waiting he kept coming nearer, always pausing on the crest of each spur to look carefully, sometimes up, sometimes down, and even behind. Finally he descended into the last canyon between us. Then came suspense for I knew that the trail divided, one branch leading directly to me, the other farther down, out of sight behind a precipice. Should he take that one, the outcome would be in doubt. Waiting anxiously, a glimpse of his horns showed that he had taken the lower trail. Having foreseen this contingency I hastened down far enough to have the trail below within shot. The risk of the descent was forgotten in the eagerness of the chase, but I was quickly reminded of the danger by slipping, and only saved myself by using the butt of the rifle.

Reaching the selected point I waited, lying flat. But when, after a sufficient time, no ram appeared on the trail, I was perplexed. Suddenly his horns came in sight above, at the spot I had recently left. He had turned from the lower trail to the upper one. Quickly he rose into full sight and stood alert against the skyline, neck swelled, horns held a little back and tipped to one side. Then he turned his head and looked directly at me, his eyes seeming to pierce me. Never shall I forget the sight of that lordly ram standing rigid and alert below the rocky cliffs and jagged crests, with Denali beyond, majestic against a sky painted with glowing colors.

My rifle shot echoed from the mountain walls; the ram jumped, staggered, recovered, took two bounds upward and sank in his tracks.

When he stood at the spot where I had been waiting so long, why did he not wind my presence and run instead of merely looking about? He was only a hundred and fifty yards away.

Dall sheep grazing —Leonard Lee Rue III photo

A Dall ram on the alert (above) and a Rocky Mountain bighorn ram (below)—Leonard Lee Rue III photos

As soon as I knew he was dead I walked a short distance around the slope and saw the ewes and the ram with compact horns. They were feeding quietly, apparently not having been frightened by the echoes of the shot. The ram stood a little apart broadside, presenting a well-defined target. He appeared to be nearly six hundred yards away; nevertheless I decided to try a shot at him—a risk I have rarely taken at such a distance. Aiming well above him I pulled the trigger. He ran somewhat wildly for a few yards, and vanished behind the point of a spur.

While working my way up to the dead ram the wind increased, the snow began to whirl and the cold became penetrating. After photographing the ram, I cut away a large cake of snow beneath him, stamped down the rest, and carefully lowered him into the depression so he would not roll down the mountain while I was taking off his cape and head. The horns were large and massive, with ten rings, and were freshly chipped at the tips, the end of the right one having been cracked and slightly splintered. He carried evidence of recent combats: two flesh wounds on the face, one on the cheek, and a cut below the left eye. His face was very dirty and his long silky winter coat was stained brownish. The lachrymal glands were greatly enlarged, the areas around the eyes much swollen, the testes enlarged, and a strong odor emanated from the body. Heavy balls of ice were attached to both den claws, and the slits between the cloven hoofs were heavily wedged with ice, indicating that he had crossed an overflow on the bar. The iris was yellow, the nose and lips dull blackish gray.

As I worked on the ram in clouds of drifting snow a jay suddenly came flying up from the distant woods and attempted to alight on the body, but quickly departed when I waved at it. After separating the ram's cape from the neck I cut off the head and examined the stomach, which contained exclusively grass, some of it green at the roots.

No less true in spirit, but much briefer, is the terse description of the Rocky Mountain bighorn by some forgotten Indian who really understood his subject:

"Mountain sheep can't hear thunder, can't smell dead horse, but can see through thin rock."

Which brings us to the wonderful Charles M. Russell, cowboy artist *extraordinaire* and Montana yarn-spinner without peer. In "Trails Plowed Under", published in 1927 by Doubleday, Page & Co., soon after his death, Russell proves his mastery of the old-time frontier idiom and relates the tale of a team of buffalo that were broken to harness—sort of. O, rare Charlie Russell!

A tall western tale

"There used to be a man on the Yellerstone," says Rawhide Rawlins, "that catches a pair of yearling buffalo. He handles them hump-back cows till they're plumb gentle — they hang around the ranch like any other cows.

"One day he decides to put them in the yoke. That bump hits back of the yoke and in all ways they are built for work. But he finds looks are deceivin' when he rigs a pole on a pair of old hind wheels, making a kind of cart — it's no sulky, 'tain't built for speed, but that's what it's used for. They ain't hard to yoke. He's whacked bulls and skinned mules, but when he gets up behind this team he can't find no team talk the pair savvies. He's usin' rope reins but they might as well be thread — he couldn't bend their necks with a canthook.

"Finally, they start. Maybe these hump-backs know where they's going, but this driver ain't got no idea. 'Tain't long til he's in a country he ain't never seen but judgin' from the sun he's going south, an' both wheels are smoking. They run over a jackrabbit and pass a band of antelope that's doing their damdest. It's afternoon when the hurry-up party hits a rut that breaks the driver's hold and he lands in a patch of buck brush. He's dam' glad of it — he's plumb tired holdin'. He don't know how far they went, but he don't get home till noon next day. About a week later his team shows up at the corral — they're still packing the yoke. They don't show no signs of being jaded.

"Next spring a neighbor talks him into breaking sod with them. He gets to thinking this over, and knowin' they got the power he hooks them onto a plow.

"This time he heads them north, but this direction suits them. It's springtime and they don't mind going north. He's got his plow sunk to the beam — it slows their gait some but he can't turn them. They started north and that's where

Buffalo team in harness —Kansas State Historical Society, Topeka

they's going. Streams don't stop them, and when he quits the handles they's still plowing north.

"He finds out that these animals travel north in the spring and south in the fall. If he could find a country with seasons no longer than this field, they'd do good for a driving team. If he was fixed so he could spend his winters in Mexico and his summers in Canada, they'd just be the thing. He hears from them through a friend late that summer—they're north of the Teton, plowing south."

Slewfoot

One of the last American frontiers was not west, but southeast, in the interior of Florida. There, in the remote fastness of palmetto scrub, wet "prairie" and forest, Marjorie Kinnan Rawlings set her superb 1938 novel *The Yearling,* published by Charles Scribner's Sons. The book is filled with remarkable vignettes of old Florida and its back-country folk and wildlife. One of the best of these is the boy Jody's finding of his pet fawn. But even more remarkable—having come from the pen of a gentle newspaperwoman—is this account of Jody and his father cornering the great bear "Slewfoot":

The morning's trailing had been a leisurely business; a pleasant jaunting rather than a hunt. Now the dark bay thicket closed in over their heads, jorees flew from the denseness with an alarming whir of wings, the earth was soft and black, and there were scurryings and rustlings on either side in the bushes. On the trail, a bar of sunlight lay occasionally where the thicket parted. The scent, for all the comings and goings, was not confused, for the taint of bear hung heavy in the leafy tunnel. The short fur of the bulldog stood on end. Old Julia ran swiftly. Penny and Jody were forced to stoop to follow. Penny swung the muzzle-loader in his right hand, its barrel tipped at an angle, so that if he stumbled and the charge went off, he would not touch the running dogs before him. A branch crashed behind and Jody clutched at his father's shirt. A squirrel ran chattering away.

The thicket thinned. The ground dropped lower and became a swamp. The sunlight came through in patches as big as a basket. There were giant ferns here, taller than their heads. One lay crushed where the bear had moved across it. Its spiced sweetness lay heavy on the warm air. A young tendril sprang back into an upright position. Penny pointed to it. Slewfoot, Jody understood, had passed not many minutes before. Old Julia was feverish. The trail was food and drink. Her nose skimmed the damp ground. A scrub jay flew ahead, warning the game, and crying "Plick-up-wha-a-a."

The swamp dipped to a running branch no broader than a

Great horned owl
—Ned Smith

178

A black bear on the prowl —Leonard Lee Rue III photo

fence post. The print of the nubbed foot spanned it. A water moccasin lifted a curious head, then spun down-stream in smooth brown spirals. Across the branch, palmettos grew. The great track continued across the swamp. Jody noticed that the back of his father's shirt was wet. He touched his own sleeve. It was dripping. Suddenly Julia bayed and Penny began to run.

"The Creek!" he shouted. "He's trying to make the Creek!"

Sound filled the swamp. Saplings crashed. The bear was a black hurricane, mowing down obstructions. The dogs barked and bayed. The roaring in Jody's ears was his heart pounding. A bamboo vine tripped him and he sprawled and was on his feet again. Penny's short legs churned in front of him like paddles. Slewfoot would make Juniper Creek before the dogs could halt him at bay.

A clear space opened at the creek's bank. Jody saw a vast black shapeless form break through. Penny halted and lifted his gun. On the instant, a small brown missile hurled itself at the shaggy head. Old Julia had caught up with her enemy. She leaped and retreated, and in the moment of retreat, was at him again. Rip darted in beside her. Slewfoot wheeled and slashed at him. Julia flashed at his flank. Penny held his fire.

Black bears —Leonard Lee Rue III photos

He could not shoot, for the dogs.

Old Slewfoot was suddenly, deceptively, indifferent. He seemed to stand baffled, slow and uncertain, weaving back and forth. He whined, like a child whimpering. The dogs backed off an instant. The moment was perfect for a shot and Penny swung his gun to his shoulder, drew a bead on the left cheek, and pulled the trigger. A harmless pop sounded. He cocked the hammer again and pulled the trigger once more. The sweat stood out on his forehead. Again the hammer clicked futilely. Then a black storm broke. It roared in on the dogs with incredible swiftness. White tusks and curved claws were streaks of lightning across it. It snarled and whirled and gnashed its teeth and slashed in every direction. The dogs were as quick. Julia made swift sorties from the rear, and when Slewfoot wheeled to rake at her, Rip leaped for the hairy throat.

Jody was in a paralysis of horror. He saw that his father had cocked the hammer again and stood half-crouching, licking his lips, fingering the trigger. Old Julia bored in at the bear's right flank. He wheeled, not on her, but on the bulldog at his left. He caught him sideways and sent him sprawling into the bushes. Again Penny pulled the trigger. The explosion that followed had a sizzling sound, and Penny fell backward. The gun had back-fired.

Rip returned to his attempts for the bear's throat and Julia took up her worrying from the rear. The bear stood again at bay, weaving. Jody ran to his father. Penny was already on his feet. The right side of his face was black with powder. Slewfoot shook free of Rip, whirled to Julia and caught her to his chest with his cupped claws. She yelped sharply. Rip hurled himself at the back and buried his teeth in the hide.

Jody screamed, "He's killin' Julia!"

Penny ran desperately into the heart of the fracas. He jammed the gun-barrel in the bear's ribs. Even in her pain, Julia had taken a grip on the black throat above her. Slewfoot snarled and turned suddenly and plunged down the bank of the creek and into the deep water. Both dogs kept their hold. Slewfoot swam madly. Only Julia's head showed above the water, below the bear's snout. Rip rode the broad back with bravado. Slewfoot made the far bank and scrambled up its side. Julia loosed her hold and dropped limply on the earth. The bear plunged toward the dense thicket. For a moment more Rip stayed with him. Then, confused, he too dropped away and turned back uncertainly to the creek. He snuffed at Julia and sat down on his haunches and howled across the water. There was a crashing in the distant undergrowth, then silence.

William Faulkner

One of the giants of American letters, William Faulkner, Nobel Prize winner, was a haunted man born to the new South but forever dreaming of the old. Throughout his work runs a deep love of the southern land, and a deep fear of its devastation. Nowhere is his profound land-love better shown than in "Go Down, Moses," published in 1940 and containing his three most vivid outdoor writings: "The Old People," "The Bear," and "Delta Autumn." In "The Old People" he is twelve years old again, waiting in the slow rain with an old half-Negro, half-Indian named Sam, and sensing the great buck moving somewhere beyond:

They went on. The boy could still hear Boon talking, though presently that ceased too. Then once more he and Sam stood motionless together against a tremendous pin oak in a little thicket, and again there was nothing. There was only the soaring and sombre solitude in the dim light, there was the thin murmur of the faint cold rain which had not ceased all day. Then, as if it had waited for them to find their

A tense moment —Karl H. Maslowski photo

Eight point white-tailed buck —Leonard Lee Rue III photo

positions and become still, the wilderness breathed again. It seemed to lean inward above them, above himself and Sam and Walter and Boon in their separate lurking-places, tremendous, attentive, impartial and omniscient, the buck moving in it somewhere, not running yet since he had not been pursued, not frightened yet and never fearsome but just alert also as they were alert, perhaps already circling back, perhaps quite near, perhaps conscious also of the eye of the ancient immortal Umpire. Because he was just twelve then, and that morning something had happened to him: in less than a second he had ceased forever to be the child he was yesterday. Or perhaps that made no difference, perhaps even a city-bred man, let alone a child, could not have understood it; perhaps only a country-bred one could comprehend loving the life he spills. He began to shake again.

"I'm glad it's started on," he whispered. He did not move to speak; only his lips shaped the expiring words: "Then it will be gone when I raise the gun—"

Nor did Sam. "Hush," he said.

"Is he that near?" the boy whispered. "Do you think—"

"Hush," Sam said. So he hushed. But he could not stop the shaking. He did not try, because he knew it would go away when he needed the steadiness—had not Sam Fathers already consecrated and absolved him from weakness and regret too? —not from love and pity for all which lived and ran and then ceased to live in a second in the very midst of splendor and speed, but from weakness and regret.

So they stood motionless, breathing deep and quiet and steady. If there had been any sun, it would be near to setting now; there was a condensing, a densifying, of what he had thought was the gray and unchanging light until he realized suddenly that it was his own breathing, his heart, his blood— something, all things, and that Sam Fathers had marked him indeed, not as a mere hunter, but with something Sam had had in his turn of his vanished and forgotten people. He stopped breathing then; there was only his heart, his blood, and in the following silence the wilderness ceased to breathe also, leaning, stooping overhead with its breath held, tremendous and impartial and waiting. Then the shaking stopped too, as he had known it would, and he drew back the two heavy hammers of the gun.

The solitude did not breathe

Then it had passed. It was over. The solitude did not breathe again yet; it had merely stopped watching him and was looking somewhere else, even turning its back on him, looking on away up the ridge at another point, and the boy knew as well as if he had seen him that the buck had come to the edge of the cane and had either seen or scented them and faded back into it. But the solitude did not breathe again. It should have suspired again then but it did not. It was still facing, watching, what it had been watching and it was not here, not where he and Sam stood rigid, not breathing himself, he thought, cried No! No!, knowing already that it was too late, thinking with the old despair of two and three years ago: I'll never get a shot. Then he heard it—the flat single clap of Walter Ewell's rifle which never missed. Then the mellow sound of the horn came down the ridge and something went out of him and he knew then he had never expected to get the shot at all.

"I reckon that's it," he said. "Walter got him." He had raised the gun slightly without knowing it. He lowered it again and had lowered one of the hammers and was already moving out of the thicket when Sam spoke.

"Wait."

"Wait?" the boy cried. And he would remember that— how he turned upon Sam in the truculence of a boy's grief over the missed opportunity, the missed luck. "What for? Don't you hear that horn?"

And he would remember how Sam was standing. Sam had not moved. He was not tall, squat rather and broad, and the boy had been growing fast for the past year or so and there was not much difference between them in height, yet Sam was looking over the boy's head and up the ridge toward the sound of the horn and the boy knew that Sam did not even see him; that Sam knew he was still there beside him but he did not see the boy. Then the boy saw the buck. It was coming down the ridge, as if it were walking out of the very sound of the horn which related its death. It was not running, it was walking, tremendous, unhurried, slanting and tilting its head to pass the antlers through the undergrowth, and the boy standing with Sam beside him now instead of behind him as Sam always stood, and the gun still partly aimed and one of the hammers still cocked.

Then it saw them. And still it did not begin to run. It just stopped for an instant, taller than any man, looking at them; then its muscles suppled, gathered. It did not even alter its course, not fleeing, not even running, just moving with that winged and effortless ease with which deer move, passing within twenty feet of them, its head high and the eye not proud and not haughty but just full and wild and unafraid, and Sam standing beside the boy now, his right arm raised at full length, palm outward, speaking in that tongue which the

The camera moves in. —Leonard Lee Rue III photo

boy had learned from listening to him and Joe Baker in the Blacksmith shop, while up the ridge Walter Ewell's horn was still blowing them into a dead buck.

"Oleh, Chief," Sam said. "Grandfather."

When they reached Walter, he was standing with his back toward them, quite still, bemused almost, looking down at his feet. He didn't look up at all.

"Come here, Sam," he said quietly. When they reached him he still did not look up, standing above a little spike buck which had still been a fawn last spring. "He was so little I pretty near let him go," Walter said. "But just look at the track he was making. It's pretty near big as a cow's. If there were any more tracks here besides the ones he is laying in, I would swear there was another buck that I never even saw."

Shore bird decoys
—Shelburne Museum photo

Slat geeese—canvas covered (below)
—Shelburne Museum photo

An early American art form

One of the first men to realize that early duck decoy carvers had, unknowingly, created an authentic American art form was Joel Barber, an amiable gentleman from Connecticut. During the 1930s when decoys were inexpensive and available (people thought duck hunting was doomed) Barber put together a massive collection. He ranged the country in person and in correspondence, making a study of the art techniques, and put what he learned into *Wild Fowl Decoys,* published by Garden City in 1934. Barber's collection is in a Shelburne, Vermont museum, and his book is a source for those who study decoys.

Data is scant but what we know to be ancient native methods were employed by white men at no very distant date. In my own collection are two duck decoys having bodies designed to receive bird-skin covering, also a snipe stool made in 1800 on which bird wings served the purpose of painted plumage. The mallard head decoy shows ancient Indian methods employed by modern sportsmen. Thus we have parallels of artifices extending back to the second period of native American culture; over a thousand years.

First methods of pursuit are also shadowy but from recorded observations it can be assumed that the earliest gunning was conducted from land, ducks and geese being attracted to shore and not killed on open water. But land shooting offered limitations that the increasing demand for waterfowl could not satisfy. The rafts of birds off shore were at once a solution and an inspiration. Some inventive colonist of unknown name and date brought forth the innovation that spread rapidly. This conjectural person constructed a floating decoy made of wood, which would ride at anchor in semblance of wild fowl feeding. In this connection, it is important to observe the radical change in construction. While

Displays at the Shelburne Museum, Vermont —Shelburne Museum photo

the Indian used materials of an impermanent character, the white man employed something relatively permanent: wood. His object was the production of a practical implement for continued and heavy service. Trifling modifications have appeared, but the great idea remains unchanged. These wooden birds of the floating type became known as "duck decoys," or "duck stools," those of the stick-up variety as "snipe decoys." Both were finished in painted plumage.

The name "decoy" was derived from European fowling. "Stool" likewise comes from old world usages. In its original meaning this term signified a movable pole or perch to which a live pigeon was fastened as a lure to entice his kind within gunshot. The bird so used was termed "stool pigeon." The live stool pigeon was employed in pursuit of the passenger pigeon, now extinct.

Decoy, stool, block and toller

Thus both "decoy" and "stool" came to designate a device to mislead unwary waterfowl. It is easy to see how these basic but foreign names were applied to the later American invention.

Along the Atlantic Coast other names appear, principally "blocks" and "tollers." Block is self-explanatory. Toller, while possibly a survival of the process called "tolling ducks," in all probability reaches back to the ancient calling or tolling of the death knell. All of these names are still used in different localities, but decoy, in its original implication of deceit and unseen operator, remains the most generally accepted name for the false bird of American tradition.

The making of decoys grew to a stage of minor coastal industry. But it was never more than a slack season trade. Beginning with gunners, it spread to scattered individuals having a peculiar knowledge and knack with tools. Practitioners went by the name of "stool-makers." The years immediately following the Civil War saw the beginning of decoys made by machinery, a separate branch of the industry which continued down to the end of unrestricted shooting.

During this period a few well-known factories supplied

Swan decoy, circa 1890
—Shelburne Museum photo

Setting decoys —Courtesy Evinrude Motors

thousands of decoys to sportsmen and gunners, principally in the south and west. But the 'longshore stool-maker never ceased production. Handmade decoys were the favorite of the experienced professional and fastidious sportsman. From this source emanated the classic decoys of American duck shooting.

Decoys were the tools of a grim profession. There is no way of estimating the number employed in the pursuit of waterfowl. In the hands of the principal users many were lost every season, broken in necessarily rough handling or gone adrift in heavy weather, never to be retrieved. Those that do survive are in the class of curios, reminders of an older order of things American which have passed out of existence.

J. Frank Dobie, Texan of the world, was a Man of the Border—*any* border, though his favorite country was the wide land drained and nurtured by the Rio Grande. He set down old *corridas,* tales from campfires, legends, myths and folklore. He wrote of *vaqueros,* Apache gold, Yaqui silver, longhorn cattle, and of life in the arid region that stretches from the Gulf of Mexico to Baja California. But he was at home in Cambridge (the English one) where he lectured on American History, on the Texas campus at Austin or on horseback in brush country.

He wrote that "not even the most scientific mammalogist can comprehend the whole animal without hospitality towards the stuff of dreams that this more than mere mammal has influenced human minds to weave around him." Such an attitude is denounced as anthropomorphism by most young game managers, and by most hunters, to the distress of James Frank Dobie.

"Sympathy for wild animals that is intellectual as much as emotional has not been a strong element in the American way of life," he wrote. " 'I was wrathy to kill a bear,' David Crockett said, and that is essentially all one learns about bears from the mightiest of frontier bear-hunters . . . Buffalo Bill derived his name from the fact that he excelled in killing buffaloes, not from knowing anything about them except as targets. . . . These are not instances of eccentricity but of the representative American way, until only yesterday, of looking at wild animals."

True sympathy with the wild "is found in the two extremes of society—savages and people with cultivated minds and sensibilities," Dobie wrote, and quoted Mary Austin's *The Land of Little Rain:* "No man has ever really entered into the heart of a country until he has adopted or made up myths about its familiar objects." And on his own: "All of the ecological, biological and other logical studies that public bureaus and private enterprises may forward still will not bring those authentic tidings of invisible things that the lifted voice of the coyote brings in the early evening while lightning bugs soften the darkness under the trees . . ."

A hunting coyote
—Leonard Lee Rue IV photo

Howling wolf
—Betty R. Thomas

Old Crip

For a story about an individual coyote, try "Old Crip" from *I'll Tell You a Tale:*

Luke Stillwell, government trapper, was silent for longer than a minute. He shifted in the rawhide-bottomed chair. A wrinkle stood on his forehead.

"I called her Old Crip," he began. "I set my first trap on this ranch the twelfth day of September. There had been trappers ahead of me, and they had caught some coyotes a lot. I began right away catching cripples escaped from their traps. I caught fourteen cripples and then there were two coyotes left. They were really educated. Finally I caught one of them and the trap held. It took me fifteen months and five days to get Old Crip.

"She had two toes off her left front foot. While I was still clearing the others out, she put her right foot into one of my traps. She pulled, gnawed, twisted and broke that foot off just above the steel jaws. What she left there was all I ever saw of her until the end. The average coyote caught in a trap becomes frantic. It bites bushes, steel, sometimes its own tail . . . another trapper told me of a coyote that chewed both front feet out of a trap and then just sat there while he came up to kill her. I am sure that Old Crip knew what she was about when she set to work to free herself.

"Within thirty days the stub had healed and she was killing sheep again. She went from one pasture to another and killed $3,000 worth of sheep during the fifteen months and five days I kept after her. I didn't let up a day. Her track was unmistakable and her habits individual.

". . . Old Crip never seemed boastful and reckless in her killing, like some coyotes. One night four bold ones came into a pasture, killed sixteen lambs, gorged, went on, met a skunk, killed him and rolled on him without taking a bite, went on, met a fat possum, killed it and left it untouched beside the trail. These coyotes were out to shoot up the town. Old Crip would slaughter sheep right and left; then she was gone. When a coyote with any sense kills a sheep, he knows he is in danger. He eats in a hurry. He takes one gulp and looks up. As soon as he is full, he makes tracks. This was the way of Old Crip . . . always on the alert. After the killing was over, she seemed never to be playful or loggy. She stayed unceasingly careful.

"She never traveled stock trail or road. Coyotes that travel that way—and it is natural to trot down a road—are easily caught. All the time I was after Old Crip, fresh coyotes were coming into the ranch. They had regular entrances, and they regularly got into traps. . . . A dead coyote seems to mean nothing to a live one—excepting the highly intelligent, and Old Crip was the most intelligent of them all. Trapping on one big ranch before I came here, I caught fifty-four coyotes in a single trap at one location, just resetting it and hanging the carcasses, one after another, near by. This was at a wire-netting fence corner. The easiest kind of coyote to trap is a young male. The females even when young are more distrustful.

"Old Crip had already depredated on the ranch for several years when I took up her trail. She would never go under a fence unless another coyote preceded her. She had probably been caught at a hole under a fence. She avoided all lures, scents and baits. I caught her that first time in a blind trap— just a naked trap hidden in the ground where I thought she might go to water. That was the night of October 31. She had miles of Los Moros creek to water in and she was not fixed by habit to any one place. After she stepped down the bank to water and had drunk, she backed out now, putting her feet in almost the exact tracks they made coming in.

"In the spring I found her den with the pups. Her mate had no doubt been caught. I set a blind trap at the den. A sheep got into it and fell into the hole, rather large at the mouth. That night that mother coyote beat a trail around the sheep and her den. I took the sheep out next morning. Old Crip never returned to her pups. The mother instinct in coyotes is strong; in Old Crip it was not blind. She plainly suspected— and she was right—that a hidden enemy would not let her pass if she stepped into her den to move her young. She left them to perish.

A coyote stalks his prey (right).
Testing the air (below).
—Leonard Lee Rue III and IV photos

"In coyote country you frequently see them moving by day, though it is their nature to be nocturnal. I never once saw Old Crip. It is my belief she never roamed during daylight. So far as I know, she never howled. Except at mating time, she ranged alone. She killed alone. She went in the night and she went in silence.

"It is a habit with some coyotes to gorge a bait of sheep meat, six pounds say, go off maybe forty or sixty yards to where there is brush and shade, and there dig a hole. Then the animal throws up the meat, still fresh and undigested, into the hole and covers it with earth, just like a dog buries a bone. The coyote that does this will almost invariably come back the next night, dig its meat out of the earth that has kept it fresh, and eat. By that time, buzzards would have ruined a carcass, provided other animals had not made away with it.

"A coyote will rob another one's cache if he finds it. The caches make good trapping places; sometimes I bury a piece of meat, round up earth over it in a natural way, and set traps. After a coyote fills up on meat for the purpose of burying it, and has buried it, he goes straight back to the carcass and eats again, either to digest the food or to carry it to the young.

"Now, if Old Crip ever buried a piece of meat, I did not know it. If she ever ate carrion, I did not know it. She had lost the scavenger habits. She was always choosy about her meat. She liked it warm and fresh, and she was particular about the cuts.

"On the night of December 17 I caught her the second time, in a blind trap on a bluff overlooking water. She must have realized she could not free herself this time. I found her drowned. She had dived off the bluff and gone under some wire netting in the water. The hook on the trap chain caught in this wire. She aimed to kill herself, so it seems to me. She had just cut the throat of a choice lamb, had eaten and was on her way to water. I examined her stomach. It contained five or six pounds of select meat—kidneys, small intestine, leaf fat, loin and tender ribs. I never heard of a lobo smarter than Old Crip. I came to admire her while she was baffling me. She seemed to belong to the hills that I belong to. I think of her lots of times in the night. I'll never forget her."

Old Mattie

To ask what dogs mean to humans is to ask a stupidly-broad question; as well demand to know why those who claim to love humanity generally hate people. But ask how a given hunter feels about a certain dog. Then Bob Lee Maddux of Cookeville, Tennessee, who set down long thoughts for long years in *The Hunter's Horn* magazine, can tell you how he, a pursuer of foxes, felt in 1932 about one particular canine. Bob Lee, nearing ninety, was living in Cookeville in 1975 and still writing.

I'm going hunting tonight but my heart isn't in it. Dewey buried old Mattie yesterday.

She had been running the night before and was returning home about sunup when struck by an automobile as she crossed the highway in front of my place. She made it to the yard but died before reaching the house. A neighbor saw the car strike her and asked Dewey, who hunts with me, if any of my hounds were hurt. He came to see, and found her lying under a cedar near the kennels.

Dewey dug the grave close to the kennel gate, putting up foot and head stones, while my wife gathered zinnias and marigolds to cover the grave. I did not attend the burial; tears are always just under my lids, and I loved Mattie. A better foxhound never lived.

Dewey and I called her the Character Witness. Many are the hounds she has discredited for lying, and many she saved from threshing by telling us it was fox. She had a mouth that was near perfection: clear, distinct, yet soft like the lady she was. In her veins was the blue blood of Kentucky and Missouri hounds blended with native mountain Tennessee stock. Her sire, Dick Martin, was a grandpup of John B. — many letters have been written by Texas hunters about his get — and of Nash's Charley, a locally famous red fox hound, and of Jeff Wall's Queen, a Goodman hound. Her dam was a Hershel matron, Hershel's dam was Mary Ann, a mate to John B.

All of which means nothing, unless it proves everything.

Big red fox were using the Low Gap, along Little Caney Fork, and round Devil's Knoll when Mattie was six months old. All that winter she followed the old dogs as they ran the ridges down into the gulches, swimming the river when it was icy cold and out of its banks. Bill and Dick were hard hounds; either could drive a fox at top speed alone, and when one of them got the fox on a straight run, you might as well try to pass a fire truck on its way to work.

Mattie wasn't any sort of field trial hound — she was too good for that. She simply refused to run roads and rabbits. But her not hunt? You could give her a search warrant and she would serve it if she had to hunt ten square miles and look all night. If fox changed feeding gounds and we had no race, if fellows were putting their hounds into the cars and the fire had about gone out, those of us who knew her would wait for Mattie. Many times she would come in hearing, running her fox when all other hounds had given up.

She never told a lie in her life. When she gave tongue, hounds came out of their beds in fence corners. Lame hounds or sore hounds would hobble after her on three feet, young ones would step in your face if you were stretched on a sheepskin for forty winks. She was my best hound. Good hunter, good trailer, good mouth, dead game, and a driving hound if there be such.

So I am bothered, being just between my good friends Dan Shaw and Preacher Burns of West Virginia. Col. Shaw threatened to quit hunting when his favorite, Highball, was killed by a car; and Preacher Burns wrote about his favorite being poisoned, dipping his pen into fire and brimstone. He didn't see how he could endure it, yet was revived and given hope by the smell of frying bacon, wafted his way by a special providence just in time to prevent self destruction.

I am not quitting, not do I blame the driver of the death car — the law of averages will finally get car and hound together if one travels highways. It is hard for me to think that anyone would intentionally kill Mattie, and I don't want to believe it.

I am glad she died here. She might have hung in a woven wire fence miles from the casting ground, to die in pain and thirst; or fallen into a sink hole on a deserted mountainside and starved.

I have hunted lost hounds for days, leaving my business, wearing out casings over impossible roads, and spending twice the cost of replacement of the dog. Then I learned a lesson. I searched not because I had to have the hound, but because it needed me.

The men whose hounds chase foxes are a mystical breed. It doesn't seem to carry over into those who pursue coons, where the name of the game is kill the prey. In some hills further west, another writer told of that sort of chase about the same time Bob Lee Maddux was setting down his views.

Coons and possums

Vance Randolph was also an octogenarian in 1975, living in Northwest Arkansas contemplating the Ozarks and their people, whom he has been observing for fifty years in print and photographs. He never made much money from his books and articles, but he gained some literary reputation for such volumes as *We Always Lie to Strangers* and *From an Ozark Holler.* He wrote of catfish, coons and "peerch catchin," or the .22 pistol for squirrel-hunting. This report on the pursuit of raccoons is excerpted from *Ozark Outdoors,* published by Vanguard Press in 1934 and dedicated to U.S. Senator Harry B. Hawes of Missouri, who loved black bass more than he did Byzantium-on-the-Potomac. The Senator has a

A bluetick coonhound treeing coon
—Leonard Lee Rue III photo

Brown Trout by Bob Hines

(On preceding page)
Pacific Marlin by Bob Hines

Brook Trout by Bob Hines

Rainbow Trout by Bob Hines

Raccoon out on a limb —Leonard Lee Rue III photo

monument above Big Spring on Current River, but none in Washington; the Ozark plaque was dedicated at an Outdoor Writers Association meeting in June, 1954.

Coons and possums are plentiful in Ozark country, and hunting these animals at night with dogs is one of the hill-man's chief recreations. Nearly every mountain cabin is guarded by two or three flop-eared coon dogs, and the man who owns a genuine red-bone bawlin'-hound is the envy of his neighbors. Scarcely a night in hunting season passed that I did not hear the full-throated coon hound music in the hills, and I had only to attend the afternoon caucus in the crossroads store to hear last night's adventures recited with enthusiam and detail.

This sort of hunting has its attractions, but I have never cared much for it. Listening to the canine chorus is pleasant enough, but galloping through black dripping forests, up hill and down, falling headlong and scrambling up again for five of my best sleeping hours is a bit too strenuous for my taste. And I do not get much thrill out of the actual killing; the coon is simply located with a flashlight and shot or shaken down to the dogs. Sometimes it is necessary to cut down trees, which does not add to my enjoyment.

My first real interest in coon hunting began when I became acquainted with Carney Peters, a tall, gimlet-eyed fellow who

—Ned Smith

wore the conventional slouch hat and went about his business in orthodox Ozark fashion.

He took little part in the conversation at the country store and he owned no dogs. He did not seem to be a trapper, either, but there were always a few coonskins drying on the north wall of his cabin, and once I noticed a row of cased possum hides on a wire in his summer kitchen. In rambles through the Holler I often met Carney, always alone, always casually friendly, but after a few words I thought best to get on about my affairs. I made it a point, too, to keep away from certain heavily wooded ravines near his cabin. This was during the Volstead experiment, when many hillmen saw fit to do some of their farm work in private.

One afternoon I was in need of meat for the pot, and out on a hardwood ridge back of Carney's place I spied a fox-squirrel in a big chinquapin tree. Resting my .22 Colt against a convenient limb, I put the tiny bullet fairly through his shoulders, and almost before he struck the ground another squirrel appeared. The little pistol cracked again, and the second squirrel came thumping down. (I usually take several shots to a squirrel and have been known to empty the magazine without touching a hair.)

As I picked up the squirrels, wishing some skeptical friends had witnessed this coup, I heard a twig snap and turned to see Carney Peters with his mouth open.

"Wal, sir," he said in the peculiar falsetto which hillmen use in moments of emotional stress, "I'll be teetotally dadgummed."

The Ozarker is a rifleman first of all, and his knowledge of one-hand firearms is limited to heavy revolvers. A hillman does not regard the pistol as an instrument of precision. I am really a very ordinary shot, but my Poot Holler neighbors thought I was a wizard because I killed small game with a pistol.

Carney examined my two squirrels with interest. Then he wanted to look at the pistol . . . we sat and talked far into the night, and as the moon rose over ragged cedars it was greeted with shrill whoo-oo-oo from the limestone ledge behind us.

"Know whut that is a-hollerin'?" asked Carney.

"Sounds like a screech-owl gone wrong," I answered.

He said it was a coon a-whickerin' and we fell into a discussion of these animals. It was long after midnight when I heard of Carney's method of hunting.

"Wal, sir, this hyar huntin' with tree-dawgs of a night is all right for them whut likes it, but as for me, I git my coon an' possum in broad daylight, an' I don't need no pot-lickers t'

194

holp me, neither. Come long with me tomorrow, I'll show ye. Fetch that leetle pistol, too. We mought meet up with a painter" — an old joke. There hasn't been a "painter" in the Poot Holler for twenty-five years, but the danger is still mentioned in talking with city hunters.

Morning sun saw us on the trail as Carney led the way to the river. Coons, said he, spend daylight in trees, and preference is given to hollow trees near water. He was scrutinizing the mud at water's edge, with occasional sallies up into the brush where he carefully examined the bark of certain trees. In some cases one can track a coon directly to the tree in which he lives, but more often one must depend upon marks which continued climbing leaves upon the trunk itself.

Sometimes there is mud on the tree, too, and a careful search may show a few hairs caught in rough bark. There are doubtless other signs — tracking is Carney's business, not mine.

My idea was that coons sought out big, hollow trees with large openings near the ground, but Carney says he has never

Perched in comfort —Leonard Lee Rue III photo

taken one in such a place. It appears that the best trees are those not conspicuously decayed, but which have a small hollow rather high up, where the opening is often not visible from the ground. The size of the best entrance was a surprise to me; even a big coon can squeeze into a small hole, while a fat possum wriggles into a cavity which appears scarcely large enough for a fox squirrel.

In a mild climate like the Ozarks many possums do not live in hollow trees at all, but lie in old squirrel nests or among matted grapevines.

We walked for at least two miles, and Carney examined twenty trees before he found one to suit him. An old white oak it was, with a hollow where a big limb had fallen off, and Carney showed me a few possum hairs in the bark.

"If it warn't such a easy climin' tree, we'd jest leave th' varmit go." He did not think it worth while to do much hard climbing for a possum. A coon, now . . . a prime coonskin was worth seven or eight dollars that winter.

Carney was up that tree and poking in the hollow with a stick. I heard a peculiar gasping snarl, and a big possum came crashing down through the branches, with Carney not far behind. From now on I had to carry the game in a gunny sack, for he was busy with other matters.

Finally he showed me an old sycamore leaning over the river; here we should certainly get a coon. He intimated that he had better take the pistol with him. I began to see why Carney was so interested in it — a pistol would be mighty useful in this tree-climbing style of hunting.

The hollow in the old sycamore was not wide or deep, and the coon jumped out before Carney expected it, and ran out on a limb like a great squirrel. Anxious to avoid further climbing, he fired several shots at it. At such short range he couldn't miss. The coon humped his back, clung for a moment, then plunged down with a great splash into the river. He sank like a stone.

It was only a few hundred yards downstream that we found the next promising place, and this time the tree looked so easy that I undertook to climb it myself. There was a wide shallow cavity in the top of a stub; when I got high enough I saw the coon peering at me with bright, beady eyes. He turned slowly and seemed in no great hurry to escape. Finally he started up over the edge, and with the loss of the other coon in mind, I shot him through the head.

At this he sprang almost into my face, then went crashing down through vines and branches. He fell just at the edge of the water but after a feeble kick he lay still. Into the sack he went and we decided to call it a day.

Have they gone?
—Photo by Don Woolridge,
Missouri Department of Conservation

196

Peaks of Otter, thought by Jefferson to be the highest point in North America
—Virginia Chamber of Commerce, Flournoy photo

DeVoto, another renaissance man

Shortly before those Japanese bombs fell on Pearl Harbor with booms still echoing in the national subconscious, the editor of Harper's Magazine was finishing up his ninth book, a study of earlier troubles. Bernard DeVoto was another of those renaissance men: a good editor and fine writer (which is a rare combination), conservationist, critic, literary figure, historian, *bon vivant,* outdoorsman.

197

Writing *The Year of Decision: 1846* he got hung up on the memory of James Clyman, a Virginia-born mountain man who survived for 89 years to die in California in 1881. Clyman was a master of the sierras and "also had literary moments;" he kept a journal in a time when most of his fellows could not read or write. Using those journals and stray letters, DeVoto wrote of the Long Hunters even better than Emerson Hough wrote of the Long Trail cowboys. Here are some of his most eloquent interpretations of that breed of men, from *Year of Decision* as published by Little, Brown in 1942.

History does not tell us whether Eric the Red and his successors traded with the Indians for furs. If they got to Minnesota, as legends say, they had to when winter closed in. Besides birds and herbs and carvings, there may have been furs in the wealth that the Admiral of the Ocean piled in Queen Isabella's throne room. Certainly, before Spain or France or England sent explorers up the tidal rivers, coasting fishermen from overseas made deals for furs with the native savages. Furs were a principal object of all explorations, no matter if one also sought Cibola or the Northwest Passage or some other sunny myth, and the Captain John Smith who took skins home to his queen got them along trade routes already old. Then half a dozen countries planted colonies in the New World, and from all these plantations men went up the rivers—whether a few miles up the James or by the St. Law-

—Betty R. Thomas

rence to the Lakes and by portage to the Wisconsin and so down the Mississippi—to trade with Indians for the only wealth the Indians had. It was these men who made the unknown known.

In all the colonies the Indian trader pushed up the streams, over the divide and down into new country. He was the man who knew the wilderness and he held the admiration of the settlements. Let there follow after him the men who built cabins; his was the edge and the extremity. The settlements saw his paddle flash at the bend or sun glint on his rifle at the edge of the forest, and then there was no word of him until his shout sounded from the ridge and he was back, with furs.

He had to live in the wilderness. That is the point. Woodcraft, forest craft, river craft were his skill. To read the weather, the streams, the woods; to know the ways of animals; to find food and shelter; to find the Indians when they were his customers or to battle them from stump to stump when they were on the warpath, and to know which caprice was on them; to take comfort in flood or blizzard; to move safely through the wilderness, to make that wilderness his bed, his table, and his tool—this was his vocation. And habits and beliefs still deep in the patterns of our minds came to us from him. He was in flight from the sound of an ax and he lived under a doom which he himself created.

Thus the Long Hunter. On May 25, 1804, Lewis and Clark, ascending the Missouri River, passed LaCharette Creek and a settlement of "seven small houses and as many poor families . . . the last establishment of whites." Here ended the fringe of civilization and the lifelong westering of Daniel Boone, seventy years old, his back to the wall, unable to go farther. The Long Hunter's farther west . . . Lewis and Clark went on up river, to winter near the Mandan village . . . so far the pirogues of rivermen were familiar, the trails known. Next spring they went on, and to about the mouth of the Yellowstone they still traveled where the voyageurs had gone before them, but somewhere hereabouts the known ended. . . . Somewhere on this side of the Shining Mountains they were seeking, Lewis and Clark brought a white man's eyes for the first time to the big unknown. They went on into the mountains, over the divide, down the Snake to the Columbia, and on to the Pacific. The next year they were coming back along their own trail—and met fur hunters already following it. The Astorians moved in, the North West Company worked westward through English lands, Americans and Mexicans came up from Taos or Santa Fe. The era of the mountain men began.

Rocky Mountain National Park —George H. Harrison photo

Solitude of the mountains

The frontiersman's craft reached its maximum and a new loneliness was added to the American soul. The nation had had two symbols of solitude, the forest and the prairies; now it had a third, the mountains. This was the arid country, the land of little rain; the Americans had not known drouth. It was the dead country; they had known only fecundity. It was the country of intense sun; they had always had shade to hide in. The wilderness they had crossed had been a passive wilderness, its ferocity without passion and only loosed when one blundered; but this was an aggressive wilderness; its ferocity came out to meet you and survival required a whole new technique. Before this there had been no thirst; now the creek that dwindled in the alkali or the little spring bubbling for a yard or two where sagebrush turned a brighter green was what your life hung on. Before this one had only to look for game; now one might go for days without food, learn to live on rattlesnake or prairie dog, or on the bulbs of desert plants, or when they failed on the stewed gelatine of parfleche soles . . . in the new country, a white man's face was three months' travel, or six months', or a year away. Finally this was the country of the Plains Indians, horse Indians, nomads, buffalo hunters, the most skillful, the most relentless, the most savage on the continent.

Mountain craft was a technological adaptation to these hazards. . . .

* * * *

Much of the routine could be repeated here from Clyman's recollections: drifting downstream with a log to escape the Aricara, watching a Dakota tear the flesh of a dead enemy with his teeth, sewing Jedediah Smith's scalp and ear in place after a grizzly had lacerated them, starving in winter canyons, purged by alkali water, feasting with the Crows on a buffalo hunt, battling the Arapaho on Green River, captured by the Blackfeet but escaping them. But the routine may be assumed.

* * * *

Of the Ashley expedition which he joined, Clyman said that "Falstaf's Battallion was genteel in comparison." Yet it included some men whose distinction did not rest entirely on their craftsmanship. There was Jedediah Smith, the Yankee whose ambition was to be a geographer, who first crossed the desert to California . . . whose reports it would have been sensible of both Polk and Frémont to look up — a Christian gentleman who became an explorer of the first rank. There were Pierre Louis Vasquez, the Spanish gentleman from St. Louis; Robert Campbell, who was to become a great Western merchant; Andrew Henry, who was a true empire builder. Elsewhere in the mountains there were men like them; Joe Meek, whose cousin by marriage, Jim Polk, was President of the United States; Lucien Fontenelle, in whose veins flowed the royal blood of France; Manuel Lisa, whose life was ambiguous and shrouded but who came from Spanish aristocracy. There were other sprigs of British, French and Spanish nobility, remittance men or younger sons or just the restless. . . .

Against such mountain men may be set off such others as Edward Rose, the crossbred white, Negro and Cherokee who had been a river pirate and became a Crow chief. Or Mike Fink, who has become immortal in our folklore. Or another Crow chief, the mulatto Jim Beckwith, who went up the river as Ashley's blacksmith and gave our literature its goriest lies. Or Bonneville's partisan, Joe Walker, who broke part of Frémont's trail, who wiped out Diggers as he would have stepped on piss-ants, and opened a trade in stolen California horses, and so gave the mountains another routine of simple theft, complicated though not made hazardous by the murder of Californians. Such irreproachables as Frémont and Kit Carson were to follow him in this commerce.

And there were those whose distinction was wholly of the trade itself. There was the French strain . . . there were the Canadians and Scots of the North West Company and the Hudson's Bay outfit that absorbed it. More particularly there were the Americans, mostly Missourians, Kentuckians and Virginians: the Sublettes, John Gant, Drips, Vanderburgh, Peg-leg Smith who cut off his own leg and whittled a stump to take its place, Black Harris, Old Bill Williams, who had been a Methodist preacher, David Jackson, Dick Owens, Dick Wooton, Hugh Glass, Greenwood, Fallon, Rube Herring, Long Hatcher . . . And finally the great triumvirate must be named: Kit Carson, the Little Chief; Tom Fitzpatrick, White Head or Broken Hand; and with drums and trumpets, Old Gabe, Jim Bridger.

* * * *

Jim Beckwith, who knew, said that though the Indian could never become a white man, the white man lapsed easily into an Indian. The mountain man's eye had the Indian's alertness, forever watching for the movement of boughs or grasses, for the passage of wild life, something unexplained floating in a stream, dust stirring in a calm, scratches on a cottonwood. His ear would never again hear church bells but was tuned to catch any sound in a country where every sound was provisionally a death warning. He dressed like an Indian in blankets, robes, buckskin and moccasins . . . he lived like an Indian in bark huts or skin lodges, and married a succession of squaws. He thought like an Indian, propitiating the demons of the wild, making medicine and consulting omens. . . .

Retreats of the mountain men

He might winter at Taos, that first of Wild Western towns; he might bring furs to St. Louis after the fall hunt, when the town would roar with war cries, rock with the pleasures of

Mount Rainier —Washington State Department of Commerce photo

behemoths, and grow quiet toward dawn when he spread his robes in some alley. But mostly he wintered at a log stockade a thousand miles from Planters' House—Bent's Fort, Fort Union, Fort Laramie; or hutted up in some basin under the peaks—Brown's Hole, Ogden's Hole, Jackson's Hole, Pierre's Hole, Bayou Salade. Mostly his only touch with the settlements was an annual debauch when the caravan came to buy his furs and get the purchase price back in tobacco and alcohol at two thousand per cent advance. For the rest, he was on the creek and among the mountains. His legs stiffened from the icy waters where he trapped beaver. Behind any ridge Blackfeet or Arapaho might be waiting for him. From the dark behind any fire he lighted might come the ultimate arrow. Any sleep might end in the rush of stampeded horses and a gurgle in his partner's throat. . . .

True enough . . . but the back trail was always there and need only be followed eastward. Few ever took it. They were, by God! the mountain men. The companies might exploit them but they were free and masters. They had usurped the Indian's technology and had so bettered it they could occupy the Indian's country and subdue the Indian. They had mastered the last, the biggest and the hardest wilderness. Give any of them a horse and a pack mule, a half-dozen traps, a couple of robes, a bag of possibles, and a rifle — and he could live comfortably among privations that broke the emigrants' spirit and safe among dangers that killed soldiers like flies in the first frost. They had learned not only to survive the big lonesome but to live there at the height of function.

The waters of Manitou held freedom and desire, both inappeasable in the American consciousness. Why else the everlasting myth of the West? . . . The seed of expansion, to answer the tug, to push over the ridge, to go it alone . . . to be a man and to know that you were a man.

And to be a free man. At any evening campfire below the Tetons, if they had paid civilization its last fee of contempt they had recompense in full, and Henry Thoreau had described it. They made their society, and its constraints were just the conditions of nature and their wills, the self-reliance in self-knowledge that Mr. Emerson commended. In the illimitable silence of the mountain night with the great clouds going by overhead, one particular American desire and tradition existed in its final purity. A company of free companions had mastered circumstance in freedom and their yarns were an odyssey of the man in buckskin who would not be commanded — what scalps had been taken along the Yellowstone, who counted coup in Middle Park, what marvels had been seen in John Colter's Hill or where stone trees lie beyond the Painted Desert or where the waters of Beer Spring make the prettiest young squaw quite unattractive for a surprising time. The stories came from a third of a continent and summed up two centuries of the American individual.

Finally there was the beauty of this last wilderness, added upon all the unspoiled natural beauties through which the individual had passed in his two centuries. The land of little rain, the Shining Mountains. It was theirs before the movers came to blemish it — rivers flowing white water, peaks against the sky, distances of blue mist against the rose-pink buttes, the canyons, the forests, the greasewood flats where the springs sank out of sight. They were the first to pass this way and, heedless of the eagle's wing they had stretched across the setting sun, they stayed here. God had set the desert in their hearts.

Alone in a stream —Tom Rost, *Field and Stream*

American angling literature

Mark J. Sosin is a lecturer on fishing, photographer, outdoor editor for a radio network and vice-president of the Outdoor Writers of America. His interpretation of angling literature between the Roosevelt presidencies is a unit in itself.

As America started its journey through the 20th Century, fishing and its literature underwent a metamorphosis. The armchair adventurer still wanted to be entertained with tales of distant places, but exciting stories set closer to home also had appeal and writers began to tell their audience about secret spots that harbored superb sport.

It must be remembered, however, that transportation systems left something to be desired and, although the Wright Brothers were about to make their historic flight, it would be half a century before low cost air travel was available to the masses. Autos were still not the most reliable conveyances, roads in the wilds were crude at best, and the railroads took time to get there. To travel, an angler not only had to have means, but he had to have time. Only the leisure class could journey to angling Edens.

More people began to take up angling and they craved information on technique. The barefoot boy with branch, string, and bent pin was

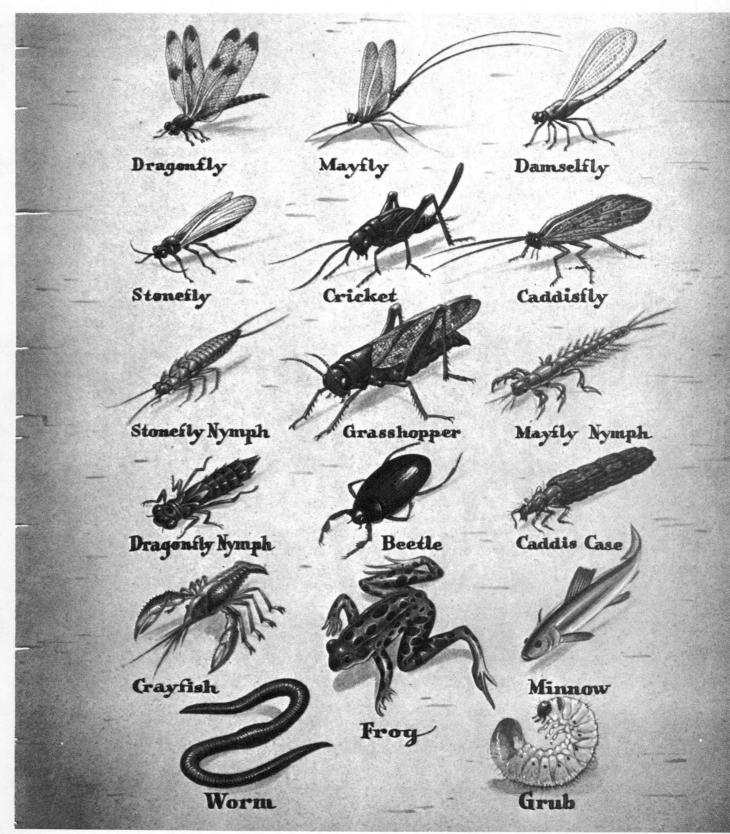

Dragonfly   Mayfly   Damselfly

Stonefly   Cricket   Caddisfly

Stonefly Nymph   Grasshopper   Mayfly Nymph

Dragonfly Nymph   Beetle   Caddis Case

Crayfish   Frog   Minnow

Worm   Grub

Favorite baits for fresh-water fishing

A fly fisherman tries his luck. —Courtesy Pennsylvania Fish Commission

already legendary. Angling was now taking a turn toward sophistication. Fly fishing for trout (a royal sport in Europe) was gaining momentum in America and men such as Gordon, La Branche, and Hewitt shared their knowledge with the reader along with their skillful manner of expression.

One might question why so much was written about the trout, while other species suffered literary neglect. Perhaps the reason is simply that the new trout fisherman was willing to buy books on the subject. Publishers were in business to make money, trout fishermen purchased books, so trout books were published.

In the early days of this century, tackle was relatively expensive. Bamboo flyrods brought a substantial price and reels, lines and gut leaders were not cheap. The angler who could afford the equipment was more affluent and tended to read more.

The interesting aspect of the outstanding literature of this period is that many of the theories advanced then are valid now. If a comparison were made, one might speculate how many more fish those angler-writers might have caught if they had the tackle available to us.

The observations on streamside entomology presented in "The Notes of Theodore Gordon" provide an excellent starting point. Not only does he describe the insect hatches, but comments on the reaction of the fish through the season:

> Nothing excites the ardent angler more than seeing a large trout rising steadily, which he cannot induce to take his flies. If the right fly is found and success follows, great is the joy of our friend. He attributes the result to his own skill and is apt thereafter to pay more attention to the natural flies that he sees on or about the water. The study of entomology would add considerably to the interest of fly-fishing, at least in many streams of New York and Pennsylvania. I know of no work upon the subject that is of much assistance to the angler, and he will often be at a loss in trying to identify an insect which he finds is attractive to the fish. The habit is formed, how-

Theodore Gordon on the Neversink around 1912
—Courtesy Crown Publishers, Inc., from *Fishless Days, Angling Nights*

ever, of noting the flies as they appear, and he will often be astonished at the numbers which hatch out when the weather is favorable. He learns to be a judge of color and size, and finds that a comparatively small assortment of flies will enable him to imitate the naturals, if he fishes in the same locality. I believe that four families comprise the major part of the insects found on cold, clear brooks and rivers of the Middle States; the Ephemeridae, to which the mayflies, red, brown and golden spinners, and the different colored duns belong; the Perlidae, stone flies, willow fly, etc; Diptera, all the black gnats, etc; and the Trichoptera, all the caddis flies. Ephemera are numerous and easily known by the upright wings and long, tapering body, curved upward at the tail and terminating in two or three whisks, which are frequently mottled.

Big stone fly as lure

Nearly everyone has noticed the big stone fly which hatches out all through the season. I have never seen this fly in large numbers, though a yellowish stone fly comes out in great force sometimes in the latter part of May or early June. As with all these insects, the temperature of air and water has everything to do with when they appear. The wings of stone flies lie flat upon the back when at rest, and are four in number. The fly itself is a fat and juicy morsel for the trout. I do not think that the fish get many of these insects in a perfect state, but when they are crawling about waiting for their wings to grow the trout have a better opportunity. I have found many in their stomachs. Everyone has seen the case which these flies leave upon the rocks after they have hatched out.

The Diptera form a very large family, the first to appear being a black gnat with clear wings, early in March. There are more or less of these little creatures about at all seasons. Some are so small as to be scarcely visible without a magnifying glass.

The Trichoptera, or caddis flies, are a host in themselves, and their numbers are, at times, almost beyond belief. The larger members of this family make their houses of sticks, and until they are seen crawling about will be thought to be sticks. Vast quantities may be found in June. The smaller caddis use small stones to build their homes, beautifully made, and smooth as satin inside. Trout when hungry will swallow the caddis, case and all. Remains of the cases can often be found in the stomachs of large brown trout. In western North Carolina the caddis is called "stick bait." The Indi-

Edward Ringwood Hewitt
—From an etching by Gordon Stevenson. Courtesy Crown Publishers, Inc., from *Fishless Days, Angling Nights*

—Ned Smith

ans of this State made use of the deer-hair hackle or buck-tail fly long before the country was settled by the whites. I cannot vouch for this, but my informant was a gentleman who was passionately fond of "The Land of the Sky."

All the water flies are quite hardy and are best observed during the early part of the season. As soon as the temperature of the water rises they cease to hatch out in any number. I say the temperature of the water, because one can find a good many flies during hot weather if he seeks the headwaters of the brook, where it is cool. The hatch will be confined to evening and early morning hours, as the hot sun is not favorable to any of these insects. I have seen great numbers of ephemera hatching out in April, and have taken a basket

Fly casting mountain waters —Leonard Lee Rue III photo

of trout while the snow was falling. Of course, I do not mean that the air was very cold; the snow melted about as fast as it fell.

At first the trout are hungry and foolish, and will take almost any fly, but they soon learn to be discriminating. Some patterns will kill more or less all through the season, but when the fish get well on to a particular color, more trout and a better average will be secured with a good copy of the natural. The color of the body is of the first importance. I remember a fly that was only good for a short time during one season, and that was a period of three weeks in August. I have seen a few in subsequent years, but only a few. The water was low and the trout shy but, thanks to a good imitation of this fly, I enjoyed excellent sport among large trout. I tried experiments with other flies and compared results with other fishermen, and this fly easily led all others while the natural was about. In the matter of size (of fish taken), the difference was remarkable.

I know so little of entomology that I do not pretend to instruct anyone. I only hope that a more competent person may take up the study of the insect life of our trout streams. I do not advise slavish following of the imitative theory, I only claim that on some streams (particularly where there is much still water), a copy of the natural fly upon the water will often give one a good basket of trout when all other artificial flies are nearly useless. Big trout that confine themselves practically to a fish diet are not often to be lured to the surface by small insects, yet may be taken by a large moth, particularly if fished at night.

To me, the ephemera, or day flies, are the most interesting. It was formerly thought that they lived only for a day, hence the name. As inhabitants of the air, their life history is short, not much more than two weeks, but as larval insects in the depths, they pass from one to two years. If water is shut off from a mill race, and the bottom proves to be composed of stones, sand and gravel, it will be interesting to appoint one-self a committee of investigation. The larvae of various sorts and kinds will usually prove surprising. Many sizes will be found; brown, dull yellow, olive and dark orange are the common colors. All have good strong mandibles or pincers to seize their food, and all those I have found of the ephemeral species are active and full of life. When the time comes for these creatures to change their habitat, they swim upward to the surface, the shell of the larval forms splits down the back and the winged insect emerges, sometimes with a rapidity that almost defies the sight, and again slowly and with difficulty.

A rainbow caught on a Mickey Finn fly
—Leonard Lee Rue III photo

George LaBranche

Fish hogs and conservationists

Some fishermen and hunters have been conservationists for a long time, their efforts documented in the history of the sport 60 years ago. Back in 1914, for example, George La Branche not only chastised anglers who were fish hogs, but he reprimanded writers who boasted of keeping more fish than was necessary. The message in La Branche's excerpt is just as valid now as it was then.

"I am brought to the consideration of the pot-hunter and the fish hog. Many angling writers there be who have not hesitated, nor have they been ashamed, to describe the taking of great numbers of trout. They feel, no doubt, that such narratives entitle them to consideration as authorities. I quote from one his bragging description of a perfect slaughter. After telling of thirty trout taken during midday, naming at least a dozen flies he had found *killing,* he concludes: 'All my trout were taken from the hook and *thrown twenty-five* feet to shore. Thirty, my friend claimed, yet when I came to count tails I found *forty* handsome trout, and all caught from six in the evening until dark, about seven forty-five. I had no net, therefore had to lead my trout into my hand. The friend claims I lost more than I caught by having them flounder off the hook *while trying to take them by the gills and by flinging them ashore.'* The italics are mine. And this fellow had the temerity to add that some poor devil annoyed him by wading in and fishing with a 'stick cut from the forest.' Had Washington Irving witnessed this fellow's fishing I doubt that he would have been moved to write: 'There is certainly something in angling that tends to produce a gentleness of spirit and a pure serenity of mind.' "

Preston Jennings —Photo by Walter Engel

The art of fly-fishing

During the Depression years, catching fish was a way to feed the family. But even dire economic times couldn't dampen the spirits of the purist who continued to increase his knowledge about artificial flies. In a clear, accurate passage, Preston Jennings summarized the differences between attractor and deceiver patterns and applied the information to the feeding habits of brook, brown, and rainbow trout.

Reduced to fundamentals, fly-fishing is the art of catching fish by means of an artificial fly which suggests to the fish some form of insect life upon which it is accustomed to feed.

Leonard West, the author of The Trout Fly, suggests that trout flies fall into one of two categories, Attractors or Deceivers. Attractors are frankly lures and are not made with the intention of being copies of any natural insect. They are designed with the idea of having high visibility and, being usually fished as wet-flies, depend upon movement rather than form and color for their attraction. The Deceivers are those flies which are patterned after natural insects and, according to West, "must be a good imitation of an individual species, or sufficiently typical to be at once mistaken for some fly or larva on which the fish are feeding."

The fact that trout take natural flies for food has been overlooked by the fly-fishers in America. There are several reasons for this, and one of the prime reasons is the fact that both of the native trout found in the streams of the eastern part of America, the Rainbow (Salmo irideus) and the Char, known as the Eastern Brook Trout (Salvelinus fontinalis), are by instinct and preference deep feeders and seem to prefer to take their food under water, instead of feeding on the winged insects on the surface of the stream.

With both of these fish, flies of high visibility such as the Royal Coachman, Silver Doctor, Parmachene Belle, etc., fished as deeply-sunk wet-flies, seem to have the desired effect in filling the creel, while the sober-hued flies, more nearly of the coloring of the natural flies found on the stream, fished as dry-flies, seem to be better for the imported Brown Trout.

The Brown Trout will no doubt be the predominant trout in the streams of the East, if it is not already. About 1882 the Brown Trout were introduced into American streams. Due to the fact that some of the first eggs of this species of trout were sent over by Herr Von Behr and Herr Von Dem Borne of Germany, the appellation German was attached, while, as a matter of fact, the Brown Trout is the native trout of all Europe and the British Isles. R. B. Marston, editor of the Fishing Gazette, London, was one of the first to ship Brown Trout eggs to this country, and it was through the endeavors of A. N. Cheney, fish culturist for New York, that these became established.

With the coming of Brown Trout to American waters, came the necessity for changing the methods of fishing, as these fish did not readily succumb to the Attractor type of fly that was commonly in use for native trout. It was not until the small sober-hued flies of the Deceiver type were fished without drag or manipulation, that these fish were taken in any appreciable quantities.

Around the turn of the century, Theodore Gordon visited England and returned enthusiastic about the dry-fly. No doubt Gordon recognized the value of tying flies suggestive of the natural insect, for the Quill Gordon, which bears his name, is an excellent representation of certain members of the Mayfly family. Gordon's friend, Roy Steenrod, also recog-

A quill Gordon
—Courtesy *Field and Stream*

213

Hendrickson fly
—Courtesy Crown Publishers, Inc.,
from *Fishless Days, Angling Nights*

nizes the value of representing the natural fly, for the Hendrickson dry-fly, which he designed and named for A. E. Hendrickson, is a fine copy of a natural fly found throughout the Catskill and Adirondack districts.

Perhaps the greatest single factor that has deterred the fly-fisher in the study of natural insects is the lack of adequate text books. The reason for this lack is that America is a tremendous country, covering a wide range of climatic conditions, which makes the task of assembling complete information the work of a number of men, each working in a different locality, and as yet no one man has collected a sufficient amount of data to write a book covering the field as a whole.

In this connection, Dr. Herman T. Spieth, who has made an exhaustive study of aquatic flies known as the Ephemeridae of Mayflies, tells the writer that at the time of the Glacial Period the northern species of Mayflies were forced to move south, where they crossbred with the Mayflies then occupying that territory, with the resulting confusion which now occurs between closely related species. In Great Britain the condition has been far simpler, as the country is small and there seems to be a smaller number of different kinds of flies.

Plug fishing for bass

With the modern emphasis on bass fishing and the introduction of countless new techniques, it is difficult to remember that casting the shoreline with a top water bait was the accepted method for catching this great competitor. Spinning tackle was unknown in the 1930s and if one didn't use a flyrod, the other choice was bait casting. Ray Bergman's introduction to plug fishing is particularly poignant to those of us who learned to cast with a steel rod armed with imitation agate guides. And this passage is a marvelous example of youngsters who take their fishing seriously. Bergman was a keen student of the sport:

Around the pot-belly stove of a country grocery store it started, three boys in a heated argument over the merits of trout and bass, myself the lone defender of speckled beauties and having a tough time because of my lack of knowledge.

"Why," accused one of the boys, "what can you say about it? You've never caught a bass in your life!"

This was the gospel truth but I did not admit it.

"You don't know what you're talkin' about. I've caught more bass than you'll ever ketch. I could go over to Rockland Lake this very minute an' take a bass before you could say Jack Rob'son. Not know anythin' about bass? You make me sick!"

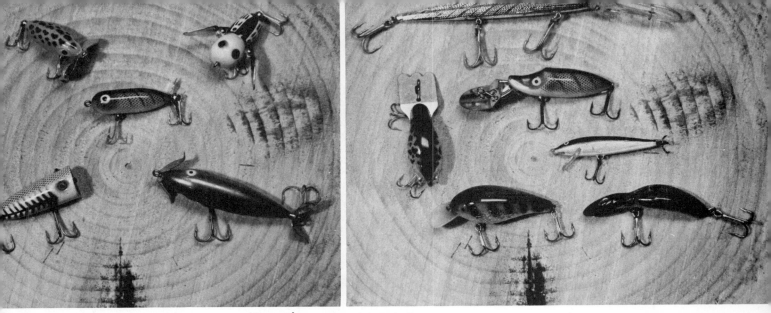

Bass plugs —Howard A. Bach photos

"Oh, is that so?" sneered Jim, my foremost tormentor. "Let's go over right now. You gotta prove it to me."

This was an unlooked-for development. I had not expected such an abrupt challenge. Furthermore I did not have a plug rod nor a plug. But I had to save my face.

"You lissen, Jim Billings," I replied heatedly. "I gotta go home and cut the grass now. But to-morrer I'll go over t' the lake with you and Al, at daylight, and I'll show ya what I kin do. I'll bet ya my best shooter against that black one of your'n that I'll trim the everlasting daylights outer ya. Don't think yor're such a much."

And with that I departed, amid the jeers of my friends. When I got home I thought things over. The boys would make my life miserable if I failed to go the following morning. If I went without an outfit they would have conclusive proof that I had been lying about my experience at plug fishing. I took account of my finances. Three dollars in my pocket. Two dollars in my dime bank. I searched through my Sunday clothes. In the trousers I found a nickel. Then in a bag of marbles I found four pennies. Five dollars and nine cents would never be enough! And then luck favored me. I found some old lead pipe, a number of discarded brass faucets and a large bundle of paper in the cellar. I loaded the stuff on my express wagon and rushed to the junk dealer. He paid me two dollars and seventy-five cents for it. I now had seven dollars and eighty-four cents.

I got a steel rod with imitation agate guides for three dollars, a fine looking multiplying reel for another three and a line for another dollar. But then came the heartrending blow. Plugs were seventy-five cents each, some of them even more!

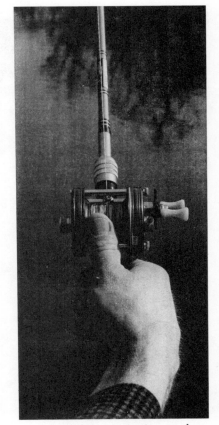

Thumbing a casting reel
—Leonard Lee Rue III photo

215

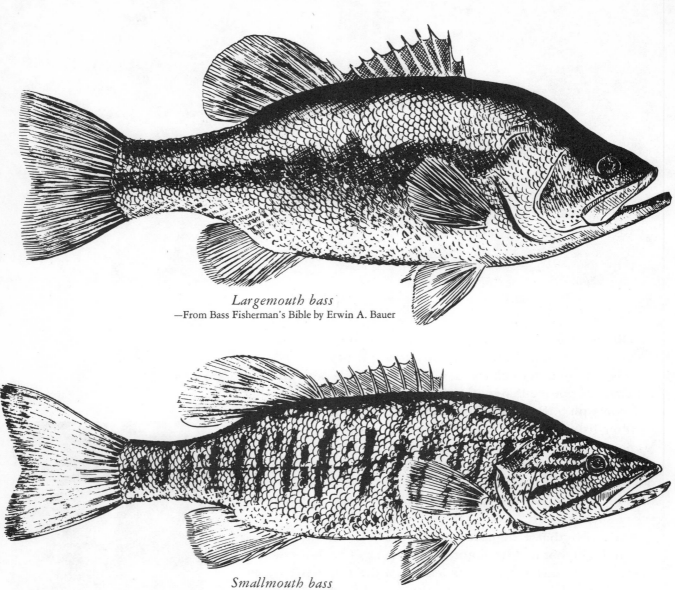

Largemouth bass
—From Bass Fisherman's Bible by Erwin A. Bauer

Smallmouth bass
—From Bass Fisherman's Bible by Erwin A. Bauer

I purchased a white body, red head tango. Then doubt assailed me. If I only had one plug the boys would be suspicious.

"Say, Mr. Carr, could ya let me have a coupla more plugs an' charge 'em on the slate? I'll pay ya for 'em Sunday outa my paper money."

Mr. Carr smiled. He was a man who assumed a bulldog gruffness but at heart he was a good scout. "Sure, son, I'll hang ya up 'til Sunday morning. What'll it be?"

In a spirit of recklessness I spent a dollar each on the two plugs. "Thanks, Mr. Carr. I'll sure pay ya on Sunday morning."

"See that ya do," he retorted, then, "Say, I gotta couple of plugs here that are sort of shop worn. Want 'em?"

I accepted them gratefully. They were dirty and scratched, as if they had caught countless numbers of bass. Now the boys would think I was an old timer at the game.

Next morning was misty and raw. I took the oarsman's seat in the boat and started rowing. Dad had told me that there was good bass fishing around the lily pads at the southwest corner of the lake and I headed there. There was method in my doing this. I wanted the boys to get fishing before I could set my rod up, to see how they did it. My plans worked splendidly. My two comrades were casting away before I got my rod together.

I had gathered the general idea of how to cast and thought that I would be able to do it without giving myself away. But I reckoned without taking into consideration the perverseness of a bait casting reel in the hands of a beginner. I managed to get the plug out all right, for a distance of thirty feet, but at what a cost! Under my thumb the line tied itself up into the worst mess you ever saw. Luckily my partners were too much interested to notice my predicament although Jim did make a wise-crack about the distance of my cast. But I knew I must do something so I started reeling in over the top of the back lash. And then it happened. Before I had turned the handle a half dozen times a large bass hit my plug with a resounding splash. I hooked him but I do not know how. The rest was easy enough. I had caught plenty of trout and knew the technique of playing a fish. Bass safely in the boat, we sat and looked at it.

"Gee, it must weigh ten pounds," marveled Jim. (Actually it weighed four.)

"Well," I boasted, "that's why I cast that plug such a little way out from the boat an' let it lay there before reelin' it in. I knew that bass was there an' I knew jus' how to get 'im." This was lying braggadocio and I am ashamed to tell it but as I have long since got over boasting about fishing, or anything else for that matter, I can appreciate the story to its fullest extent.

Then I thought of the badly tangled line. I knew that it would give me away for the fraud I was if I disentangled it before the boys and I knew that I could not expect anything but disastrous consequences if I tried to cast with it the way it was. So without saying anything I started rowing back to the dock.

"Hey, where y goin'? There ain't no fish over that way." The boys were greatly agitated.

"I know it," I said, "but I promised Ma I'd be back for breakfast an' finish that job I started yesterday afternoon an' I gotta leave right now."

Landing a bonefish
—Courtesy *Field and Stream*

Bonefish
—Mark J. Sosin photo

Bonefish as game

Much of the writing on the marine scene during the first part of the century centered around so-called glamour species that were the impossible dream for most anglers, who only knew of these species through outdoor magazines or from books. Skillful writing and the aura that surrounded these fish vaulted them into a lengendary world that heated the imagination of those who had to settle for typical coastal fare.

To make everything believable for the angler who wasn't able to travel (and that meant most), Van Campen Heilner established his credentials early in this piece so that his comparisons would have validity.

Of all the fish which I have had the pleasure of pursuing in a lifetime of angling for everything from brook trout to swordfish, my favorite is the bonefish. Trout, salmon, black bass, muskies, pike and others were old stories to me before I caught my first bonefish. For thirty years I have averaged a month a year surf fishing for channel bass and stripers. With Zane Grey, William Scheer, Fred Alexander, Bob Davis and others we fought the great tuna off the Jersey coast. When the Overseas Railroad had crossed from the mainland of Florida to Key West, I wrestled with great leaping tarpon along the viaducts and the freshwater rivers. Yet to none will I yield the palm of fighting fury possessed by the bonefish.

My brother anglers will look upon these statements with amusement. But I am not alone, and all those who have concentrated on bonefish over a period of years are just as "nutty" as I. We belong to a select fraternity of maniacs who get a tremendous kick out of their insanity, and if the rest of the angling fraternity choose to regard us as demented, we are perfectly satisfied.

For fifteen years I had a camp on North Bimini in the Bahamas and there I have had an excellent chance to study the elusive bonefish. With some of the world's finest marlin, tuna, and reef fishing at my door I have concentrated on the bonefish. It occurs in warm seas all over the globe. In any part of the tropics you are almost sure to run across bonefish. In Florida and the Bahamas it has been angled for extensively, and from these records and experiences most of our knowledge is derived.

In appearance he is a sort of cross between a carp and a grayling. His head is sharp and mean-looking. His color is silvery white shading to greenish blue on the back. His dorsal fin looks like a shark's as it cuts the water, and the upper lobe of his caudal sticks from the surface almost as high. In size he runs from a pound to sixteen pounds.

When bonefish are small they run in large schools, but as

A bonefish catch —Courtesy *Field and Stream*

they grow older they break up into pairs or become solitary. The largest I have ever caught, or seen caught, were alone or part of a pair. Frequently schools of small bonefish will form what is known as a "mud," a large patch of discolored water in the center of which the fish are feeding. If the angler can locate a mud and get ahead of it, as the fish move with the tide, he can catch bonefish as fast as he throws out his bait. If no undue noise is made, the fish do not take alarm and the mud can be followed for long distances.

Bonefish are lovers of shallow water. As soon as they feel the first thrust of incoming tide they move in over the banks searching for the tiny "ghost" crabs or other succulent bait hidden in the grassy bottom. They will force themselves into such shallow water that they can navigate only with the greatest difficulty and I have seen them struggling with half their backs out of water to pass over some particularly shallow bank.

As the tide continues they work further and further in until at high water they are scattered about among the mangroves and sometimes up in the heads of creeks which are dry at low water. As the tide falls off, they start to come off the banks: at this stage they do not seem so hungry. Sometimes they will pass over bait without noticing it, or pick it up to drop it immediately. However, there are no set rules for bonefish because they will never react the way you expect them to. They continue to back off the banks as the tide drops lower, until at dead low water you will find them settled off in deep holes or in the channels waiting for the never ending cycle of tides to repeat.

The Solunar Theory

John Alden Knight delighted readers with his coverage of many outdoor topics, but he is best known for his Solunar Theory. First appearing in *Sportsman* magazine in 1935 under the title of "Ocean Tides and Fresh Water Fish," the Solunar Theory is subscribed to by many anglers today. Oddly, although not every fisherman is willing to follow the theory with fervor, few totally ignore it. One may not believe, but hardly anyone disputes that it *could* be true.

Unquestionably, the phases of the moon affect the lives and habits of all living things. The extent to which the moon's influence is felt depends upon the order of development of the individual, be it insect, bird, animal, or fish. It is difficult, however, to lay down hard and fast rules regarding the effects of the moon upon the feeding habits of fish. Too many other factors enter into the problem to permit anything other than generalities.

Anglers have learned that fish are usually more active during the dark of the moon (the new moon) and the first quarter, and that they are less active during the full moon and the third quarter. Many anglers of the Middle West believe that the best night fishing is to be had during the full moon and the best daytime fishing during the dark of the moon. Most salt-water anglers agree with this belief. Another rule of the moon's effects, used mainly by salt-water anglers, has to do with the apogee and perigee phases of the moon. Fishing is presumed to be at its best when the moon is in perigee (at the point of its orbit which is closest to the earth). The fish are supposed to be least active when the moon is in apogee (farthest away from the earth). For generations, hunters and fishermen in many of the Southern states have considered that the time of the south moon under (the time of the moon's transit on the opposite side of the globe during the

—Courtesy Mrs. Richard Alden Knight

221

dark of the moon) marks the period of outstanding activity among the creatures of the wild.

While all of these beliefs have considerable truth in them, they cannot be accepted as absolute rules of behavior. The very fact that there are four or five of these rules is in itself ample testimony that none of them is infallible. None the less, they are of sufficient importance to warrant some thought on the part of the angler with an inquiring mind. The fact that most of the record catches are taken during the sunlight hours of the days at the time of the new moon is evidence enough to show that they deserve some study. Fishing calendars which indicate the best days for fishing of each month are formulated according to one or more of these rules of the moon. The next time one of these comes to hand, just for the fun of it, get your almanac and find out to what school of thought the author of that calendar belongs.

Since Biblical times and, no doubt, before, salt-water anglers have been planning their fishing trips according to the stages of the tides. Here again, however, we find inconsistencies. In the various better-known bays, estuaries, and passes along the coastlines of Long Island and New Jersey, there are only a few spots where the same stage of tide marks the best time for fishing. It seems to me that if a certain stage of tide indicates the best time for fishing at Moriches Bay, that rule should apply also at, say, Montauk Point. Such, however, is not the case.

Years ago I learned from a Florida guide that the market hunters and fishermen of Florida and Georgia planned their excursions according to moon up and moon down. In other words, they had learned from long experience that fish would feed and game would be on the move when the moon was directly overhead or directly underneath. He told me that he had been taught these things by his grandpappy when he was a kid in Georgia and that he had been applying this system to his fishing and shooting ever since. To prove his point, he showed me some of the best bass fishing I ever hope to see right under a hot July sun at high noon. Like most fishermen, I had always been under the impression that the best fishing was to be had early in the morning or just after sundown. Thinking back over past years, however, I could remember some days when I had found very excellent fishing at odd hours during the day. It seemed to me that this moon up and moon down idea might possibly be the key to these odd-hour periods of good fishing. Surely the experience of my guide pointed in that direction.

For the next year or so I kept a careful watch of moon positions every time I went fishing. The system worked quite

—Courtesy Mrs. Richard Alden Knight

222

well for several days of each month. Then the schedule would go awry and would not return to normal for about ten days. This happened with such regularity that I concluded that the moon, of itself, could not be the complete answer. Finally, through devious methods of reasoning, the thought came to me that there might be some connecting link between the feeding cycles of fresh-water fish and their cousins the salt-water fish.

The general belief of salt-water anglers is that the tides bring food to the fish and thus arrange the feeding periods. Thinking on the matter, however, it hardly seemed logical that off-shore schools would find any variation in their food supply because of a change of tide. Finally the idea came to me that there was a possibility that instead of the tides themselves being the contributing factor, the cause or causes of the tides might have something to do with it. If this were the case, then it might well be that these same causes would constitute the prompting stimuli behind the odd-hour feeding periods of fresh-water fish.

This involved taking the sun into the calculations, as we know that tides are caused by the combined gravitational pull of sun and moon. Equipped with tide tables and a Nautical Almanac, I made up a tentative schedule of feeding periods. This schedule proved to be much more accurate than the moon up, moon down method, but it still was far from perfect. Finally, by discarding the tide tables and doing my own calculation of the actuating force by charting the resultant of the solar and lunar forces as applied to the earth, I found that the schedule could be made fairly accurate. In so doing, the name "Solunar" was coined—purely as a convenient term for describing the force in question. Thus was the Solunar Theory born.

Crusading angler-writers

It is impossible to reflect forty years with a handful of passages representing the angling writing of the period. One could argue validly for the inclusion of other writers and different excerpts. But each writer during the first part of the 20th Century contributed something to the sport of fishing. Each article, poem, and book was a building block upon which writers who followed could start their own careers.

Charles L. Cadieux, 1973–74 president of OWAA, has written three books and many articles while working for federal and state wildlife agencies in the Dakotas, New Mexico, Texas and Washington, D. C. His analysis of the conservation movement between World Wars I and II focuses on what was then the key conservation magazine of the period.

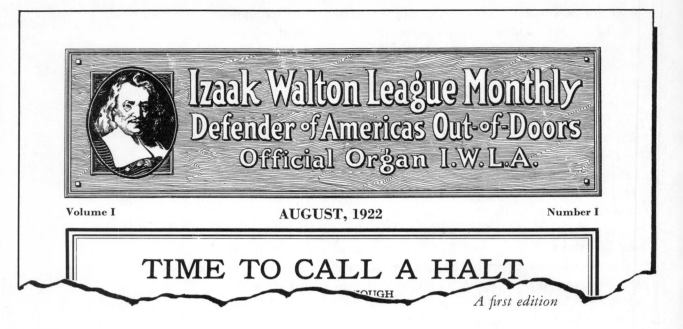

Izaak Walton League Monthly
Defender of Americas Out-of-Doors
Official Organ I.W.L.A.

Volume I   AUGUST, 1922   Number I

TIME TO CALL A HALT

A first edition

The masthead of the *Izaak Walton League Monthly* in 1922 reads like a Who's Who of well-known writers interested in conservation and the out-of-doors.

Managing Editor Will H. Dilg could call on contributing editors like Dr. James A. Henshall, source of the famed description of black bass as . . . "inch for inch, and pound for pound, the gamest fish that swims"; a multimillionaire writer of Western novels named Zane Grey who was also one of this nation's big game fishing experts; Emerson Hough, the famed novelist whose nature writing greatly influenced the National Park system; Ozark Ripley, who wrote as much instructional material on the out-of-doors as any man dead or alive; Travers D. Carman; Bob Becker; M. L. Gochenour; Thomas Ambrose and Marguerite Ives — all widely acclaimed in the first decades of the century.

These writers believed in crusading; they were hardly optimistic but they wanted to go down with their verbal guns blazing. Emerson Hough, often quoted, vowed to *League Monthly* to lend its cause his name "after fifty years of love and labor in and for outdoor America — fruitless labor — none the less with an undiminished love and a hope not yet wholly faltering that the needed miracle even yet may come."

Sometimes the journalistic style of the Izaak Walton League's monthly became swollen with hyperbole. An example is Zane Grey's reaction to the Emerson Hough vow. Zane wrote:

"If a million outdoor men who have sons, will think of those sons, and band together to influence other men who have sons — then we may save something of America's outdoor joys for the boys. There is no other way. Commercialism has laid its sorid hand on the soul of the nation. Bolshevism is rampant, not only in labor circles, but in politics, in business, even in literature. If the real Americans do not rise in a body, we are doomed."

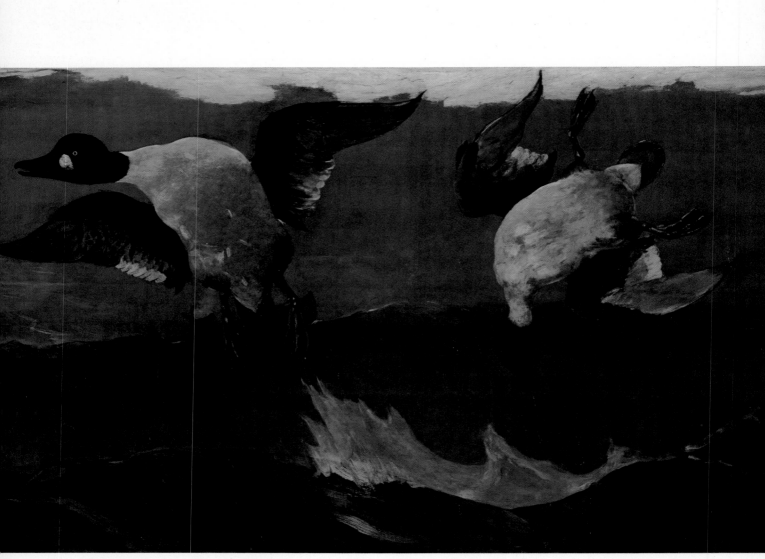

—From a painting by Winslow Homer (1836-1910)/National Gallery of Art, Washington, gift of the Avalon Foundation

Right and Left

(On preceding page)
Wild Turkey by Lynn Bogue Hunt
—Courtesy Field and Stream Publishing Company

Cooper's Hawk

Goshawk

Peregrine Hawk

Marsh Hawks (Harrier)

*National Wildlife Federation Conservation Stamps—the first set,
drawn in 1938, by founder Ding Darling*

(At right)
1898 Winchester calendar by A. B. Fro.

Quails, Partridges,
and Pheasants

BOBWHITE

SCALED
QUAIL

HARLEQUIN
QUAIL

CALIFORNIA
QUAIL

GAMBEL'S
QUAIL

MOUNTAIN
QUAIL

GRAY PARTRIDGE

CHUKAR

RING-NECKED
PHEASANT

RING-NECKED
PHEASANT

—FROM PAINTINGS BY ROGER TORY PETERSON
FROM "A FIELD GUIDE TO WESTERN BIRDS"
PUBLISHED BY HOUGHTON MIFFLIN COMPANY

Flycatchers

WIED'S CRESTED FLYCATCHER

OLIVACEOUS FLYCATCHER

THICK-BILLED KINGBIRD

ASH-THROATED FLYCATCHER

CASSIN'S KINGBIRD

WESTERN KINGBIRD

TROPICAL KINGBIRD

EASTERN KINGBIRD

KISKADEE FLYCATCHER

SULPHUR-BELLIED FLYCATCHER

—From paintings by Roger Tory Peterson
From "A Field Guide to Western Birds" Published by Houghton Mifflin Company

—From a painting by Roger Tory Peterson/courtesy Mill Pond Press

Great Horned Owl

Gene Stratton Porter

But even 50 years ago male scribes had no stranglehold on outdoor writing. Famed novelist Gene Stratton Porter, who died in 1924, but is still selling today, contributed an eloquent account of the ravaging of the continent. Here is a part of her article titled, "All Together, Heave!":

Grand Canyon walls —George H. Harrison photo

The Everglades —George H. Harrison photo

This world has never known a country equal to ours in size, having greater natural beauty of conformation, diversity of scenery and wealth of animals and plant life. Three hundred years ago, in the days of our beginnings as a nation, places that are now known as Niagara Falls, Mammoth Cave and the Everglades, were practically untouched. The prairies really rolled, the mountain ranges towered, the Garden of the Gods, the Grand Canyon, the Petrified Forest, Muir Woods, Yosemite, the entire stretch of Atlantic and Pacific seaboards, lay in nearly natural state while we had the unique advantage of having ice on our heads and our feet in tropical heat. We were a land of great placid lakes. We knew the sweep of mighty winds, our ears were attuned to running water. We had lakes bordered with true lotus lilies, and the biggest trees in all the world. We had magnolia, tulip, poplar and the like literally mantled with bloom every spring, ferns of all varieties, flowers from the bloody red snow flower of the mountains to fragile orchids of southern trees, from bog lilies to pastel cacti of the scorched desert. There were uncounted herds of buffalo, elk and moose. There were deer and bear, seal and beaver. The trees and waters were aflame with gaudy birds, parrots to flamingoes, painted warblers to equally painted wood-ducks.

Only as a day in the evolution of the world is three hundred years, and after this length of time we, today, are called upon to answer for our stewardship of this plethora of riches and beauty. We admit that we have handled these natural wonders, this profusion of riches, in a spirit of insane recklessness. During my own childhood, I recall the ascending smoke of countless burning log heaps, and those heaps composed of golden oak, walnut, red cherry, bird's-eye maple and hickory, treess that were suitable to be sawed into thin slabs for veneering of less expensive woods. Yet, I saw them cut by the acre, stacked and burned where they fell in order that the land upon which they stood might be used for the cultivation of crops. There was no one with vision to erect warehouses and save for us today untold billions that went up in the smoke of the most wanton waste this world ever has known.

The animal life receded before the destruction of the forests; the buffalo ranging in countless herds are now practically extinct. The splendidly beautiful wood-duck, extremely rare. The wild pigeon that once broke down branches of forest trees with the weight of their numbers now gone forever.

—Drawing by Bob Hines
from *Crusade for Wildlife*

Birth of Outdoor America

By 1927, the monthly magazine of the Izaak Walton League had been retitled *Outdoor America,* and had reached an eminence of influence in forming public opinion along conservation lines. That year's May issue listed such authors as Kenesaw Mountain Landis, Nash Buckingham, Ben Thompson, Robert Page Lincoln, Mark Catlin, Seth Gordon, Herbert Hoover, Lee W. Sturges and Struthers Burt — leaders to guide the conscience of America. Then, Seth Gordon wrote with clarity of wildlife management from his post as director of the Pennsylvania Game Commission. Professor Aldo Leopold, head of wildlife studies at University of Wisconsin, was a contributor. Dr. Ira Gabrielson, who still campaigns vigorously for the things he believes, followed efforts of an earlier Iowan to organize sportsmen into a force for good, when he replaced Ding Darling as head of the Biological Survey, which became the Fish and Wildlife Service.

Consider a paragraph from Leopold. Writing about the extinct passenger pigeons, he said:

—By William Harnden Foster,
courtesy Charles Scribner's Sons

"For one species to mourn the death of another is a new thing under the sun. We, who have lost our pigeons, mourn the loss. Had the funeral been ours, the pigeons would hardly have mourned us. In this fact, rather than in nylons or bombs, lies evidence of our superiority over the beasts."

In 1934, an illustrator took command of the federal government's work in wildlife management when J. N. "Ding" Darling, Pulitzer Prize cartoonist and wildlife crusader, became director of the Biological Survey. Through his conservation cartoons syndicated by the Des Moines (Iowa) *Register*, Ding had become known as "the best friend ducks had," and as an organizer of sportsman's clubs. President Franklin Roosevelt asked him to head the Survey when it was at low ebb in morale, manpower and funds. He restored it, got the Duck Stamp program going, expanded the refuge system—and resigned in two years, to resume his cartooning crusades and to work toward a truly national wildlife federation.

Standing room only—Courtesy Ding Foundation

228

Nash Buckingham

As the public became aware of conservation crusaders, tactics of the leaders changed. Thus Nash Buckingham had used his pen as a war-trumpet to marshal forces of good against legions of evil. But now this gifted journalist and great gentleman used a more subtle approach, a word-painting of the joys of outdoor life, or perhaps a homely bit of eloquence which fit man in his place as another creature of Nature instead of the be-all of creation. A good example of his writing, which did so much to instill the conservation ethic in an America still seeking to understand that Daniel Boone was dead, is in his piece from *Outdoor America* of August 1937, entitled "While There's Life." Read it slowly, tasting it with your mind.

My friend Henry's farm slopes from a coniferous Maryland ridge down to the broad Potomac river; just beyond which, in Virginia, reposes historic Mount Vernon, countryseat and home-close of George Washington. As Squire and General, George Washington used to cross the Potomac and attend divine worship in a brick chapel still in use for such Godly purpose, at the head of Broad creek, just around the point from Henry's plantation. A countryside rich in panoply of this nation's cradling, and, when waterfowl are migrating, fur-bearers prime, fish striking and bobwhites awing from embrowned and frosty coverts, one with meed for sport.

For all his association with Big Business, Henry is a true dirt farmer, bred from pioneers of remote soil. Never having lost touch with nature, its human elements are pretty well catalogued in Henry's mental files. With him the milk of human kindness is always on tap. Character and straight shooting are bred in Henry's bone. Withal, a gentleman-sportsman worthy of the title, and a far-seeing proponent of practical conservation. All of you know such men as my

—By William Harnden Foster, courtesy Charles Scribner's Sons

friend Henry. There are more of them in this disturbed nation of ours than you think.

When zero gripped the country, Henry and I spent a weekend at his farm. Getting there was no easy matter, but Henry was determined to know that all was well with his bird dogs and Chesapeake Bays, that cattle and stock fared sumptuously, and that grain was being distributed for game birds and songsters. The neighbors, too, must be visited, for Henry is the kind that instills his own spirit into a community.

Sitting around the living room hearth that night, Ed, Henry's plantation manager said: "Mister Henry, when lightning struck the grand old oak down by the spring, it was almost like losing a grandfather—but its stove and firewood have carried us through about the toughest winter I recall." He was talking about a patriarchal oak close by a magnificent cold spring gushing from the hillside. A landmark, that ancient oak, cynosure of all eyes that dwelt upon the landscape, and said by examining authorities to be more than three hundred years old.

"Ed," replied Henry, "how long have you and I cropped this place?"

"Pretty close to twenty-five years," replied Ed.

"We've planted many a tree, too, haven't we?"

"Yes, sir, there's a handsome stand of young stuff on the east fifty, and them down along the c'rick forty are doing fine, too." They puffed their pipes awhile. I had an idea what Henry was thinking. We used to lie under that giant oak in summertime, while a watermelon chilled in the spring, and try to recapture interludes in the life of that vast tree. When Indian lodges dotted hereabouts, game trails criss-crossed the land, and the Potomac's tidal waters lay unpolluted by civilization's slime and crimes against nature.

"Ed," mused Henry, "it's just as well we've planted so many trees. Did you stop to think that it took more than three hundred years to grow that old oak? Then, in the twinkling of an eye, just like floods and droughts have a way of happening, Nature tore it to pieces? You can't lick Nature, Ed. We can give it the runaround and get away with it for what seems like a long time to us, but amounts to nothing whenever Nature decides to change things. But, Ed, the wood from that three hundred year old tree kept our bodies warm for three months. Think of that, for only three months. And, but for the Grace of God, it might have been the Last tree." Ed repeated, half to himself, and very soberly — "more than three hundred years to grow — and three months to keep warm by."

"But," Henry continued, "the lightning dissolved a wonderful partnership — between the oak and the spring — we've still got its pure, life-giving water. Why, it has never even slowed down during the drought; it still serves us, and the neighbors, and all Nature hereabouts. It gives us something to remember our old friend, the oak, by, too." Ed's face brightened.

"I've attended to that, too, Mister Henry. The kids and I missed the oak so much I sawed its stump off smooth and planted a flower garden atop of it — with sweet peas and roses all down around its roots. And I've put a guard fence around it, too." Henry said he was glad, and thought that was a fine thing to do. He called his big pointer, Jim, over to him and scratched gently behind his ears. Jim always liked that.

Aldo Leopold's "shack" —George H. Harrison photo

Aldo Leopold, pioneer and martyr

The major outdoor philosopher of the period between World Wars was Aldo Leopold, who set his conclusions down in one slim volume that sums it all up thirty years later. Ray Heady, a Life Member of the Outdoor Writers Association and the thoughtful, perceptive outdoor editor of the *Kansas City Star* for 15 years before retiring in 1973, wrote of him for this book:

I never met Aldo Leopold the man; I know him only as Aldo Leopold the writer, naturalist and conservationist. But this I do know: no collection of outdoor writing would be complete without quotations from *A Sand County Almanac,* which probably is the bedrock of modern philosophy in regard to land and wild creatures. Simply stated, Leopold holds that man should not live off the land; he should live with it.

I never read *Almanac* until a few years after Leopold's death in 1948, and then I cried bitterly when I learned he had died fighting a grass fire in his beloved Wisconsin. By then I was middle aged but I tearfully protested to God that men like this should not be taken from us. We need them so desperately on what remains of this green earth.

I tried to conjure up some justification for such a tremendous loss in what might have been a minimal blaze, but there was no rationalization possible. Was he setting a backfire to outflank the main blaze? Was he protecting his shack in the woods? A mallard's nest in a marsh? I never really pushed for an answer, because somehow the picture of Leopold

Aldo Leopold's Sand County bench
—George H. Harrison photo

Upland sandpiper
—Charles Schwartz

White-tailed deer and fawn
—Charles Schwartz

Mallard duck and brood
—Charles Schwartz

233

giving up his life to fight a grass fire puts a heroic stamp on his departure—almost as if after carving out his commandments of reverence for the earth he was wrapped in wings of flame and recalled to another glory.

Oh, Leopold the duck hunter and forest ranger would have hooted at such a comparison, but no matter, that's where I rank him, right up there with Moses trying to lead his wandering tribe out of a wilderness of wastefulness.

As an outdoor editor, I reviewed some 200 to 300 books a year for the *Star.* Some of them were important and impressive; some were fly-by-night productions that never should have had paper wasted upon them. But none even approached *Sand County Almanac.* It is the book to measure other books by. It wrapped up all the loose ends of our random thoughts on conservation into an ethic. It gave us a measuring stick. To reach this standard of judgment, I applied a simple formula: a book was to be judged by what it said, and how it said it. Leopold scored high on both counts. He said a lot and he said it beautifully in simple words.

Even the opening lines of the foreword are classical: "There are some who can live without wild things and some who cannot. These essays are the delights and dilemmas of one who cannot."

That opening ranks right up there with another great lead: *In the beginning God created the heaven and the earth . . .* And with: *Four score and seven years ago:* and: *When in the course of human events . . .* which are great declarations of principles of man.

But the earth came before man. Why has so little been written on the rights of that earth which supports man?

I am trying to make two points. First that some of the greatest stories were written in simple, beautiful words. Second, that man has completed his conquest of the earth. And the earth has taken just about all the despoilation it can take. Now is the time for understanding and love of the planet we live on.

Leopold left us a legacy of only 399 pages of words in type, not counting his technical volumes on game management that have so shaped scientific wildlife teaching. There are 226 pages in my edition of *A Sand County Almanac* (Oxford University Press, 1949), and 173 pages in *Round River* (Oxford University Press, 1953), enough to permit me to say I feel that I know him. His philosophy takes roots and grows within his readers. The total output in pages is not impressive but his total impact is immeasurable.

Round River does not match *Almanac* in philosophy or depth. It is mainly a collection of notes and observations on hunting and fishing trips that Leopold made during his younger and formative years afield. They are as down-to-earth as a soot blackened coffee pot, but they give a keen insight into his early perceptions of nature and wildlife. This volume was edited by a son, Luna B., after his father's death.

The Leopold family—father, mother, five children and two of Aldo's brothers—was an outdoor family. They camped, hunted, fished and

Raccoon and young
—Charles Schwartz

Bobwhite quail and chicks
—Charles Schwartz

canoed together. If Aldo was too busy to write up the day's log some evening, other members of the family kept the journal up to date.

Consider these quotes as an insight to the Leopold philosophy and style:

"Conservation is a state of harmony between man and land. By land is meant all of the things on, over or in the earth. Harmony with the land is like harmony with a friend; you cannot cherish his right hand and chop off his left. That is to say, you cannot love game and hate predators; you cannot conserve the waters and waste the ranges; you cannot build the forest and mine the farm. The land is one organism . . ."

Or: "Have we learned this principle of conservation: to preserve all the parts of the land mechanism? No, because even the scientist does not recognize all of them . . ."

Or: "Clean farming, to be sure, aspires to rebuild the soil, but it employs to this end only imported plants, animals and fertilizers. It sees no need for the native flora and fauna that built the soil in the first place . . ."

Or: "Conservation is getting nowhere because it is incompatible with our Abrahamic concept of land. We abuse land because we regard it as a commodity belonging to us. When we see land as a community to which we belong, we may begin to use it with love and respect. There is no other way for land to survive the impact of mechanized man, nor for us to reap from it the esthetic harvest it is capable of contributing to culture."

And: "There are two spiritual dangers in not owning a farm. One is the danger of supposing that breakfast comes from the grocery, and the other that heat comes from a furnace."

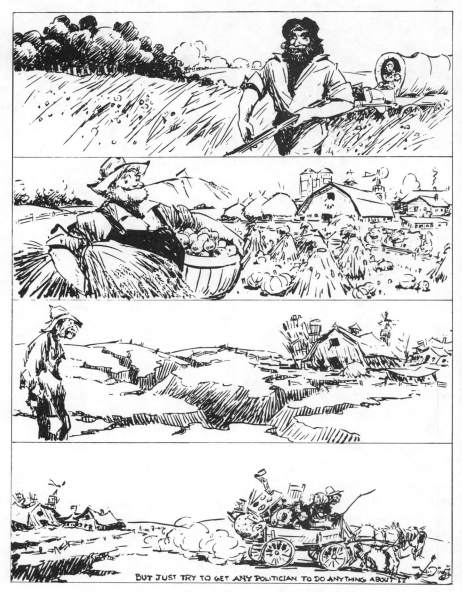

Ding's conservation ethic —Courtesy Ding Foundation

Leopold's "Conservation Esthetic"

But trying to summarize Leopold in brief quotations is rather futile. He has to be read thoroughly and repeatedly to get his full impact. Each new reading brings new insights — year after year. For his *Sand County Almanac* is the greatest outdoor book of this century. Choosing a single essay to typify the Leopold whole is like choosing one act to celebrate Shakespearean drama. But some of his most pertinent utterances for the present (and past and future) are in "Conservation Esthetic."

Barring love and war, few enterprises are undertaken with such abandon, or by such diverse individuals, or with so paradoxical a mixture of appetite and altruism, as that group

236

of avocations known as outdoor recreation. It is, by common consent, a good thing for people to get back to nature. But wherein lies the goodness, and what can be done to encourage its pursuit? On these questions there is confusion of counsel, and only the most uncritical minds are free from doubt.

Recreation became a problem with a name in the days of the elder Roosevelt, when railroads which had banished the countryside from the city began to carry city-dwellers to the countryside. It began to be noticed that the greater the exodus, the smaller the per-capita ration of peace, solitude, wildlife and scenery . . .

The automobile has spread this once local predicament to the outermost limits of good roads — it has made scarce in the hinterlands something once abundant on the back forty. . . . Like ions shot from the sun, week-enders radiate from every town, generating heat and friction as they go. A tourist industry purveys bed and board to bait more ions, faster, further. Advertisements on rock and rill confide to all the whereabouts of new retreats, landscapes, hunting grounds and fishing lakes just beyond those recently overrun. Bureaus build roads into new hinterlands, then buy more hinterlands to absorb the exodus accelerated by the roads. A gadget-industry pads the bumps against nature-in-the-raw; woodcraft becomes the art of using gadgets. And now, to top the pyramid of banalities, the trailer. To him who seeks in woods and mountains only those things obtainable from travel or golf, the present situation is tolerable. To him who seeks something more, recreation has become a process of seeking but never quite finding, a major frustration of mechanical society.

The retreat of the wilderness . . . is no local thing; Hudson Bay, Alaska, Mexico, South Africa are giving way; South America and Siberia are next. Drums along the Mohawk are now honks along the rivers of the world. Homo sapiens putters no more under his vine and fig tree; he has poured into his gas tank the stored motivity of countless creatures aspiring through the ages to wiggle their way to pastures new. Antlike he swarms the continents.

Take a look at any duck marsh. A cordon of parked cars surrounds it. Crouched on its reedy margin is some pillar of society, automatic ready, trigger finger itching to break, if need be, every law of commonwealth or commonweal to kill a duck. That he is already overfed in no way dampens his avidity for gathering his meat from God.

At some nearby resort is another nature-lover, the kind who writes bad verse on birchbark. Everywhere is the unspe-

Early migratory bird hunting stamps
—U.S. Fish and Wildlife Service

cialized motorist whose recreation is mileage, who has run the gamut of National Parks in one summer, and is headed for Mexico City and points south. Lastly, there is the professional, striving through countless conservation organizations to give the nature-seeking public what it wants, or to make it want what he has to give.

Why should such a diversity of folk be bracketed in a single category? Because each, in his own way, is a hunter. And why does each call himself a conservationist? Because the wild things he hunts for have eluded his grasp, and he hopes by some necromancy of laws, appropriations, regional plans, reorganization of departments, or other form of mass-wishing to make them stay put.

The ethics of recreation

Recreation is spoken of as an economic resource . . . committees tell us in reverent ciphers how many millions the public spends in its pursuit.

It also has an ethical aspect. In the scramble for unspoiled places, codes and decalogues evolve. We hear of "outdoor manners." We indoctrinate youth. We print definitions of

—Drawing by Bob Hines from *Crusade for Wildlife*

"What Is a Sportsman" and hang a copy on the wall of whosoever will pay a dollar for the propagation of the faith.

It is clear that these economic and ethical manifestations are results, not causes of the motive force. We seek contacts with nature because we derive pleasure from them. . . . The duck-hunter in his blind and the operatic singer on the stage, despite the disparity of their accoutrements, are doing the same thing. Each is reviving, in play, a drama formerly inherent in daily life. Both are, in the last analysis, esthetic exercises.

Public policies for outdoor recreation are controversial. Equally conscientious citizens hold opposite views on what it is . . . the Wilderness Society seeks to exclude roads from hinterlands, and the Chamber of Commerce to extend them,

—Drawing by Bob Hines from *Crusade for Wildlife*

both in the name of recreation. The game-farmer kills hawks and the bird-lover protects them. . . . Such factions label each other with short and ugly names when, in fact, each is considering a different component of the recreational process. . . . It seems timely to segregate the components and to examine the distinctive characteristics of each.

We begin with the simplest and most obvious: the objects that the outdoorsman may seek, find, capture and carry away. In this category are wild crops such as game and fish, and the tokens of achievement such as heads, hides, photographs and specimens.

—Drawing by Bob Hines
from *Crusade for Wildlife*

All these things rest upon the idea of trophy. The pleasure they give is in the seeking as well as in the getting. The trophy, whether it be a bird's egg, a mass of trout, a basket of mushrooms, the photograph of a bear, the pressed specimen of a wild flower, or a note tucked into the cairn on a mountain peak, is a certificate. It attests that its owner has been somewhere and done something—has exercised skill or discrimination in the age-old feat of overcoming, outwitting, or reducing-to-possession.

But trophies differ in their reactions tó mass-pursuit. The yield of game can, by means of propagation or management, be increased . . . however, when carried too far, this stepping up of yields is subject to a law of diminishing returns. . . . Consider, for example, a trout raised in a hatchery and newly liberated in an over-fished stream. No one would

Oldtimers down at the creek —Courtesy Evinrude Motors

Fifty years of hunting licenses—Courtesy Pennsylvania Game Commission

claim that this fish has the same value as a wholly wild one caught out of some unmanaged stream in the high Rockies. Its esthetic connotations are inferior, even though its capture requires skill.

All intergrades of artificiality exist, but as mass-use increases it tends to push the whole gamut of conservation techniques toward the artificial end, and the whole scale of trophy values downward.

Damage to plant life usually follows artificialized management of animals—for example, damage to forests by deer. . . . On English heaths, reproduction of trees is inhibited by rabbits over-protected in the process of cropping partridges and pheasants. On scores of tropical islands both fauna and flora have been destroyed by goats introduced for

241

meat and sport. It would be hard to calculate the mutual injuries by and between mammals deprived of their natural predators and ranges stripped of their natural food plants. We generalize by saying that mass-use tends to dilute the quality of trophies like game and fish, and to induce damage to other resources such as non-game animals, vegetation and farm crops.

The same dilution and damage are not apparent in "indirect" trophies such as photographs. A piece of scenery snapped by a dozen tourist cameras daily is not physically impaired thereby, nor does any other resource suffer when the rate increases. The camera industry is one of the few innocuous parasites on wild nature.

We have, then, a basic difference in reaction to mass-use as between two categories of physical objects pursued as trophies.

The wilderness controversy

Let us consider another component which is more subtle and complex: the feeling of isolation in nature. That this is acquiring a scarcity-value . . . is attested by the wilderness controversy. . . . Out of every dozen wild areas opened up, one may be proclaimed "wilderness" and roads built only to its edge. It is then advertised as unique. Before long its trails are congested, it is being dolled up to make work for CCCs, or an unexpected fire necessitates splitting it with a road to haul firefighters. Or the congestion induced by advertising may whip up the price of guides and packers, whereupon somebody discovers that the wilderness policy is undemocratic. . . .

In short, the very scarcity of wild places, reacting with the mores of advertising and promotion, tends to defeat any deliberate effort to prevent their growing still more scarce. It is clear that mass-use involves dilution of the opportunity for solitude; that when we speak of campgrounds, trails and toilets as "development" of recreational resources, we speak falsely . . . such accommodations for the crowd are not developing (in the sense of adding or creating) anything. They are merely water poured into already-thin soup.

We come now to another component: perception of the natural processes by which the land and the living things upon it have achieved their characteristic forms (evolution) and by which they maintain their existence (ecology). That thing called "nature study," despite the shiver it brings to the spines of the elect, constitutes the first embryonic groping of the mass-mind toward perception.

—Drawing by Betty R. Thomas from *A Conservation Saga*

The outstanding characteristic of perception is that it entails no consumption and no dilution of any resource. The swoop of a hawk is perceived by one as the drama of evolution. To another it is only a threat to the full frying-pan. The drama may thrill a hundred witnesses; the threat only one — he responds with a shotgun.

To promote perception is the only truly creative part of recreational engineering. This fact is important, and its potential power for bettering the "good life" only dimly understood. When Daniel Boone first entered into "the dark and bloody ground," he reduced to his possession the pure essence of "outdoor America." He didn't call it that, but what he found is the thing we now seek, and we here deal with things, not names.

Recreation, however, is not the outdoors but our reaction to it. Boone's reaction depended not only on the quality of what he saw but on the quality of mental eye with which he

*Ivory-billed woodpecker,
now thought extinct*
—Photo by Arthur Allen,
Bird Photographs, Inc.

243

saw it. Ecological science has wrought a change in the mental eye. It has disclosed origins and functions for what to Boone were only facts. . . . The incredible intricacies of the plant and animal community — the intrinsic beauty of the organism called America, then in the bloom of maidenhood — were as incomprehensible to Daniel Boone as they are today to Mr. Babbitt. The only true development in American recreational resources is the development of the perceptive faculty . . . the other acts we grace by that name are attempts to retard or mask the process of dilution.

Let no man jump to the conclusion that Babbit must take his Ph. D. in ecology before he can "see" his country. The Ph. D. may become as callous as an undertaker to the mysteries at which he officiates. . . . The weeds in a city lot convey the same lesson as the redwoods; the farmer may see in his pasture what may not be vouchsafed to the scientist in the South Seas. Perception cannot be purchased with learned degrees or dollars; it grows at home as well as abroad; and he who has a little may use it to as good advantage as he who has much.

There is, lastly, the sense of husbandry. It is unknown to the outdoorsman who works for conservation with his vote rather than with his hands. . . . Its enjoyment is reserved for landholders too poor to buy their sport, and land administrators with a sharp eye and ecological mind. The tourist who

Early Hawk Mountain slaughter —Richard Pough photo, Hawk Mountain Sanctuary

Building a lookout tower, Harney National Forest, South Dakota —Civilian Conservation Corps photo

buys access to his scenery misses it altogether; so also the sportsman who hires the state to be his gamekeeper. The Government, which essays to substitute public for private operation of recreational lands, is giving away to its field officers a large share of what it seeks to offer its citizens.

Scientists have an epigram: ontogeny repeats phylogeny. What they mean is that the development of each individual repeats the evolutionary history of the race. This is true of

245

—By William Harnden Foster,
courtesy Charles Scribner's Sons

mental as well as physical things. The trophy-hunter is the caveman reborn. Trophy-hunting is the prerogative of youth, whether individual or racial, and nothing to apologize for.

The disquieting thing is the trophy-hunter who never grows up, in whom the capacity for isolation, perception and husbandry is undeveloped. He is the motorized ant who swarms the continents before learning to see his own back yard, who consumes but never creates outdoor satisfactions. For him the engineer dilutes the wilderness and artificializes its trophies. . . . To enjoy he must possess, invade, appropriate. Hence the wilderness that he cannot personally see has no value . . . hence the assumption that an unused hinterland is rendering no service to society. To those devoid of imagination, a blank place on the map is a useless waste. (Do I need a road to show me the arctic prairies, goose pastures of the Yukon, the Kodiak bear, the sheep meadows behind McKinley?)

It would appear that the rudimentary grades of outdoor recreation consume their resource base; the high grades, at least to a degree, create their own satisfactions with little or no attrition of land or life. It is the expansion of transport without a corresponding growth of perception that threatens us with qualitative bankruptcy of the recreational process. Development is a job not of building roads into lovely country, but of building receptivity into the still unlovely human mind.

Thus thought and spoke Aldo Leopold, just before CCC camps were replaced with infantry posts and air bases. He was the last great outdoor thinker of the era between the wars; though he lived to see the victory of World War II's allies, his most creative life was finished before Pearl Harbor. But even in 1976, his ideas and eloquence are alive, and modern writers quote him without remembering the source.

—By William Harnden Foster, courtesy Charles Scribner's Sons

Seagulls and the primeval sea at Monterey Peninsula, California —Courtesy David Muench Photography

Salt-water lures, rod and reel
—Frank Woolner photo

Spinning lures
—James Bashline photo

Fly reel—James Bashline photo

THE POSTWAR OUTDOOR WORLD 4

Nearly there —John Bosak photo

As we tumbled unceremoniously from the depression of the thirties into the global war of the forties, few Americans had time to think about outdoor journalism. Survival consumed most of their time.

Conservation in all its ramifications, sport hunting and fishing, and the writing of it didn't seem all that important. The war effort created jobs and money for those who were not in the armed forces. The additional pollution of our waters, skies and soil seemed patriotically sound in that hour of world folly.

A few outdoor typewriter punchers who had weathered the storms of the twenties and thirties were visible, still doing their best to educate and entertain, but nothing much of value happened until Germany and Japan finally said, "Enough!"

Returning GIs who vowed never again to sleep under the stars, carry a gun or do anything more outdoorsy than mow the lawn discovered, curiously, that they were more interested in woods and streams and, in general, the "outdoor experience." A long spell of shortages in non-essential goods — and sporting items were definitely in this category — caused a buying spree that went on for twenty-five years. Firearms com-

Winchester Model 12
—Courtesy Winchester Arms

panies switched from M1 rifles to pump action shotguns. Tackle firms began to crank out the then strange fiberglass fishing rods. Gadgets and gimmickry ran amuck and the whole country seemed to go on an outdoor binge.

There's still good news and bad news in this trend. The good is that more people are learning about the geography around them and, hopefully, appreciating it. The bad news is that, as more people want to use the land for more diverse outdoor pursuits, it's difficult to accommodate them. These widely divergent approaches form the boxes that today's outdoor journalist finds himself in. Depending on the medium he is working in, the writer has to make some sort of decision about what kind of journalist he wants to be.

249

AUDUBON
National Wildlife Federation
Sierra Club

By JACK PARRY

Sportsmen's Den

OUTDOOR EDITOR

Although the U.S. Weather Service has been issuing Lake Michigan water temperatures just below the 50 degree mark recently, it is apparently somewhat warmer than that off Northwest Indiana.

"A mile and a half off Burns Ditch we found th[e] water temperature at 53 degrees," Capt. Bob Cash [of] the charter boat "Raindrops," repor[ted.] "But, it wa[s] [unt]il we hit 47 degree water [...]

In medicine, engineering, physics and a host of new sciences that were scarcely dreamed of in our preceding 200 years, we are in the age of the specialist. There is simply too much new technology these days for any generalist to absorb it all. And so it is with the "outdoor writer," a term that has become a catchall for all who hunt, fish, camp, nature look or watchdog the forces which would upset the environment . . . and then write about it.

A proliferation of conservation organizations collectively crank out a blizzard of news releases and position papers on an almost daily basis. Equipment manufacturers are constantly introducing a new something or other that is scientifically proven to catch more bass, find more buried treasure, or lure more ducks to your blind.

To defend himself, the outdoors "communicator" has become a specialist. It began before 1940, of course, when magazines decided to create departments and named specialists as *shooting editor, fishing editor, camping editor,* and the like. After the war, this specialization became even more refined. *Salt water editors* were created and *skeet shooting columnists* emerged. People who wrote only about dogs became common while bird watching was an identifiable specialty. A few freelancers continued to write about a combination of subjects but, little by little, their areas of interest had to be reduced. The newspaper columnist is probably an exception but even here, most practicing columnists today write for their readership. If you live in Tucson, you don't write much about muskellunge.

It's against this background that some working journalists, mostly specialists, have been brought into this offering as Associate Editors. In some cases they have been asked to make comments on authors who are not within their outdoor orbit. In other cases quite the opposite is true.

Of guns and dogs

If one thing has created the attitude and character of Eastern gunning, it is the fact that we hunt a lot for a little. Years ago the Eastern gunner began an emphasis on what we might call the ancillary facts of the sport. We grew very involved with the guns themselves, and a man's shotgun, if finances permitted, became a blend of beauty and function — with beauty often taking the edge.

With his dogs, the same thing happened. And still today, it isn't rare to see an enormous Blue or Orange Belton strolling through a New England grouse cover as if he'd just stepped out of some old-time calendar depicting the familiar scene of the pipe-smoking flannel-shirted sport, in front of a log fire with his faithful friend curled up on the rug, with a rack of gleaming doubles in the background.

What a man needs a lot of in this part of the country is Yankee wit and philosophy. And much of our outdoor writing is, thankfully, well spiced with it. The writing selected is intended to span a variety of our

—By William Harnden Foster,
courtesy Charles Scribner's Sons

interests as well as opportunities afield. Good writing should be a well-constructed mirror of many things.

It is ponderously hard to transpose into words the deep feelings that a bird hunter has for his favorite shotgun. The nonhunter will never understand it. Some hunters don't! It's not quite the same with dogs; they can respond in an almost human way. Shotguns, particularly those used for wing-shooting, have a way of transmitting feeling too. It's a strange sort of osmosis that mysteriously passes through steel and well worn walnut into the flesh of the hands that hold it and the cheek that fondles it. William Harnden Foster in "New England Grouse Shooting" understood this perfectly.

"The Little Gun" was finished in the dusty little plant down in Meriden in November 1889. It was in the first vintage of relined sixteen gauge American breech-loaders and was billed to Mr. D. W. Parker, then treasurer of the Parker Company. That gentleman probably kept his eye on "The Little Gun" as it grew in the works for it must have been a sweet gun in those days. Yes, and it is a sweet gun now, clean lined and truly balanced and more; it has surrounded itself with the sentiments of nearly fifty years of family gunning tradition. I know because "The Little Gun" worn bright and smooth by the hands of my people holds a place of honor in my gun room.

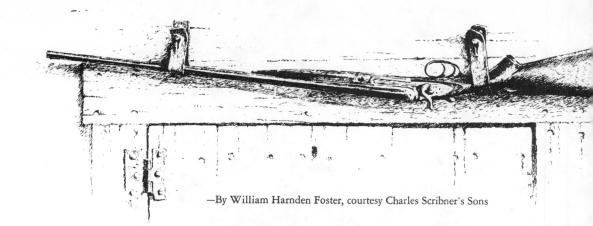

—By William Harnden Foster, courtesy Charles Scribner's Sons

The silt of time has obliterated most of the devious channels by which "The Little Gun" reached the square New England farmhouse at the cross-roads, that, years before, had served as a stagecoach tavern on the old Boston and Lowell turnpike. But there it came, after, I imagine, some careful figuring in which the prices of spring "muskrat" pelts and hand-picked cranberries were involved. It was about 1893 that "The Little Gun" became the prized possession of Everel Harnden, farmer, stone mason, trapper, and market hunter by occupation, redoubtable fox hunter by natural preference. Everel Harnden was my grandfather.

Seated in what was then the heart of a grand upland game country, the old white homestead became a veritable sporting

—By William Harnden Foster,
courtesy Charles Scribner's Sons

camp when the first frosts of early New England autumn painted with gaudy colors the Shawsheen meadow maples. Along with other dependable signs of approaching fall came Hub Cox from Reading, and Elbridge Gerry from Stoneham to stand the runways between Hannah Dam and the Brown place with grandfather Harnden, while slow-driving hounds sent up their jubilations as they ran the red fox. And there were the bird hunters who came to gun the North Ground and Kendall's Run with Uncle Gene. One day it would be Gard and Allen Eames, or Frank and Fin Killam. The next it might be the Curtis boys or Jim Baxter or Martin Holt. Pa'tridge hunters, everyone, that crowd, pa'tridge hunters of the old school.

The creaky barn door opened to a medley of noises, and smells. Chained in a bay were Elbridge Gerry's old-fashioned black-and-tans with their twenty-eight ear spread and bellowing voices. In one of the vacant stalls was grandfather Harnden's diminutive Bell; she who never grew big enough to give a fox a respectable shake, but the queen of local fox hounds, nevertheless. In another stall were Web and Tick, uncle Gene's pointers. The latter was a great grandson of Champion Graphic, although no one seemed especially interested in the fact.

And the guns. Some stood in the corners of the kitchen. The old Hapgood hung in straps over the back entry door. Some favorite occupied a worn wooden box under the "settin' room" sofa. What a place was the old homestead at the Tewksbury cross-roads for a gunstruck boy born to upland gunning traditions that dated back to the passenger pigeon days.

Then came "The Little Gun." It was the first sixteen that my grandfather ever saw. Just why he laid aside the old Tonks and the more modern ten gauge, side-snap Hollis, and bought a sixteen to shoot foxes with, no one knew. Perhaps it was the craving for innovation, perhaps he sensed its practical value, but I would guess that it was the same motive that causes us, in these days, to study and dream and suffer temptation before a showcase of fine guns: pride of ownership. Be that as it may, he bought the sixteen, defying Elbridge Gerry's grunts and what modern youth would call the wise cracks of Hub Cox. Local fox hunting gossip had it that Ev Harnden was probably losing his grasp on good judgment, to put it delicately.

"She don't weigh nothin'"

As the news of "The Little Gun" spread through the neighborhood lanky men dropped in of an evening to "heft" it and

—By William Harnden Foster, courtesy Charles Scribner's Sons

253

speculate on its practical value. "Gee-rifus, Ev!" they'd say, "she don't weigh nothin', does she?" Then they'd set the front log in the fireplace to sizzling to add impressiveness to the statement. George Sims "calc'lated" after squinting first one way and then the other at the size of the muzzles that he'd stand back-to and let anybody shoot at him at "twenty rod" for a couple of russet apples. But Ev Harnden just said nothing, as was his custom, although I have a notion that he knew more about what we call shotgun ballistics than his colleagues, and I am quite sure he knew more about what "The Little Gun" would do than he disclosed. In fact, I have a distinct recollection of his asking me to roll an apple barrel across the road and turn it around head-to. I remember seeing him stand back about forty-five yards and start the dust off the stone wall behind the barrel, and then seeing him, after studying both sides of the head for some time, chop it up and put it in the wood-box behind the kitchen stove. It is an unusual man who destroys favorable evidence, but grandfather Harnden was an unusual man in many ways.

Then, as the fox-hunting season began, and Bell's silvery tonguing rose on the frosty air, there would come a report from up Strongwater or across Heath, different in volume and tone from the roar of the old Hollis, and then Bell's song would stop. Pretty soon Ev Harnden would come down the Billerica road with "The Little Gun" in the hollow of his arm, his hound at heel, and an old dog fox hanging out both sides of his weather-bleached hunting coat.

"How fur, Ev?" Elbridge Gerry would ask in due time.

" 'Bout nine rod."

"By mighty!" Hub Cox would ejaculate. "She must drive 'em something tremenjous, mustn't she Elbridge?"

And Elbridge would look the fox over a time, turn his gaze on "The Little Gun" and finally say:

"Yup, she must, Hub."

There was a very definite reason why any gun that Ev Harnden used attained the reputation as a long killer. As "The Little Gun" produced results its reputation spread, quickened by grandfather's statement that "she was the hardest shootin' critter he ever see." But the fame of "The Little Gun" became immortal the morning that grandfather and Elbridge Gerry stood in the same cart-road and Bell and the two black-and-tans drove a fox right along the ege of Deacon Pillsbury's woodlot. Mr. Gerry swung onto him his twelve bore Scott, hitherto the small-bore of the neighborhood, when the fox came opposite. Then, deciding it was a hopeless chance, lowered it without shooting. Ev Harnden, twenty rods farther on, had the fox at the same distance, a lit-

—By William Harnden Foster,
courtesy Charles Scribner's Sons

254

tle farther if anything, waited for him to stretch out at the top of a jump, and dropped him in a heap, using only the left barrel. Elbridge Gerry paced it off, slowly and somewhat dolefully.

"Ev," he said, "that was nigh on to fifty-four honest yards, and, by the power o' mud, that was the thunderin'est shot I ever hope to see."

So local gunners continued to drop in and "heft" "The Little Gun" and speculate on the secrets of the wonders it performed. But "The Little Gun" did not confine its talents to Middlesex County foxes. The younger generation of bird hunters used to get hold of it whenever they could, and there was some plain and fancy pa'tridge shooting done in which the reputation of "The Little Gun" was amply maintained.

"The Little Gun" weighed six and a half pounds, nearly a pound and a half lighter than anything carried by local gunners. "I tell you, you can get on 'em quicker with a light gun," was the verdict of those who used it. Sixteen gauge talk became common, for the small bore spark was struck.

Uncle Gene Harnden, ace-high pa'tridge hunter, had, of course, used "The Little Gun." In fact, he had got in some pretty busy days with it. At that time he was firing the "Bay State" from Boston to New London and back every other day. Off days he gunned; quite a neat arrangement for a Harnden, forsooth. At any rate, he came home by the way of Kirkwood's one night with a new gun that created further furor in Tewksbury gunning circles. It was another sixteen gauge but this time a hammerless weighing six pounds and two ounces. The night that Uncle Gene brought that gun home was a black one for the pa'tridge tribe from Ashburnham to Epping. But the important point, so far as I was concerned, was that, with the advent of the new Pigeon Grade hammerless, the demands on "The Little Gun" were somewhat relieved.

—By William Harnden Foster, courtesy Charles Scribner's Sons

Old enough to gun

I reached the ripe age of twelve in July. On the first of September of the same year it became the consensus of the male members of the family that "William was old enough to gun." I had been along many times but usually in the capacity of transportation manager in charge of heavy-footed old Dick and the democrat wagon. My job was to leave whoever went at the head of a "run," take the shortest road around and wait at the bottom until they came out. Later in the season, when the leaves were off and the birds had worked out on the edges, I usually managed to do my waiting where I could see something of what went on, often the climax of the entire doings in the run. I had, therefore, seen a number of pa'tridge shot and had a pretty fair idea of how it should be done.

Like most people, I have had my moments of self-importance, but never, in later years, anything that compared with those when I drove out of the door-yard, wedged in between two of the best pa'tridge shots in the county, with a half dozen light loads in my pocket and with "The Little Gun" wrapped up in a horse blanket under the seat.

I wasn't very hard on either ammunition or game that first fall. They only let me load the right barrel and I was pretty much afraid to shoot that. I wasn't afraid of the gun, but of missing. All the shooting practice that our family had was on game, and if it so happened that you hadn't shot any flying game, why, you didn't know very much about the art of wing-shooting, that's all. I worried a good deal about it and on the first few trips passed up a number of good shots.

But the day did come and I remember the details as if it were but yesterday, and it was all over before I knew what had happened. We were down back of Mary Orcutt's and I was on the outside and a little ahead as usual. My right barrel was cocked and I was all keyed up like an E-string.

Uncle Gene was going along inside and I could follow his progress as he occasionally spoke to Tick.

Then, from down in the cover:

"Look out, William, there she comes!"

I don't remember hearing anything else, not even the gun, but I saw a pa'tridge, one of the rusty-brown ones, break out of the low white pines. I saw its head, its ruffs, its tail fanned up as it turned down the edge of the cover. I saw a gray cloud in the air over me and a feather or two floating down as the bird set its wings and scaled out into the open field.

"Did you stop her?"

I replied in a rather quavering voice that I didn't know but that she'd lit out in the lowbush blackberry vines "right in the open." The older generation of Harndens weren't given to excessive talk, but they always did a lot of silent chuckling and, although I did overhear my uncle relating the incident to some of his old cronies, it was only after more seasoning that I saw anything amusing or queer about it. It did not take Uncle Gene long to get out to where I stood and I showed him where the pa'tridge came down. I had visions of being set to my greatest shooting test, a shot in the open with a master critic at my elbow. But at the moment, it was just, "Don't load your gun, now — Tick, dead bird." And then Tick made a short cast into the briars and suddenly turned himself

—By William Harnden Foster,
courtesy Charles Scribner's Sons

—From a painting by Bob Kuhn

Bull Moose

(On preceding page)
Autumn Transitions, Elk Creek Canyon
—Photograph by David Muench

Cougar

—From a painting by Bob Kuhn

Grizzly Bear

—From a painting by Bob Kuhn

Polar Bear of the Arctic
—From a painting by Charles Livingston Bull
Courtesy Glenbow Alberta Institute

(At left)
Cowbird stealing an egg
from chestnut-sided warbler's nest
—Photograph by Hal H. Harrison

(Below) Skimmers
—From a painting by Don Eckelberry
courtesy the Frame House Gallery

—By William Harnden Foster,
courtesy Charles Scribner's Sons

into a letter U when he had nearly run over the bird that seemed to rise up from nowhere, spread its tail and try to skulk away.

When we drove in that night I had my bird that had been carefully smoothed and kept apart. The menfolks were all sitting in the kitchen going over the day. A square of bricks extended out onto the floor in front of the brick oven and that was the temporary place for all game brought in during the day. Often enough there would be a fox, sometimes a mink or a fall muskrat. Once a season, an otter, from time to time quail and woodcock and always, I guess, pa'tridges. Rabbits didn't count.

With a hopeless attempt at nonchalance, into the kitchen I walked, set "The Little Gun" in its corner, and with a feigned air of indifference tossed my first pa'tridge onto the heap, noting, at the same time, where it landed. My grandfather said nary a word. He just got up slow-like, fished out his worn purse of the many compartments, and handed me sixty-five cents. Then he sat down again. I wish I might see him do it over again—now. I'd look for the twinkle in his calm blue eyes that I know was there that big night when I was twelve.

"The Little Gun" had begun to uphold its reputation in the trembling hands of the third generation.

—By William Harnden Foster,
courtesy Charles Scribner's Sons

Exit Laughing

BY ED ZERN

L ately I've been getting some complaints about this column, and am overjoyed to learn that somebody is reading it; the original idea was simply to put something back here that would keep the back cover from sticking to the ... For instance, I met a guy ... I spent ...

Spin casting a quiet river
—Leonard Lee Rue III photo

It seems as if Ed Zern has been writing "Exit Laughing" for *Field & Stream* for one hundred years. Actually, it has been much less than that. From time to time, Zern writes something serious but his place in outdoor literature will be more secure because of his outrageous whoppers. Here's one from "The Hell With Hunting."

Gollup Kuhn's hunting accident

Some people don't know when they're well off, but Gollup Kuhn isn't one of them. With his wife and small daughter he lives in the white frame house where he was born, with one of the best bass pools of the upper Delaware River within plug-casting distance of his front porch, the dark trouty waters of the Lackawaxen swirling almost outside his kitchen window, and all of Pennsylvania's Pike County for his back yard. Gollup has been up and down and across the United States, and seen a lot of choice countryside, but he figures that for a man who likes to hunt and fish and raise a family and cut up a little at the Saturday night square-dance, he has got a pretty good location, and he aims to hang on to it.

There are all kinds of ways to make a living in Pike County, and Gollup has tried most of them. As a kid, he used to pick up a hundred-odd dollars a year catching live rattlesnakes and selling them at fifty cents a head. He has farmed some, and run eel racks, and harvested wild honey, and guided hunters and fishermen, and navvied on the railroad, and lumberjacked, and trapped, and gathered ginseng root, and excavated Indian relics, and generally managed to reconcile the business of making a living with his love of the outdoors.

I first met Gollup when I saw him walking down the Lackawaxen road carrying a small sack, and offered him a lift, which he accepted. "Many rattlesnakes around here?" I asked, by way of making conversation.

"There's three in this car, that I know of," Gollup said, poking the sack with his foot and watching it squirm angrily. In Pike County, if you ask a man a direct question, he gives you a direct answer.

"Many deer?" I asked.

"Yup," Gollup said.

"Much hunting done?" I asked.

"Yup," Gollup said.

"Ever do any?" I asked.

"Not since my accident," Gollup said, filling his corncob pipe with cut plug and lighting it. When he saw I was going to wait him out, he kind of settled back and said, "It was two years ago, the second day of the season. I had drove for some city fellers on opening day, but this day I was still-hunting

White-tailed getaway —Wilford L. Miller photo

back up of the bear swamps, where I knowed there was an old twelve-pointer stomping around. I was coming upwind over a ridge when that big buck jumped up facing me not more than ten yards away, and I snap-shot him in the chest. I was shooting a .30/40 because my brother Ralph had wanted to use the .30/30, and by God, that buck wheeled around so fast that that there high-powered bullet come right out of his hindquarters and wounded me in the shoulder. Still bothers me some on cold days."

Gollup struck a stove match on his pants and relit his pipe. "That's my place right there," he said. "You can drop me by the gate, and much obliged. Are you staying around here someplace?"

I said I was staying at the hotel in the village, but that this was my first day in that part of the state.

"It's real nice country up here," Gollup said, "but don't pay too much attention to no stories you hear. There's some terrible liars in Pike County."

Gene Hill, who assisted in making the selections in this section, has, in a few short years, made his end-of-the-book offerings in *Sports Afield* magazine a must for a million or more readers. He wouldn't make this selection so the editors took the liberty of doing it themselves. This selection is from his "Mostly Tailfeathers."

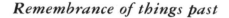

—Drawings on pages 260, 261
and 262 by John Scott

Remembrance of things past

My days spent on the Eastern Shore are all too few. And no matter how good the gunning ever is, the memory of how it used to be makes my "three dead in the air" seem a mockery of what the word "waterfowling" used to mean to the men of the Chesapeake Bay.

I've listened to the old-timers wistfully recalling the nights they took ducks outlined in flight against the full of an ice-white moon. I've heard them talk about the sinkboxes surrounded by more than 300 decoys and how they would lay there wet, frozen and often frightened of a running sea and a ten-knot wind. I've heard the baymen talk softly amongst themselves about the live tollers, blacks and mallards and Canadas, that they used to train. I've seen their guns from "O" bores to the "little" ten-gauge side-by-side. Yes, I've listened to the talk and seen their boats and held their guns, but I know nothing of the meaning of their words.

I will never see the thousands upon thousands of canvasbacks on opening day along the Susquehanna flats. I will never thread a boat, shipping water from the weight of mallards, with a sculling oar at one end and a gunning light at the other.

I will never know the bellow of a half-pound of sixes tamped down in front of black powder and oakum. I'll not likely take in my lifetime as many as some of these men have often taken in a single day.

They tell of the nights so filled with music; the whistling of pintails, the grunting of geese, the tuk-tuk of mallards that two men in a blind had to talk to each other by kicking and poking.

They let me hear their words, but it is really to each other that they talk of another time—and not to me.

I will never know their Currituck, their Pamlico, their Nags Head, their Smith and Tangiers islands.

But the one thing I know is their mind. I can imagine what it must have been like to set out with a case of hand-made shells and expect, on a very good day, to use the whole batch up. And I wish I could have done it—just one time.

They—the old gunners and baymen—talk about the hardness. They talk about the cold and the wet and the days that came and went without sleep, and I see their hands and I understand. Hands that lived in ice and around oars and push-poles and rope and frozen netting and hatchets, draw knives and files. Hands that brought canvasbacks and ruddies and brant alive from cedar logs. Hands that crafted deadeyes, and sneak-skiffs and pungeys. Hands that tell me more of what they're saying than the words.

But it's the eyes that give them away. It's the looking backward to the day they stared down the barrel of an old Remington Model 11 with a ten-shot extension on the magazine

261

more than 500 times a day—on more days than one. And I see an excitement there that I wish I'd known firsthand—just once.

We are the same, these old men and me. Separated a bit by time and fortune, but imagination stirs my gunning blood the same—and when I close my eyes I can see it all . . . I can feel the cold, duck-riding wind on the back of my neck. My hands, still frozen from helping set out more than a hundred blocks, are tucked up in my armpits for warmth. I would have had my ten-gauge hammer gun reamed out about to almost cylinder bore for the first shot, and a touch more choke for the second. It is still night, the reluctant winter sun imperceptible yet behind the heavy banks of scudding clouds that promise snow before noon. But I can hear them overhead pouring through the dark from sheltered bays on the first flights to the flats where the wild celery grows. And I wait . . . not for any legal shooting time . . . . but just for light enough to silhouette the sculpture of the canvasback over a gun barrel.

And at last, as it always must, it happens. I have heard the cans dropping in amongst the decoys for the last half-hour and now with light, I stand and shoot. Three fall with the first barrel as they blossom up from the water and then a pair of drakes tumble with the second. (I always shoot beautifully in my imagination.) And as fast as I can load and shoot they drive in to the stool. My pick-up man is standing by until I'm done — and by the time the other working men are at their jobs, I'm through.

Ducks of all sorts nearly brush our caps as we retrieve and pick up the handmade decoys from the freezing chop. Who could have ever stood there then and guess that in less than 30 years these skies would be near silent and a box of shells would last the average gunner a month? Who would then have ever said that his great-grandchildren would likely never know the smell of roasting canvasback and a daily limit of other ducks could be carried in just one hand?

I can't find it in myself to condemn the old-time gunners. It is indeed a tragedy that they did not realize the havoc that they wrought — but a tragedy born of ignorance rather than intent. And lest we too hastily blame them for being ignorant, let me remind you of the atomic clouds that still circle the atmosphere, DDT, Thalidomide, leaded gasoline, mercury wastes, phosphates, just to name a few — that in the last years have done more to affect our living environment than the short span of time that was the heyday of the commercial gunner.

And what about you? I'd like to bet that I could find you any morning of the gunning season dressing in your union suit of scratchy wool by the light of a smoky kerosene lantern. Your good wife downstairs in the kitchen making oatmeal, some fried home-cured ham and a blue enamel pot of boiled coffee, and maybe a buttermilk biscuit or two to tamp the whole thing down. Along about half-past three, with the second cup of coffee in your hand, you'd be out on the porch smelling the wind like an eager hound. Your wife sees the timeless excitement in your face and takes pleasure in the fact there's still a lot of boy that's living in the man she married years ago. I hope she'll be the one to hear my horse's hooves striking sparks from the frozen road and come out to say hello when I stop to pick you up — with a hot cup and maybe a biscuit or two.

You take the reins while I light my pipe and tuck Old Maude's blanket in a little tighter around my knees; seems the mornings are a little brisker than they used to be. The horse forces herself into a tiny trot, pretending she's as excited as we are, and we just sit there staring at the cold blue sky — not saying much, just sort of puffing our pipes at each other as certain men are apt to do when they know for sure that there's no place in the world they'd rather be.

Give Maude a little flick of the reins, it won't do much good, but it flatters her.

The Road to Tinkhamtown

The pitfalls of becoming enthralled with a particular author are many and dangerous when piecing a book like this together. Nash Buckingham, Havilah Babcock, Archibald Rutledge and a host of others can set an editor to dreaming and before he knows it he's lulled away from the purpose of the book. Corey Ford is like that. Perhaps best known for his "Lower Forty" tales, which appeared in *Field & Stream* for many years, Ford also contributed a great many articles to *Readers Digest* and dozens of other periodicals.

A collection of Ford's best will be done some day but for our purposes let's read "The Road to Tinkhamtown". It was his epitaph. Rejected by one magazine and almost forgotten by another, it appeared in the 75th Anniversary Issue of *Field & Stream,* June 1970. It was tried, without success, to extract a portion of this story for space saving reasons. It couldn't be done; it's all here. If you're a grouse hunter or know one well and haven't read this before, brace yourself.

It was a long way, but he knew where he was going. He would follow the road through the woods and over the crest of a hill and down the hill to the stream, and cross the sagging timbers of the bridge, and on the other side would be the place called Tinkhamtown. He was going back to Tinkhamtown.

He walked slowly at first, his legs dragging with each step. He had not walked for almost a year, and his flanks had shriveled and wasted away from lying in bed so long; he could fit his fingers around his thigh. Doc Towle had said he would never walk again, but that was Doc for you, always on the pessimistic side. Why, now he was walking quite easily, once he had started. The strength was coming back into his legs, and he did not have to stop for breath so often. He tried jogging a few steps, just to show he could, but he slowed again because he had a long way to go.

It was hard to make out the old road, choked with alders and covered by matted leaves, and he shut his eyes so he could see it better. He could always see it when he shut his eyes. "Yes, here was the beaver dam on the right, just as he remembered it, and the flooded stretch where he had picked his way from hummock to hummock while the dog splashed unconcernedly in front of him. The water had been over his boot tops in one place, and sure enough, as he waded it now his left boot filled with water again, the same warm squidgy feeling. Everything was the way it had been that afternoon, nothing had changed in ten years. Here was the blowdown across the road that he had clambered over, and here on a knoll was the clump of thornapples where a grouse had flushed as they passed. Shad had wanted to look for it, but he

—From a painting by Howard Terpning

had whistled him back. They were looking for Tinkhamtown.

He had come across the name on a map in the town library. He used to study the old maps and survey charts of the state; sometimes they showed where a farming community had flourished a century ago, and around the abandoned pastures and in the orchards grown up to pine the birds would be feeding undisturbed. Some of his best grouse covers had been located that way. The map had been rolled up in a cardboard cylinder; it crackled with age as he spread it out. The date was 1857. It was the sector between Cardigan and Kearsarge Mountains, a wasteland of slash and second-growth timber without habitation today, but evidently it had supported a number of families before the Civil War. A road was marked on the map, dotted with X's for homesteads, and the names of the owners were lettered beside them: Nason, J. Tinkham, Allard, R. Tinkham. Half the names were Tinkham. In the center of the map — the paper was so yellow that he could barely make it out — was the word "Tinkhamtown."

He had drawn a rough sketch on the back of an envelope, noting where the road left the highway and ran north to a fork and then turned east and crossed a stream that was not even named; and the next morning he and Shad had set out together to find the place. They could not drive very far in the jeep, because washouts had gutted the roadbed and laid bare the ledges and boulders. He had stuffed the sketch in his hunting-coat pocket, and hung his shotgun over his forearm and started walking, the setter trotting ahead with the bell on his collar tinkling. It was an old-fashioned sleighbell, and it had a thin silvery note that echoed through the woods like peepers in the spring. He could follow the sound in the thickest cover, and when it stopped he would go to where he heard it last and Shad would be on point. After Shad's death, he had put the bell away. He'd never had another dog.

Silence of the woods

It was silent in the woods without the bell, and the way was longer than he remembered. He should have come to the big hill by now. Maybe he'd taken the wrong turn back at the fork. He thrust a hand into his hunting coat; the envelope with the sketch was still in the pocket. He sat down on a flat rock to get his bearings, and then he realized, with a surge of excitement, that he had stopped on this very rock for lunch ten years ago. Here was the waxed paper from his sandwich, tucked in a crevice, and here was the hollow in the leaves where Shad had stretched out beside him, the dog's soft muzzle flattened on his thigh. He looked up, and through the trees he could see the hill.

He rose and started walking again, carrying his shotgun. He had left the gun standing in its rack in the kitchen when he had been taken to the state hospital, but now it was hooked over his arm by the trigger guard; he could feel the solid heft of it. The woods grew more dense as he climbed, but here and there a shaft of sunlight slanted through the trees. "And there were forests ancient as the hills," he thought, "enfolding sunny spots of greenery." Funny that should come back to him now; he hadn't read it since he was a boy. Other things were coming back to him, the smell of dank leaves and sweetfern and frosted apples, the sharp contrast of sun and cool shade, the November stillness before snow. He walked faster, feeling the excitement swell within him.

He paused on the crest of the hill, straining his ears for the faint mutter of the stream below him, but he could not hear it because of the voices. He wished they would stop talking, so he could hear the stream. Someone was saying his name over and over, "Frank, Frank," and he opened his eyes reluctantly and looked up at his sister. Her face was worried, and there was nothing to worry about. He tried to tell her where he was going, but when he moved his lips the words would not form. "What did you say, Frank?" she asked, bending her head lower. "I don't understand." He couldn't make the words any clearer, and she straightened and said to Doc Towle: "It sounded like Tinkhamtown."

"Tinkhamtown?" Doc shook his head. "Never heard him mention any place by that name."

He smiled to himself. Of course he'd never mentioned it to Doc. Things like a secret grouse cover you didn't mention to anyone, not even to as close a friend as Doc was. No, he and Shad were the only ones who knew. They had found it together, that long ago afternoon, and it was their secret.

They had come to the stream—he shut his eyes so he could see it again—and Shad had trotted across the bridge. He had followed more cautiously, avoiding the loose planks and walking along a beam with his shotgun held out to balance himself. On the other side of the stream the road mounted steeply to a clearing in the woods, and he halted before the split-stone foundations of a house, the first of the series of farms shown on the map. It must have been a long time since the building had fallen in; the cottonwoods growing in the cellar hole were twenty, maybe thirty years old. His boot overturned a rusted ax blade and the handle of a china cup in the grass; that was all. Beside the doorstep was a lilac bush, almost as tall as the cottonwoods. He thought of the wife who had set it out, a little shrub then, and the husband who had chided her for wasting time on such frivolous things with all the farm work to be done. But the work had come to nothing, and still the lilac bloomed each spring, the one thing that had survived.

Shad's bell was moving along the stone wall at the edge of the clearing, and he strolled after him, not hunting, wondering about the people who had gone away and left their walls to crumble and their buildings to collapse under the winter snows. Had they ever come back to Tinkhamtown? Were they here now, watching him unseen? His toe stubbed against a block of hewn granite hidden by briars, part of the sill of the old barn. Once it had been a tight barn, warm with cattle steaming in their stalls, rich with the blend of hay and manure and harness leather. He liked to think of it the way it was; it was more real than this bare rectangle of blocks and the emptiness inside. He'd always felt that way about the past. Doc used to argue that what's over is over, but he would insist Doc was wrong. Everything is the way it was, he'd tell Doc. The past never changes. You leave it and go on to the present, but it is still there, waiting for you to come back to it.

He had been so wrapped in his thoughts that he had not realized Shad's bell had stopped. He hurried across the clearing, holding his gun ready. In a corner of the stone wall an ancient apple tree had littered the ground with fallen fruit, and beneath it Shad was standing motionless. The white fan of his tail was lifted a little and his backline was level, the neck craned forward, one foreleg cocked. His flanks were trembling with the nearness of grouse, and a thin skein of drool hung from his jowls. The dog did not move as he approached, but the brown eyes rolled back until their whites showed, looking for him. "Steady, boy," he called. His throat was tight, the way it always got when Shad was on point, and he had to swallow hard. "Steady, I'm coming."

Waiting for the grouse

"I think his lips moved just now," his sister's voice said. He did not open his eyes, because he was waiting for the grouse to get up in front of Shad, but he knew Doc Towle was looking at him. "He's sleeping," Doc said after a moment. "Maybe you better get some sleep yourself, Mrs. Duncombe." He heard Doc's heavy footsteps cross the room. "Call me if there's any change," Doc said, and closed the door, and in the silence he could hear his sister's chair creaking beside him, her silk dress rustling regularly as she breathed.

What was she doing here, he wondered. Why had she come all the way from California to see him? It was the first time they had seen each other since she had married and moved out West. She was his only relative, but they had never been very close; they had nothing in common, really. He heard from her now and then, but it was always the same letter: why didn't he sell the old place, it was too big for him now that the folks had passed on, why didn't he take a small apartment in town where he wouldn't be alone? But he liked the big house, and he wasn't alone, not with Shad. He had closed off all the other rooms and moved into the kitchen so everything would be handy. His sister didn't approve of his bachelor ways, but it was very comfortable with his cot by the stove and Shad curled on the floor near him at night, whinnying and scratching the linoleum with his claws as he chased a bird in a dream. He wasn't alone when he heard that.

He had never married. He had looked after the folks as long as they lived; maybe that was why. Shad was his family. They were always together—Shad was short for Shadow—and there was a closeness between them that he did not feel for anyone else, not his sister or Doc even. He and Shad used to talk without words, each knowing what the other was thinking, and they could always find one another in the woods. He still remembered the little things about him: the possessive thrust of his paw, the way he false-yawned when he was vexed, the setter stubbornness sometimes, the clownish grin when they were going hunting, the kind eyes. That was it; Shad was the kindest person he had ever known.

They had not hunted again after Tinkhamtown. The old dog had stumbled several times, walking back to the jeep, and he had to carry him in his arms the last hundred yards. It was hard to realize he was gone. He liked to think of him the way he was; it was like the barn, it was more real than the emptiness. Sometimes at night, lying awake with the pain in his legs, he would hear the scratch of claws on the linoleum, and he would turn on the light and the hospital room would be empty. But when he turned the light off he would hear the scratching again, and he would be content and drop off to sleep, or what passed for sleep in these days and nights that ran together without dusk or dawn.

Once he asked Doc point-blank if he would ever get well. Doc was giving him something for the pain, and he hesitated a moment and finished what he was doing and cleaned the needle and then looked at him and said: "I'm afraid not, Frank." They had grown up in town together, and Doc knew him too well to lie. "I'm afraid there's nothing to do." Nothing to do but lie here and wait till it was over. "Tell me, Doc," he whispered, for his voice wasn't very strong, "what happens when it's over?" And Doc fumbled with the catch of his black bag and closed it and said well he supposed you went on to someplace else called the Hereafter. But he shook his head; he always argued with Doc. "No, it isn't someplace else," he told him, "it's someplace you've been where you want to be again." Doc didn't understand, and he couldn't explain it any better. He knew what he meant, but the shot was taking effect and he was tired.

He was tired now, and his legs ached a little as he started down the hill, trying to find the stream. It was too dark under the trees to see the sketch he had drawn, and he could not tell direction by the moss on the north side of the trunks. The moss grew all around them, swelling them out of size, and huge blowdowns blocked his way. Their upended roots were black and misshapen, and now instead of excitement he felt a surge of panic. He floundered through a pile of slash, his legs throbbing with pain as the sharp points stabbed him, but he did not have the strength to get to the other side and he had to back out again and circle. He did not know where he was going. It was getting late, and he had lost the way.

There was no sound in the woods, nothing to guide him, nothing but his sister's chair creaking and her breath catching now and then in a dry sob. She wanted him to turn back, and Doc wanted him to, they all wanted him to turn back. He thought of the big house; if he left it alone it would fall in with the winter snows and cottonwoods would grow in the cellar hole. And there were all the other doubts, but most of all there was the fear. He was afraid of the darkness, and being alone, and not knowing where he was going. It would be better to turn around and go back. He knew the way back.

And then he heard it, echoing through the woods like peepers in the spring, the thin silvery tinkle of a sleighbell. He started running toward it, following the sound down the hill. His legs were strong again, and he hurdled the blowdowns, he leapt over fallen logs, he put one fingertip on a pile of slash and sailed over it like a grouse skimming. He was getting nearer and the sound filled his ears, louder than a thousand church bells ringing, louder than all the choirs in the sky, as loud as the pounding of his heart. The fear was gone; he was not lost. He had the bell to guide him now.

He came to the stream, and paused for a moment at the bridge. He wanted to tell them he was happy, if they only knew how happy he was, but when he opened his eyes he could not see them anymore. Everything else was bright, but the room was dark.

The bell had stopped, and he looked across the stream. The other side was bathed in sunshine, and he could see the road mounting steeply, and the clearing in the woods, and the apple tree in a corner of the stone wall. Shad was standing, motionless beneath it, the white fan of his tail lifted, his neck craned forward and one foreleg cocked. The whites of his eyes showed as he looked back, waiting for him.

"Steady," he called, "steady, boy." He started across the bridge. "I'm coming."

Another form of fox hunting

With the exception of New England fox hunting, the fox in most regions of the U.S. is not killed. It is merely chased. But oddly, this version of fox chasing has drawn relatively little attention from outdoor writers, despite McKinlay Kantor's fine novel, "The Voice of Bugle Ann," probably because it is a truly contemplative sport. Nothing much happens; the "hunters" sit around a fire listening to their dogs chase a fox, preferably a red fox, then at dawn they put out the fire and round up the hounds. The idea is not to catch the fox at all, just listen to the hounds baying as they pursue a worthy quarry. This attitude causes consternation in a goal-oriented society.

Thus most writing about this split-rail-flavored pastime has been done by people who do not make a living by communicating with a large public. They have sought to explain the inexplicable: the lure of pursuing creatures that you never see with dogs that serve no purpose except to bay in dark pursuit. The explanation is rarely successful, or literate.

But an assistant attorney general of Missouri resolved the issue in his own way 20-odd years ago. Hugh P. Williamson dealt in pure mystique to explain the phenomenon in a series of fantasies about hounds, foxes and men who listen on crisp nights. He located his tales in the Kingdom of Callaway, a half-real region along the Missouri River, a spooky land that Judge Williamson let "old Seth Robards" describe.

—Drawing from the *Missouri Conservationist* magazine

Everybody who knows anything knows about the Kingdom of Callaway. An a plenty who don't hardly know nothin else knows about it too. It's a land an a people which God created an then went off an left alone. They got along good, the land an the people did, til foreigners come an things got theirselves unsettled, 'ceptin in places. Down in Auxvasse Creek part of the country things has changed mighty little since grandpappy's time.

I aim to tell you all about them old days, an that I shall now do. I shall tell you about a fox hunt in the time when my daddy was young. That was long enuf agone, fer we berried him seventy-three years ago come January 7. The snow flew level with the ground that day, an it covered his grave like a quilt ere the mourners went away.

Well, in those days, there was a passel of fox hunting over the Kingdom. In them times foxes was foxes an dogs was dogs. An they run. They run like a wind in the night. An the men, back when my daddy was young, they followed them, easy and swift like a deer, through the woods an prairie land. An they never was tired in them times I am tellin about.

Well, in 18 an 59 it was, in the fall of the year, my daddy an his brothers an their daddy, one evenin at sundown, taken their foxhorns an blowed. They blowed like trumpets blowed at Jericho . . . they blowed like the shepherds of Canaan blowed fer the lost sheep, sweet an low, but long.

Some who heard it said twas surely the Big Horn soundin to wake the dead on Resurrection Morn. An surely that will be a pleasant thing to hear, an to see the folks that has been gone this many a day, like my children that the fever took, an the boy that drownded himself over Callanan's girl. But when they blowed here, the dogs come, our'n an the rest, come like leaves pitchin down a hillside, like sunbeams on water. They come round my daddy an set awaitin. My daddy cupped his hands before his mouth, like this, and called "Go find him!" an they went away with a sound like a whisper. An the men, they follered.

Then the hounds begun to talk to the men. They talked like a fiddle aplayin; like a child or a woman acryin in night; like the call of that witless girl as once wandered here. The things that touches heartstrings was in their call, an the men follered them into the night.

Well, stars come out an then the moon rose over yon ridge an a wind come up. The hounds was way away. But the men follered, leapin creeks, climbin ridges, runnin the glades, for they never wasn't tired. Nobody never tired in them days, when my daddy was young, when this was truly the King-

dom, sir. An they wasn't nobody never growed old.

The stars moved across, an the moon climbed high, but the wind lay. An it seemed like there wasn't nobody in all the world exceptin the hounds an the men—an the fox. The men never seen the hounds or the fox, but the hounds talked to the men all through the night, their voices soundin like church music, or like a violin playin an old, sad song. Or like a child afeared. Sounds that takes a man's soul an compels him to foller the sound.

After a long while, the bellin of the hounds faded an was lost in the dark, like a child that is gone, or, a fiddle that stops playin; like a hope that has fleeted away. Then the stars an the moon, they faded an was no longer seen in the sky; an light come on the men as they stood lookin at new-come day; an their hearts were empty of trouble like a dipper with water poured out.

An the men lay down on the leaves in the little holler where they stood, an slep long into the day.

The fox, you say? No, they never once seen the fox.

Was there a fox, you say? Well, there mayn't never have been no fox. It may be, you know, that none of the things men follers is ever there.

So spoke old Seth Robards, when I was young in the Kingdom of Callaway.

—Drawing from the *Missouri Conservationist* magazine

Escudilla

Aldo Leopold was more than a scientist; more, even, than "the father of modern game management." He was also a philosopher and one of our most beautifully expressive outdoor writers. His clear, disarmingly simple prose is a superb distillation of mood and wisdom. Professor Leopold not only knew the outdoor world as few men do, but had the gifted ability to reduce profound concepts to brief, crystalline expression. There was none like him before. It is unlikely that there will be another. Herewith, the sketch "Escudilla" from "A Sand County Almanac."

Life in Arizona was bounded under foot by grama grass, overhead by sky, and on the horizon by Escudilla.

To the north of the mountain you rode on honey-colored plains. Look up anywhere, any time, and you saw Escudilla.

To the east you rode over a confusion of wooded mesas. Each hollow seemed its own small world, soaked in sun, fragrant with juniper, and cozy with the chatter of piñon jays. But top out on a ridge and you at once became a speck in an immensity. On its edge hung Escudilla.

To the south lay the tangled canyons of Blue River, full of whitetails, wild turkeys, and wilder cattle. When you missed a saucy buck waving his goodbye over the skyline, and looked down your sights to wonder why, you looked at a far blue mountain: Escudilla.

To the west billowed the outliers of the Apache National Forest. We cruised timber there, converting the tall pines, forty by forty, into notebook figures representing hypothetical lumber piles. Panting up a canyon, the cruiser felt a curious incongruity between the remoteness of his notebook symbols and the immediacy of sweaty fingers, locust thorns, deer-fly bites, and scolding squirrels. But on the next ridge a cold wind, roaring across a green sea of pines, blew his doubts away. On the far shore hung Escudilla.

The mountain bounded not only our work and our play, but even our attempts to get a good dinner. On winter evenings we often tried to ambush a mallard on the river flats. The wary flocks circled the rosy west, the steel-blue north, and then disappeared into the inky black of Escudilla. If they reappeared on set wings, we had a fat drake for the Dutch oven. If they failed to reappear, it was bacon and beans again.

There was, in fact, only one place from which you did not see Escudilla on the skyline: that was the top of Escudilla itself. Up there you could not see the mountain, but you could feel it. The reason was the big bear.

Old Bigfoot was a robber-baron, and Escudilla was his castle. Each spring, when the warm winds had softened the

A mallard drake—Leonard Lee Rue III photo

Escudilla against the Arizona sky —George H. Harrison photo

shadows on the snow, the old grizzly crawled out of his hibernation den in the rock slides and, descending the mountain, bashed in the head of a cow. Eating his fill, he climbed back to his crags, and there summered peaceably on marmots, conies, berries, and roots.

I once saw one of his kills. The cow's skull and neck were pulp, as if she had collided head-on with a fast freight.

No one ever saw the old bear, but in the muddy springs about the base of the cliffs you saw his incredible tracks.

A silver tip grizzly —Leonard Lee Rue III photo

Bigfoot's mountains —George H. Harrison photo

Seeing them made the most hard-bitten cowboys aware of bear. Wherever they rode they saw the mountain, and when they saw the mountain they thought of bear. Campfire conversation ran to beef, bailes, and bear. Bigfoot claimed for his own only a cow a year, and a few square miles of useless rocks, but his personality prevaded the county.

Those were the days when progress first came to the cow country. Progress had various emissaries.

One was the first transcontinental automobilist. The cowboys understood this breaker of roads; he talked the same breezy bravado as any breaker of broncos.

They did not understand, but they listened to and looked at, the pretty lady in black velvet who came to enlighten them, in a Boston accent, about woman suffrage.

They marveled, too, at the telephone engineer who strung wires on the junipers and brought instantaneous messages from town. An old man asked whether the wire could bring him a side of bacon.

One spring, progress sent still another emissary, a government trapper, a sort of St. George in overalls, seeking dragons to slay at government expense. Were there, he asked, any destructive animals in need of slaying? Yes, there was the big bear.

The trapper packed his mule and headed for Escudilla.

In a month he was back, his mule staggering under a heavy hide. There was only one barn in town big enough to dry it on. He had tried traps, poison, and all his usual wiles to no avail. Then he had erected a set-gun in a defile through which only the bear could pass, and waited. The last grizzly walked into the string and shot himself.

It was June. The pelt was foul, patchy, and worthless. It seemed to us rather an insult to deny the last grizzly the chance to leave a good pelt as a memorial to his race. All he left was a skull in the National Museum, and a quarrel among scientists over the Latin name of the skull.

It was only after we pondered on these things that we began to wonder who wrote the rules for progress.

Since the beginning, time had gnawed at the basaltic hulk of Escudilla, wasting, waiting, and building. Time built three things on the old mountain, a venerable aspect, a community of minor animals and plants, and a grizzly.

The government trapper who took the grizzly knew he had made Escudilla safe for cows. He did not know he had toppled the spire off an edifice a-building since the morning stars sang together.

The bureau chief who sent the trapper was a biologist versed in the architecture of evolution, but he did not know

The prowling pack ignores a brief skirmi

that spires might be as important as cows. He did not foresee that within two decades the cow country would become tourist country, and as such have greater need of bears than of beefsteaks.

The Congressmen who voted money to clear the ranges of bears were the sons of pioneers. They acclaimed the superior virtues of the frontiersman, but they strove with might and main to make an end of the frontier.

We forest officers, who acquiesced in the extinguishment of the bear, knew a local rancher who had plowed up a dagger engraved with the name of one of Coronado's captains. We spoke harshly of the Spaniards who, in their zeal for gold and converts, had needlessly extinguished the native Indians. It did not occur to us that we, too, were the captains of an invasion too sure of its own righteousness.

Escudilla still hangs on the horizon, but when you see it you no longer think of bear. It's only a mountain now.

Quetico and far places

Sigurd F. Olson sings of the North — the lake wilderness of the Quetico and the far places beyond. He is a superb writer and when you read him, believe him. He's been there. When I first met Sig, two things impressed me: his gentle quietness, and the north-country map of wrinkles that he wears in his face. It's a face that has looked across many lakes and into much weather for a very long time, and no living writer celebrates the northern solitudes as eloquently as he. In his 1972 edition of "Singing Wilderness", he speaks of wolves:

The eyes of a hunting wolf
—George H. Harrison photo

Durward L. Allen photo

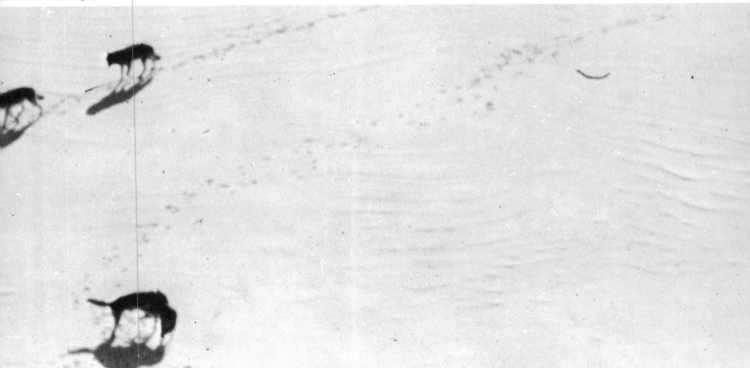

The prey is spotted.
—George H. Harrison photo

I could hear them plainly now on both sides of the river, could hear the brush crack as they hurdled windfalls in their path. Once I thought I saw one, a drifting gray shadow against the snow, but it was only a branch swaying in the light of the moon. When I heard the full-throated bawling howl, I should have had chills racing up and down my spine. Instead, I was thrilled to know that the big grays might have picked up my trail and were following me down the frozen highway of the river.

It was a beautiful night for travel: cold and still, the only sound the steady swish and creak of my snowshoes on the crust. There was real satisfaction in knowing the wolves were in the country and that it was wild and still big enough for them to roam and hunt. That night the wilderness of the Quetico-Superior was what the voyageurs had known two hundred years before.

Some months before, I had had the same kind of experience on a pack trip in the Sun River country of Montana. In the bottom of a canyon I saw the fresh track of a big grizzly in the soft muck beside a glacial creek. Although I did not see the bear, I knew it was nearby. Those tracks changed the country immediately for me. From that moment on, it was the land of Lewis and Clark, the land of the mountain men of the last century, a valley of the Old West.

The river ahead narrowed down to where two points of timber came out from either bank, and as I approached, I sensed instinctively the possibilities of attack. I was familiar with the wolf lore of the Old World, the packs on the steppes of Russia, the invasion of farms and villages, and had I believed the lurid tales of our early settlers and explorers, I might have been afraid. To the best of my knowledge, however, including the files of the U.S. Fish and Wildlife Service, there has never been a single authenticated instance of unprovoked attack on man.

But still there was a feeling of uneasiness and apprehension, and I knew that if the animals were concerned with anything but satisfying their curiosity, the narrows would be the place for a kill. A swift rush from both points at the same time, a short, unequal scuffle in the snow, and it would be all over. My bones would go down with the ice in the spring, and no one would ever hear the story and no one would be able to explain.

As I neared the points of spruce, I sensed the crash of heavy bodies against the windfalls and brush. Weighing 100, even as much as 120 pounds or more, timber wolves are huge and powerful, can bring down a caribou or a moose, have nothing to fear on the entire continent but man. This was not the first time I had felt they were playing their game of hide-and-seek with me. On other lone midwinter expeditions I had sensed they were close—a hunch perhaps, but as instinctive a reaction when in their immediate range as though I had actually seen them. As I hiked along that night, I knew I was being watched, a lone dark spot moving slowly along the frozen river.

That very morning I had seen where they had pulled down an old buck on the ice of a little lake, and how they had run the deer to exhaustion, sliced at his hamstrings, flanks, his throat; seen the long crimson spurt where they had ripped the jugular, the bits of mangled hide on the snow. He had been large and his horns were broad and palmate, but in the trampled, bloody circle where he had made his last stand he had not lasted long. He might have died slowly of starvation or disease, but he died as he should when his time had come, fighting for his life against his age-old enemies, like the valiant warrior he was out on the open ice.

An age-old dependency

The wolves had not eaten much, only the entrails and the viscera, but they would return, I knew, to satisfy themselves again. Such was the habit of their kind until we interfered with poison and trap and taught them caution and fear. When that happened, they learned to leave the carcasses after the first feeding and killed more than they would have normally. That kill was part of the age-old cycle of dependency between the wolves and the deer. The predators, by the elimination of the old, the weak, and the diseased, improved the character of the herd and kept the younger and more virile

The chase is on. —Durward L. Allen photo

breeding stock alert and aware of danger. The deer provided food when there was no other source, when the heavy snows hid the small rodents, frogs and snakes, grubs and berries and birds that gave the wolves sustenance during all other seasons of the year. There on the ice was evidence of the completed cycle, and though all kills are gruesome things, I was glad to see it, for it meant a wilderness in balance, a primitive country that as yet had not been tamed.

Once I saw a kill being made. I was paddling down the Basswood River on the way to Crooked Lake when I saw a deer running leisurely along a barren, rocky slope paralleling the river. To my surprise a wolf loped behind it, keeping a distance of some thirty yards from its prey. It moved without effort, drifting along like a shadow, then suddenly dashed forward, closed the gap, and with a movement as though in slow motion caught the deer by its nose. The stricken animal turned a somersault and struck the ledge, breaking its back. Instantly the wolf was upon it and the struggle over. I turned toward shore, jumped into the shallows, and ran up the slope to the dead animal, an old doe. The wolf circled warily and once I had a glimpse of it.

I remembered this as I approached the narrows where the spruces stood tall and black against the sky. The shores now were only a stone's throw apart. I must walk straight down the center, must not run or break my pace. I was suddenly aware that, in spite of reason and my knowledge of the predators, ancient reactions were coming to the fore, intuitive warnings out of the past. Regardless of what I knew, I was responding to an imagined threat like a Stone Age hunter cut off from his cave.

Far ahead, far beyond the dangerous points, two shadows broke from cover and headed directly down the river toward me. I stopped, slipped off my pack, and waited. Nearer and nearer they came, running with the easy, loose-jointed grace that only the big timber wolves seem to have. A hundred yards away they stopped and looked me over. In the moonlight their gray hides glistened and I could see the greenish glint of their eyes. Not a movement or a sound. We stood watching each other as though such meetings were expected and commonplace.

As suddenly as they appeared, they whirled and were off down the river, two drifting forms against the ice. Never before had I been that close, possible never again would I see the glint in timber wolves' eyes or have such a chance to study their free and fluid movement. Once more came the long howl, this time far back from the river, and then I heard them no more.

Ready for the kill
—George H. Harrison photo

The "white buffalo"

A. B. Guthrie, Jr. celebrates mountain men, and does so with a flavor of truth that can come only from sympathy and tireless research. In *The Big Sky* he has Boone Caudill starving in the Rockies, but allows Boone to save himself by killing a mountain goat. Aside from the vivid writing, and its effective contemporary style, this has always interested me because it reveals the unfamiliarity of the mountain man with the white goat of the peaks. Yet, this was apparently the case. In fact, it was well into the 19th Century before scientists had proof that there really was a "white buffalo" of the high country. It's doubtful, however, that they were more surprised and pleased than Caudill himself:

Inside the lodge Jim was going on with his talk to Summers, to old Dick Summers who maybe might know what to do if he was around. For a flash Boone saw him, too, the keen face with the tracks of fun in it and the gray eyes glinting and the half-sad understanding. For a flash he saw him standing on the Mandan's passe avant above the Little Missouri, saw him pointing to a bighorn, saw him trying to talk, trying to say something, trying to come across the years with his voice. His words were a whisper lost in time, a murmuring lapped out by the water sliding along the keel. Speak up, Dick. A man can't hear you, so much has come between. How's that? How's that? It's comin' now. Go on! Go on! "They ain't a buffalo proper, nor a white antelope. . . .They keep to the high peaks, they do, the tiptop of the mountains, in the clouds and snow. . . .Come a fix in the mountains, I do believe I'd set out for one."

. . .It was queer, not thinking of the white buffalo before, only it wasn't a white buffalo exactly or a white deer but more like a rock goat. It had taken old Dick Summers to jar his mind—old Dick Summers yelling through the years, reminding him there was game high up that a hunter hardly ever saw from below, or hardly ever hunted, either, for the going was so rough.

Boone winked his sight clear. Yon way between the peaks and over the saddle, like as not a little valley hung. Like as not the white ones played there. He held up, waiting for wind, waiting for his heart to quit hammering at his ribs, while he saw Jim lying in the shelter and Peabody sitting bony-faced by the fire and Beauchamp staring with a crazy hunger. Sneaked out, Beauchamp did, and pawed the snow off and lifted the stones away and raised himself man meat. Must be he left it out afterward and a varmint got to it, so's he didn't get all the good out of Zenon, else he wouldn't be so hungry yet and the flesh melting off him and his eyes

The mountain men's "white buffalo"
—Leonard Lee Rue III photo

283

sharp as a weasel's. Peabody would have to watch. Beauchamp was two men now, himself and Zenon chewed to one, and Peabody less than half a man.

It was too cold to breathe, almost. The air caught at a man inside as if to freeze his pipes up, and his lungs. There wasn't any good in it; there wasn't any strength to it. The chest sucked it down and blew it out and had to suck quick for more, and the knee balked before a lift and trembled at the end of it. Boone didn't know him for himself. He was like another man, far off and dim to the senses. By and by he might wake up and find himself warm and Teal Eye lying by him and meat aplenty in the pot.

He watched his feet push out. Each step was something done. Every one was one behind him and one less lying ahead. He rested again, feeling the warmth die in his clothes and the cold come creeping in. A man not on the move would freeze stiff before he knew it.

He rested again when he topped the saddle, seeing ahead a valley cupped in the rocks. A lake lay in it, probably, but it was all snow now except for one patch of twisted trees, all snow walled in by steep faces of stone. His gaze traveled high up the side until rock and sky met and the dazzle brought the tears a-running. When his heart had quieted he set out again, pointing for the timber, while he made his eyes study the ledges and come down and explore the small basin. He could look just so long into the glitter and then his eyes blurred and he had to squeeze the water out with his lids.

The timber was no more than a spot of runty trees growing toward the head of the valley, probably where snow water fed into the lake. At the far edge of it, where the wind had scoured the snow thin, he halted, for ahead of him a set of tracks stepped along, a set of split-hoof tracks not neat and pointed like the big-horn's but splayed out at the front. He sent his eyes from one print to the next, seeing them veer off to the side and lose themselves among snow-covered rocks that had broken from the cliff. He studied the rocks and the sheer face of the cliff, taking a little piece at a time but seeing nothing anywhere except stone and snow and the blinding sky arched over.

Tracks among the rocks

He flexed his right hand to limber his finger. He made sure of his rifle. Then he shuffled on, following the tracks, going slow and cautious as a cat on the hunt. It was movement that scared animals more than the thing itself. The tracks wound among the rocks. They led over a slanting shoulder butted up

(At left) A mountain goat peers at an invader.

Kids on the alert

—Leonard Lee Rue III photos

(Below) Female with a kid grazing
on a mountainside

against the cliff. He saw where the snow had been pawed away and a bit of moss taken. And then he topped the shoulder and looked down, and it was like seeing two black wings up and nothing in between, two black wings thin and raised and barely moving, and then two spots as dark as coal, two spots like eyes under wings like horns. Lines swam and took shape around them, white as snow against the snow.

He heard his lips whispering. "Goddam it! Whoa, critter, whoa!" The rifle was too heavy for a man to lift. It came up hard and stubborn. He got the butt of it on his shoulder. The barrel raised and trembled so he couldn't hold an aim, close as the target was. He couldn't shoot offhand; he'd have to have a rest. He let the rifle down and lowered himself to one knee, going as slow as if he was sinking into the earth. Even so, the goat sensed danger. Its head lifted and its ears came up and its black eyes shone with looking. It was facing him, almost, but it didn't raise its gaze. It kept it lower, on the rim and cup of the valley, as if enemies always came from below.

Boone got to the other knee and started to flatten out, and the knee slipped and he half-fell forward. The black eyes lifted then and bored straight at him. He lay still as a dead man, his rifle out before him but not raised to shoot. The goat would run. It would jump in a wink. It would be gone while his hands fumbled at the rifle and his arms tried to raise it and his blind eye searched for sights. Whoa, critter, whoa!

The goat sat down on its tail like a dog, its long face dull and curious under the spiked horns, the hair hanging in a beard from its chin, hanging in an apron across its front. It wasn't a buffalo or a deer or a goat. It wasn't a creature at all. It was something grown out of the snow; it was something a crazy mind made up; it was an old spirit man from the top of the world and a bullet wouldn't hurt it and it would fade from sight directly like a puff of smoke.

The rifle sounded loud as any swivel. The crack of it went out and struck the high rock and rattled up the mountains until, far off, Boone heard the dying echo of it. The goat sat back farther on its tail, a look of slow surprise on its face. After a while it just lay down and kicked once and was still except for the long hair that the breeze played with.

Boon lay watching it, hearing his lips make words, seeing himself bringing meat to Jim and Jim tickled and his jaws working on it and strength going into him. After a while he got up and reloaded, still talking while his hands poured out powder and patched the ball and drove it home with the wiping stick.

As he started ahead he caught a flash of movement and, turning, saw another goat high on a ledge where nothing but

A goat scrambles on his rocky domain —Leonard Lee Rue III photo

a bird could get. He pulled out his wiping stick to use as a rest and sank in the snow and tried to get it through his sights. It moved as he aimed, going along a face of stone a man couldn't hang to, but at last he had it on the bead. It fell when he fired, coming down slow like a diver to water and making a splash in the snow. . . .

A man could do so much and then no more. When all of him was spent he could only sit while the cold worked into him and sleepiness came on, and him too tired to move. With meat to shoot, his spirit lifted for a little time and strength came to him, and then the weakness took hold again and the dead tiredness. He thought about moving his hand or foot but he didn't move it. He only looked at it and thought maybe he would move it after a while.

Winchester Model 1873, one of 1000 (detail below).
—Courtesy Winchester Arms

The art of gunwriting by Richard Dietz

In a volume dedicated to the finest outdoor writing of our history, there was some question as to how one particular species of the genre should be viewed.

The category is gunwriting.

The question touched on two points—whether technical gunwriting is indeed a form of outdoor writing, and further, whether such writing could be worthy of special recognition.

We have in mind not the occasional piece by an outdoor writer devoted to some experience with a gun or group of guns. One need only read William Harnden Foster's classic chapter, "The Little Gun" in *New*

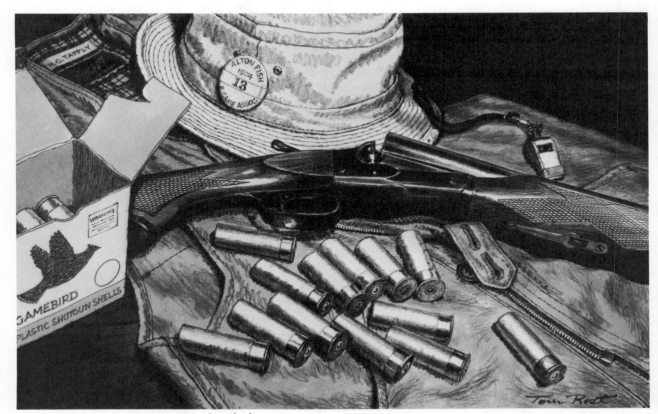

Tools of the sport —By Tom Rost, courtesy *Field and Stream*

England Grouse Shooting for an example of literary excellence on firearms. There are others of comparable merit.

Rather, we are concerned with that writing dispensed over the years on the technical aspects of sporting arms and ammunition. By its nature, such writing leaves little room for the verbal artistry that can earn literary recognition. To establish some significance to a body of work, a point of view becomes necessary. Arbitrarily, we have chosen the concept of *contribution*.

Outdoor writers, in their finer examples, have made outstanding contributions to the art of writing and to the enjoyment of discriminating readers. Inherent in such writing have been the elements of narration, beauty of description, humor, nostalgia and, when appropriate, ringing evangelism. The reward for readers has been entertainment and vicarious pleasure. For the essence of such good outdoor writing has been to transfer in print the enjoyment of an experience the reader has not actually had.

Is this enough? If it were, we have wasted ninety percent of the paper and ink expended on books, magazines and newspapers.

For writing has another function, the only one that would survive were it limited to one purpose. That purpose is to *inform*. And information, much information of a certain sort, is the contribution of the gunwriter.

Even within his restricted role, the gunwriter has served a trio of needs. He has fed the appetite of the pure hobbyist for technical fodder on the design, construction, quality and performance of arms and ammunition. And he has helped develop and disseminate knowledge on propulsion, or ballistics—a science, incidentally, that contributed to man's achievement of landing on the moon.

But the gunwriter's third role is most responsible for his significance in the outdoors. He has bestowed upon American hunters and shooters the gift of expertise. More than that, he has created a historic lore of guns that is nonexistent with the appurtenances of any other sport.

When, for example, have you ever heard a group of people spend hours describing, praising or damning the merits of 30-year-old tennis rackets, golf clubs or, even among purists, old fly rods?

But firearms? By the time they reach their teens, many gunners are steeped in knowledge of the sport's classic heirlooms. Ask one of these youngsters how and where he learned the finer points of a 1½-frame, DHE Parker shotgun made fifty years before he was born. He will mention names. The names will be those of gunwriters.

Let us make another point, one that may disturb those well versed in outdoors literature. If you request the names of fine outdoor writers from these people, they will provide several without hesitation—some of whom appear in this book.

But visit a shirtsleeve sportsman's club and ask *there* the names of the best outdoor writers. Don't be surprised if they mention the gunwriters. Why? Because these are the names, writing about the same subject,

Cockbird in full flight —By Tom Rost, courtesy *Field and Stream*

Elmer Keith
—Photo courtesy of Guns & Ammo

they have been reading for years. Those who deal in fact and strong opinion develop a fiercely loyal following.

Nevertheless, general outdoor writers usually surpass gunwriters in literary performance *when they are not themselves writing in a technical manner.*

The point is this: it is unlikely that anything written on the technical side will ever receive literary acclaim. This kind of writing doesn't lend itself to the glitter of literary excellence. The objective here is information, not art.

Page and O'Connor vs Keith

Who then are, or have been, the best gunwriters? The question is too subjective. But there are names that turn up with frequency when one discusses the field. In terms of their contribution to the lore, and the following they have attracted over the past thirty years, three in particular demand mention. They are Elmer Keith, Jack O'Connor and Warren Page, in alphabetical order.

Page and O'Connor are well-educated, highly literate individuals, at home in virtually any company, who taught English before taking up writing as a profession. Both had distinguished careers as shooting editors of major outdoors magazines. Both became experts on the technical aspects of firearms and their use in competitive shooting or hunting. And both are men of strong opinions with no reluctance to express them.

Although they differ strongly at times, Page and O'Connor as a pair are largely responsible for the modern trend in hunting toward smaller bullets of high velocity and extremely flat trajectory. If Jack O'Connor or Warren Page says so, most American hunters believe it — unless they happen to be followers of Elmer Keith.

Keith is a throwback to an earlier time that is possibly the richest part of our history — the settlement of the west when every man supposedly wore and knew how to use a six-gun. Keith still does, though his quarry has been game and not blackhats. Elmer was essentially a relatively unschooled cowboy who loved guns, loved hunting and has been writing about both for almost fifty years.

His forte is long-distance shooting, whether handgun, rifle or shotgun. With them, he has possibly taken more game than any man alive. Consequently, Elmer doesn't deal in opinion. His statements are, to him, simply facts based on an astounding amount of experience. In opposition to Page and O'Connor, he has spent a lifetime defending slow-moving, big-bullet calibers against their cult of high velocity.

O'Connor and Page are polished writers. Keith's prose tumbles down at you like rocks in a landslide, each statement positive and definite, but piled up unendingly. He has almost total recall and pours out his thoughts in Joycean stream-of-consciousness. Let editors punctuate thoughts into sentences and paragraphs. Elmer's recollections are too rapid for commas and periods. And the tales about him are the stuff from which legends are made. He lends character and color to a field where such traits are more manufactured than natural.

Of course, there are others besides these three. Larry Koller, expert gunsmith and knowledgeable writer, was equally expert at fishing and must rank as one of the finer outdoor writers in recent history. Pete Brown knows and taught as much as any, with less flamboyance. However, Page, O'Connor and another still-active veteran, Col. Charles Askins, come closest to a truly creative writing style within strictly technical boundaries.

While the legacy of the gunwriters remains information, some have departed, on occasion, from the realm of nuts and bolts. When this occurred, one sometimes found writing talent of very high caliber.

The gunwriter's place in American outdoor writing is deservedly permanent. The good ones remained gunwriters because this was their preference. We have profited from that preference.

The perils of duck hunting

Without a doubt Gordon MacQuarrie in his job as Outdoor Editor of the *Milwaukee Journal* was one of the most beloved figures in outdoor writing. Everybody knew and liked the pleasant redhead. But in his sto-

*Jack O'Connor with
Dall sheep trophy, 1945*

Warren Page

Getting the decoys out early.—Don Wooldridge photo, Missouri Department of Conservation

ries, most of which appeared in the 1940s in *Field & Stream,* he elevated outdoor writing, especially humorous writing, to a height that none will surpass. He invented a fictional society, the Old Duck Hunter's Association Inc. (the Inc. stood for incorrigible) and placed Mr. President (in true life his father-in-law) squarely in charge. Mr. President loved life, loved duck hunting and in Mac's skillful hands practiced his art with unforgettable verve and jest. Zack Taylor collected the best of his stories in a book and was personally responsible for the last two. When Zack joined *Sports Afield* as a young associate editor, he remembered the delightful stories and wrote to MacQuarrie to get the stories going again. Unknown to Zack, Mac had quit the yarns because his father-in-law had died but with the invitation he passed the mantle to his new outdoor companion, another Mr. President equally in love with life.

The shot had brought the marsh alive with tip-up feeders. Blacks and mallards mostly, big devils hovering over the fringed rice, uncertain whether to flop back into the feeding-troughs below or pick up and move on. A dozen, too curious, wheeled in close, and there was no time then to lay a bet. They hung in front of us in a 30-mile wind, not close, but close enough. When they had side-slipped away, three more lay out in the rice, and the President reminded me hurriedly that he always shot 1¼-ounce loads and for me not to hand him in payment any piddling ounce loads that I carried around.

Many of the departing ducks fled over the high hill, and soon we could hear the biddies stridently advertising the succulence of this new paradise. We hauled out the skiff and retrieved the down birds, during which Mister President politely requested me to stay down-wind from him—"There's nothing like a dill pickle, though, with a hot dog!"

Anyway, there were other things to occupy us, not to mention the pickle barrel. It was not easy searching out the fallen birds. When it was done and we were adjusted in the blinds, Mister President sniffing the heavy odor of salt vinegar and cucumbers which emanated from me, said it was a good thing that ducks couldn't smell, else there would be no shooting on the marsh that day. He also said he wished he had a clothes-pin to hang over his nose. There are few idle moments in duck blinds with the President.

Curiosity got the better of the puddlers over the hill, and they began drifting back into the bigger rice bed. The Bible says that the fool returneth to his folly as the dog to his vomit; and while we would be the last to assert that a mallard is a fool, certainly these mallards were not post-graduate locals. Our blinds were perfect, except for the odor which emanated from mine. There was not a sign of anything above ground but natural growth. Not even the old felt hat of Mister President, the band of which was festooned with twigs.

The day wore on, and it rained. It rained, and I missed ducks. I have missed ducks before and will miss them again, but seldom have I missed them like that. These travelers of the little flight had me stopped cold. Maybe, I thought, it was the light one-ounce loads, but light one-ounce loads will kill ducks, and I know it. So did the President know it. He borrowed a couple and killed a couple of ducks.

The wait begins.—Wisconsin Natural Resources Department, Madison, Wis.

Blind and decoys
—Massachusetts Division of Fisheries & Game

Toward the end of the day I waded the shore line to get into the high hill behind us and have a look-see. Hundreds of mallards got up from the smaller rice bed when I came too close, and one of them choosing the hill course, was tumbled with a thump to the soggy, acorn-strewn growth on the hilltop. It felt good to pick one out like that. Too bad the President didn't see it, in view of the performance he had witnessed from my pickle barrel.

The others milled over the rice, against a dark, wet, ragged sky. It was a wild and lovely moment—even lovlier when speedsters running the blockade at the blind came in range and I heard the deliberately spaced booms of the President's automatic.

Back in the oaks over the high hill there was less rain and wind. The forest floor underfoot was a silent carpet of yellow and bronze. A man can often flush a deer in there after the acorns have fallen. I saw one, a furtive doe quietly slipping away. She never dreamed she was seen. Snowshoe rabbits were already changed from brown to white. I walked back with my lone duck.

"Only one?" snorted Mister President. "I saw a million get out of there—well, two hundred, anyway. That's more'n a million."

"He was the only one that came in range."

Mister President pointed to his own comfortable pile, close to a limit. Just as I was about to insert myself in the pickle barrel my eye caught a piece of shell-box cardboard. The President had stuck it on the rim of the barrel and had writ-

Here they come. —Massachusetts Division of Fisheries & Game

ten thereon: "TO LET—One smelly old pickle barrel. Only good duck shots need apply. Owner going out of business. Chance for a good man to build up thriving trade."

After the laughter had been swallowed up in the tamaracks and I had missed another bird and the President had declared a halt—"for fear you'll get the habit permanently"—we picked up and headed for the car. Nosing out of the sand trails through the dripping woods, I acknowledged his masterminding anent the little flight.

"But," I insisted, "I can't figure out why I couldn't hit 'em. You suppose that pickle barrel had anything to do with it?"

He snorted and half turned beside me to deliver his dictum with full impact: "Boy, your shooting and that pickle barrel both smell the same to me."

Waiting for the feathered ones—Massachusetts Division of Fisheries & Game

The era of the market hunters

The era of the market hunter is part of duck hunting's fascinating history. In many ways the fight to save the ducks in the 1930s was a battle against man as well as nature. The drought dried up the pot hole breeding grounds but desperate men in the depression continued a relentless and illegal slaughter. It is black history, of course, but like piracy or the conquistadors, fascinating as well. The methods and equipment are ingenious. The risks the illegal gunners faced were stagger-

In the days of unlimited duck shooting —Arkansas Game and Fish Commission

ing. Not merely was the law a constant threat; they challenged open waters at night, in fog and ice and usually won.

Dr. Harry Walsh is an Easton, Maryland, doctor who made the definitive study of the illegal gunners, mostly on Chesapeake Bay, but the techniques and equipment could be duplicated almost anywhere in the country during the 1930s where ducks and geese could be found. Walsh's collection of the outlaw's gear, gathered at a time when it was just starting to disappear forever, has been preserved in a special building of the St. Michael's, Maryland Nautical Museum. Though "Outlaw Gunner" is his only book, the following section shows how ably he portrayed the skills of those colorful hunters.

As the sun set, Ander skiffed down its blood-red path through loose ice to the low-bluffed islands that were his hunting grounds. At the edge of dark, the sky had assumed an ominous expression. The storm will come with the tide — and from the northwest, thought Ander; still plenty of time for a good hunt.

In the calm of the dark of the night, he adjusted the focal point of the light against the bank; just enough light to remain hidden, and no more. The beam was fixed on the water at ideal range.

The night was hardly aware of Ander's presence as he glided like the fog across the water. He shoved along on the hard sandy bottom, never making a sound. The leading edge of the paddle cut clearly through the water — rarely leaving it and always pointing aft. In the darkness, his inborn directional system told him where he was.

Ahead, the "meowing" of the redheads could be heard. Their catlike sounds mingled with the guttural croaking of the canvasback. As the skiff drew nearer, the multitude of sounds combined in a rising, undulating wave of sound — a strange but familiar chorus to the night hunter.

The soft light fell upon a small flock of feeding canvasback, and immediately they began to swim for deep water. They're too fast and too few, thought the hunter.

The main flock lay ahead. Barely did the skiff move, but the distance between it and the ducks gradually diminished. The closer and more alert ducks noticed the light, but were not alarmed. Slowly the flock gave way toward the ice floe against which Ander was driving them.

Their ranks thickened as they became compressed along the ice. In mild alarm, they milled about, extended their necks, and made a better target.

Those closest to the light made a move to swim past the boat. As they did, they were looking directly into Ander's gun barrel. Carefully, the light was swung from ahead onto the leading birds. As they stopped and the others jammed in from behind, Ander pulled the trigger.

With a shot, the light went out and hell's cauldron erupted. The night was suddenly out of control in a hysterical symphony of discord. The weird, strident cough of dying birds never to rise again mingled with the convulsive screams of the living. A thousand wings beat the air and water with the reverberating echo of the shot. The world was

A morning's shooting on Beards Lake in 1930 —Arkansas Game and Fish Commission

upside down, its horizon tipped, as birds flew into the ice, the water, the boat, and each other. Panic spread as waterfowl elsewhere added their voices to the wild cacaphony.

Then all was still. Ander relit the light and as its rays flooded the water, he picked up over fifty limp, silent forms.

The hunter's attention now shifted to some geese whose feeding could be heard over the great void of water. Like the prowling shark, he headed his skiff in their direction.

The wind had now begun to make little tracks in the sea. Soon, parallel ranks of waves laced the surface, prophesying the approaching storm. Just time for one more shot, thought the hunter.

Slaughter and escape

With the wind at his back, Ander's approach to the geese was far too fast. The purr of their feeding ceased and was replaced by a low warning call. Each gander became the spokesman for his flock.

Like a thief in the night, Ander retreated. With the light held steady, the hunter bided his time until feeding resumed.

Now the slow, deadly stalk began. On the perimeter of the light, a few indistinct, ghostlike forms appeared. Several brant materialized, feeding on the surface. They wiggled their tail feathers in Ander's face; he could have caught them as they obstructed his path. Finally, the unwanted companions faded into the night and the chase continued.

The first geese to "loom" into the light appeared like a flock of sheep. They swam hesitantly before the light. Gradually the feather details became visible and the eyes and markings under the jaw could be discerned.

The hunter knew the geese would take no more. They turned into the wind, necks extended as flight was imminent.

The shot was like cutting a path through a field of golden wheat. "I put a hole in them that time," thought Ander, as he shot.

Ander was subduing the last of the geese and securing them to the bitter end of his anchor line, when a large ice flow, several acres across, came charging into the warning rays of his light. The wind which had freed the floe was now driving it along a path of destruction. The hunter desperately gave way toward deep water and the open Bay beyond. Neither he nor the boat could long survive in the dangerous seas. All efforts to return to shallow water and safety were blocked by the floe.

The first flakes of snow arrived with increasing winds heralding their approach. The storm had given ample warning.

Ander knew that he was in serious trouble. In a desperate bid for life, he found a safe passage directly into the mouth of the storm. A small island should lie ahead and it had to be reached before the full fury of the storm struck. If the hunter were wrong, no one would ever hear his story.

The black, murky depths of the sea swelled up about Ander as if anxious to devour him. The storm grew in power and fury. The seas rocked the skiff and its flat bottom slapped them in return. Flying clouds of spray began to freeze, fill the boat, and dull its action.

The blade of the shoving paddle no longer found the bottom to give it strength. Though the oar clawed deeply into the water, it could find little purchase against the buffeting wind.

The night played tricks on the hunter's eyes while the driving snow nearly blinded him. No sailor ever sought land with more hunger.

Ander's light had been burning brightly through it all. It swung with the bow like some giant cyclops casting its eye about, as though it, too, were searching. There was nothing but the black night, laced and lashed with snow.

The hunter was about to alter his course to destruction when from an unsuspected compass came a faint and fleeting glimpse of shore. The faithful light had shown the way.

The seesaw battle continued as Ander worked frantically for his life. His paddle finally found the bottom and began driving the skiff forward.

The tempest now reigned supreme over the land and voiced its authority with an angry, shrieking wind. Storm waves lashed the island's high, red banks, and their life's blood stained the water. Each wave that rose too high promptly had its head blown off. Spray blanketed the island, freezing where it struck.

Ander quickly found shelter under a bank and his skiff. A large pyramid of wood fueled by the kerosene of his lamp roared into flame. The hunter's clothes were soon steaming, while he sat like a smoked mackerel—one side fried and the other frozen.

A snow-wrapped, ice-encrusted world of fantasy greeted sun and hunter in the morning. Spears of light came shooting through the heavy clouds and were bursting with dazzling brilliance on the world of icy emeralds. The storm had passed and carried with it the unpleasant memories of the previous night.

The hunter loaded his skiff and began shoving across the ice with his game in tow. Daylight was burning and Ander had work to do.

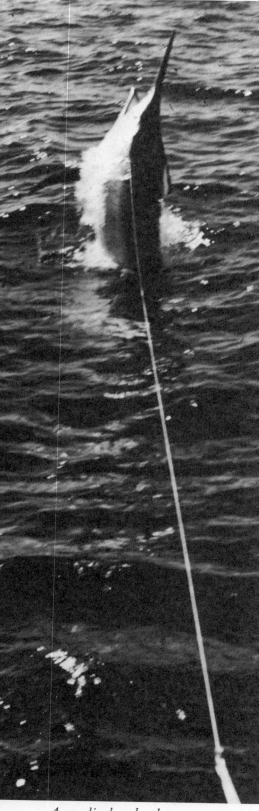

A marlin breaks the water.
—Courtesy *Field and Stream*

Big game fish

Writing of the sea and its creatures has retained its flavor for centuries. Melville's "Moby Dick" is read today with as much enjoyment as the day it was written. Men have always been fascinated with the huge game fish of the oceans and yet it was not until the turn of the century that big-game fishing and writing about it became popular.

The development of stout rods and big-game fishing reels—such as those made of German silver by the Vom Hoffe brothers of Brooklyn, New York, in the late 1890s—suddenly made it possible to play and land billfish and tuna. Soon pioneer anglers Zane Grey, Charles Belder, and Mike Lerner were hauling in the big horse mackeral off Nova Scotia and Newfoundland, broadbill swordfish off Montauk and Catalina Island, and billfish from Florida and the Bahamas.

Jack Samson, who edits *Field and Stream* magazine between fishing trips, assisted in making selections dealing with big-game fishing. Curiously, while outdoor writers and editors are known generally for possessing large egos, he did not select any of his own writing. The editors did, and following Jack's choice is a passage from his book, "Line Down."

Discussing the selections he chose to include in this book, Samson reflected, "Catching the great fish and writing about them are two different things. I do both, so have had the chance to find that out. I firmly believe catching a 700-pound bluefin tuna is a whole lot easier than trying to relate the experience later on paper! But for the purposes of this book I chose some samples of what I consider outstanding writing on big-game fishing. Each man had his own individual style and each was famous not only for his fishing prowess but as a writer."

Van Campen Heilner is one of the best fishermen-writers in the sport. The following is from his book *Salt Water Fishing*.

Marlin sport fishing as such originated at Avalon, Santa Catalina Island, California, where in the spacious and luxurious rooms of the Tuna Club emanated the beginning of big game angling which has since spread to the four corners of the world.

No fish has helped more in the spread of this wonderful sport than the marlin. Occurring in practically all tropical and semitropical seas and in colder waters in certain seasons of the year, he furnishes for the big game angler the most spectacular and giant fish he can hope to take on rod and reel. Without doubt the marlin represents the Ultima Thule of the angling world.

When I lived in California (and I hope to die there) I never missed a season at Avalon. The marlin used to show up in August and September and sometimes the sea would be alive with them. When the waterfront at Avalon became at times

A marlin on the flying gaff —Courtesy *Field and Stream*

too crowded with Adonises and Venuses in one-piece bathing suits, we used to go over to San Clemente, a sister island, for some peace and quiet. Clemente was uninhabited. It was wild and lonely with great cliffs and jagged coves into which the Pacific boomed with never ending reverberations. There was a man who ran a camp there, a half a dozen tents with board floors and a cook tent. We stayed there and we loved it. It was as comfortable as the Ritz in Paris, only better. The nights were studded with stars and the days flooded with sunshine and the salt-sweet wind that billowed along the wild oat slopes. The great Pacific at our feet literally boiled with fish, marlin, tuna, albacore and yellow tail. Some days we didn't go fishing at all. Just sat on the rocks and gazed at the sea. It was never the same; it never is, and it gave you a chance to cleanse your soul.

We had a funny experience there. I had a large wooden teaser that my friend, Ivar Hennings, of the South Bend Bait Company had given me to try out. It was something new. Grey and I had the first ones ever seen on the Pacific Coast. This was the first time I'd ever tried mine and I didn't know

*Zane Grey and his
1922 record bonefish*
—Photo courtesy George Reiger

Hal Lyman fighting a bluefin
—Courtesy *Field and Stream*

if it would work. We left the cove at Clemente one morning and we hadn't gone over a mile, I suppose, when there was an enormous splash back of the boat where we'd been trolling the teaser on a hand line. We pulled in the hand line and the teaser was gone. We couldn't figure it out because there wasn't any hook on it and finally came to the conclusion that whatever it was had swallowed it. We thought surely he must spit it out and cruised around a while looking for it, but saw nothing.

The next day about five miles out from land what should we come upon but our teaser resting peacefully on the placid bosom of the Pacific. It was all scarred up with big teeth marks and must have been through a terrible experience.

Then one day we ran into the marlin. They seemed to be everywhere. No matter in which direction we went we raised fish. If I've ever seen the sea alive with fish it was that day. Maybe we were in the midst of a big migration. Whatever it was, from the moment we left our anchorage in the morning we started to raise fish, and when we got back to it again that late afternoon we had, the two of us, hooked and played twelve big marlin, four of which we landed. That was a day I will always remember. Those great fish following along behind the bait, their dorsal and sometimes the upper lobe of their caudal out of the water, then the sudden surge and strike, the dropback, setting the hook, and that first grand rush and leap! How those babies can leap! You can close your eyes and see them now, thrashing about on the surface, their great swords wagging tails, or coming out in clean greyhound jumps that sometimes carry them and all your line out of sight on the horizon. There's absolutely nothing like it anywhere on earth or in the waters over the earth. It's marvelous, breath-taking, terrific!

Hooking a record marlin

Kip Farrington is another fisherman-writer Samson chose to include. This passage is from *Fishing with Hemingway and Glassell.*

After an hour and fifty-five minutes the leader came out of the water, but I refused to let the crew touch it. The fish then sounded again. The sea was very rough, and it was getting dark. The marlin had taken us about six miles north and some three miles inshore. We were off the Organos, high rocky boulders that resemble the pipes of an organ. Condors were circling the Organos, and playing around our boat were boobies and man-of-war birds, and an occasional penado petrel. My leader wire again came out of the water, and again I cautioned the crew not to touch it. The gaffs on either side were ready. Bates was prepared to do the gaffing on the port side, and McGill was set to take the leader. Louis had my chair and was ready to handle the gaff on the starboard side. Captain Hajus, at the up-top controls, was doing a wonderful job piloting the boat. When the leader emerged the third time, McGill grabbed it—and was yanked right around the stern. My heart was in my throat. The sea was building up, and the tremendous weight of the fish was exerting an appalling strain. Suddenly he broke loose again. Five minutes later the leader again came out, and this time I put both Louis and McGill on it, with Tom Bates as the gaffer. The fish went under the stern once, and I thought it was goodbye. I thought the cable leader would break across the stern, but it went clear by some miracle. The boys held the fish off and began to lift him. (The leader was 20 feet 4 inches long—10 feet under that specified by the rules of the International Game Fish Association.) Steadily they worked the fish up, inch by inch. The big marlin was rolling in the turbulent sea. Anxiously I looked shoreward, wondering if I should tell the boys to let him go. I thought I might lead the fish in, where it was calmer close to the beach. I looked at the crew and they seemed to have control, and the fish was still coming up,

Marlin fins cutting the water —Photo courtesy Field and Stream

303

slowly, steadily, inch by inch, and McGill and Louis grimly held on. We were soaked to the skin by heavy water, and the wind was still increasing. Up, up, up, the huge fish came, while Tom Bates waited, holding my favorite gaff—the one engraved "To Kip from Phil," a gift in 1940 from Phil Swaffield, ex-president of the Catalina Tuna Club and one of my closest California friends until he passed away. It had been used to gaff my 853-pound swordfish in Chile and my big Nova Scotia tuna and, with luck, it was about to be put to good use again.

The marlin came up, leading better, and Tom Bates cracked him on the inside with an underwater jab. The motors were shut off, the block and tackle on the big gin pole were lowered, and the tail rope was rigged. The fish was bleeding, dyeing the water, and I couldn't see where he was hooked. I stood up, keeping the leader attached to the rod and reel and holding it to help the others adjust the tail rope. We began to pull in on the gin pole and it was tough work. One of the ropes fouled the top, and Tom Bates went up to clear it. It took all five of us to get the fish up. The gin pole was 14 feet high, and the fish was longer. Captain Hajus turned the boat into the wind and it took our combined strength to pull the marlin's head into the cockpit. Then the rest of him slid in and we got him straightened away. The tip of his wonderful tail, the largest I've ever seen, touched the

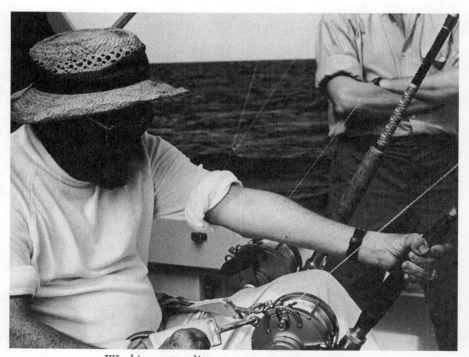

Working a marlin —Photo courtesy Field and Stream

engine box, and his bill — very short for a big black marlin — was smack up against the counter. He fitted snugly on one side.

Tom Bates and the crew crowded around me, shaking my hand.

"Boy, you've got yourself a fish!" Tom said. "I think it's easily a new record."

"I'm not after records," I said. "All I can say is I'm thankful to have got two black marlin in one day, and thank God you were with me!"

Our catch looked awfully good with the light from the gin pole shining down on him. It was now pitch dark, and we started to run back to port. I sat down and looked at my fish. He was long and beautifully proportioned.

We made the mole around 7:30 and there was Dick Norris, once more awaiting my return. He bawled me out for staying out after dark, but he relented when he saw my marlin.

The crane crew was standing by, and when they lifted the black marlin out of the boat, he looked enormous. They never look more majestic than during that long lift up the mole.

"This is it," Norris said, fetching the scales. I waited, wondering if it was possible I had caught a 1,000-pound fish after my many years of fishing.

Norris weighed him three times, and each time that splendid marlin weighed 1,135 pounds, and that was his final and official weight. He measured 14 feet 8 inches long, had a 6-foot girth, and the great tail had a width of 4 feet 10 inches.

The crew paddled in from the boat in their balsa raft and looked up at me inquiringly. "UNO UNO TRES CINCO!" I called down to them. I'll never forget their expressions.

Norris and Bates congratulated me and took me up to the El Alto Club, where I drank three great Peruvian beers with great relish.

Samson's first marlin

The editors selected another marlin fishing story. This one from Jack Samson's *Line Down.*

The marlin came up about thirty minutes later. It came up fast and I never saw it — since we were trolling slightly east and the late-afternoon sun glinted off the water where the plugs skipped. The first thing I knew was when the skipper let out a scream. "Right rigger!" he shouted. "Billfish!"

I couldn't see the fish and I couldn't remember where the right outrigger was — thinking my right was the left facing forward.

Rex Flinn (with rod) shows off one of the first broadbill swordfish landed on Atlantic coast on rod and reel. With him are Skipper Bill Hatch (with gaff) and outdoor writer Harlan Major (left). Catch took place at Montauk Point in 1932.

—Photo courtesy George Reiger

305

Jack Samson and a striped marlin —Courtesy *Field and Stream*

Samson fighting a big one
—Courtesy *Field and Stream*

"Marleen!" yelled the mate, and I heard the line snap from the rigger clip.

"Line down!" yelled the captain at the top of his voice. "Goddammit, somebody grab that rod!"

The mate, thank God, grabbed the correct rod from the gunwale and shoved it into my hands. I jammed it into the seat gimbal, and as everything suddenly began to go into slow motion—as it always does with me and the big fish—I remembered to point the rod tip at the fish.

I felt the old boat surge forward and the skipper jammed his throttle full ahead to take up any slack. I was just beginning to feel a bit of weight when I heard the captain.

"Hit him, hit him, for Christ's sake hit him!"

To my everlasting credit I did exactly as I had been told and struck three times. That was the last move I made that made any sense to me. Right after that I saw the most beautiful fish I had ever seen come out of the sea behind me—and I can see it today silhouetted against that rugged coast of Hawaii, hanging in the air, twisting and writhing with rage at the bite of the hook.

"He's on! He's on!" screamed the skipper, slowing the boat down. "Don't let him get any slack. They don't swallow these plugs. Reel, reel!"

It never occurred to me to do anything except stare at that great leaping, thrashing fighting monster that was throwing spray over the ocean surface.

I didn't have to reel to take up slack, fortunately. That marlin made one towering leap after another, tearing line off the old Ocean City reel as though it were sewing thread. The reel had been set at strike drag, probably at about 30 pounds.

"Aiieee!" screamed Kioshi. "Marleen . . .look at heem go!"

That battle, which they told me later lasted about forty-five minutes, was a complete blur to me. I still remember parts of it—my right arm going dead cranking that big reel handle and continuing to crank long after all feeling had left it. I didn't know enough then to keep my left arm straight and let the kidney harness and my legs absorb the punishment. I kept trying to gain line by pulling on the rod with my left arm at the same time I was reeling—not knowing enough to crank as the rod is lowered rather than while it is being raised. It didn't matter. The mate kept swinging the chair to face the fish, which made several greyhounding runs and Lord knows how many more leaps before the skipper backed down on it in the choppy sea.

I dimly remember—through the pain of my arms and back—seeing the double line and big brass swivel come up several times and catching a glimpse of the wire leader. But each time the fighting fish would thrash across the surface and the mate would have to let go of the line.

Finally there was the blur of a gaff, the sound of the skipper landing on the deck to help and the shower of water over me as the marlin was gaffed again and held against the side of the hull. I didn't know enough to help tail-rope the fish and just sat in the chair, exhausted, as the two hauled the fish over the starboard gunwale. It landed with a slithering thump on the deck and the mate whacked it several times on the forehead with a wooden club.

And after that everything was a melee of slaps on the back, handshakes, whoops, grins, shouts and the headiest feeling I had ever felt, up to that day, in my entire life.

A bluefin tuna from Bahama waters
—Courtesy *Field and Stream*

The evolution of angling writing

World War II stopped the hands on the piscatorial clock temporarily and the writing during the early days of this period reflected the world crisis. Most of the young men were in uniform and scattered around the globe. People on the home front faced gas rationing coupled with other transportation problems. It wasn't easy to go fishing in those days and, if you were fortunate enough to wet a line, it was usually very close to home. Tackle makers were busy supplying the G.I.s who worshiped any item of equipment as a brief respite from their more serious duties.

In spite of obstacles, fishing continued in some fashion as it always had and probably always will as long as a single fish fins in the current.

An old salt-water reel
—Frank Woolner photo

Salt-water lures and equipment
—Frank Woolner photo

The War, however, kept new writers from joining the ranks until 1946. That year marked the start of an angling revolution in many ways. Millions of servicemen returned home with the desire to make up for lost time. Coincidentally, the spinning reel also came across the ocean and fiberglass fishing rods were introduced in the marketplace.

Spinning opened the angling floodgates and millions took up the sport as their primary form of recreation. This, in turn, created a demand for more reading material and many returning veterans suddenly became outdoor writers. Publications grew larger and new ones shouldered the classics for breathing room on the newsstands. Book publishers turned their attention to this swelling market and angling literature continued its climb.

Travel became much easier in the decade from 1950 to 1960 and angling pioneers began to explore new territory and different techniques, concentrating their efforts on species of fish that were always considered out of reach. During this period, light tackle fishing in the Florida Keys for tarpon and bonefish started to flourish once more and visitors from around the nation began to visit that angling paradise.

In the last quarter century, the trend has been toward more sophisticated tackle and innovative techniques that produced fish. Electronic equipment found its way into the market and the scientific fisherman started to emerge. Equally important, fleets of airplanes from jets to single engine bush models stood ready to take the angler to any waters of the world, often within 24 hours. The back country opened up, new camps were established, and the province of the wealthy became commonplace for the middle class citizen.

Playing a bonefish —Courtesy *Field and Stream*

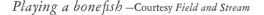

Mixed bag of mountain trout—James Bashline photo

Outdoor writing during this period changed continuously to keep pace. The adventure story for the armchair reader doesn't receive the emphasis or the editorial space it once did. Instead, magazine and book buyers want to know how to catch more fish and how to master advanced techniques. When an adventure is related, it must also include information on how to get there and how to duplicate the trip, because the reader just might be on the next airplane.

In spite of the modern approach undertaken by many of the magazines and some book publishers, there is still a market for the classical type of writing that has been a source of comfort to the trout and salmon purist for generations. And, since these anglers buy more books than others, there are still many tomes that follow the traditional approach.

As life returned to a more normal pace following World War II, people had time to reflect on why they went fishing and what it meant to them. Roderick Haig-Brown offered his own philosophy in "A River Never Sleeps."

I do not fish, as I understand some people do, for fresh air and exercise; no doubt I pick up a share of both when I go fishing, but they are unearned increment—I am not really looking for them. I do not fish for fish to eat; having to eat fish is one of the penalties of having been out fishing and with this penalty in mind I probably fish a little less often and less painstakingly than I otherwise would. I do fish to catch fish—at least, that is an idea not too far in the back of my mind while I am fishing; but I have fished through fishless days that I remember happily and without regret. I want fish from fishing, but I want a great deal more than that, and getting it is not always dependent upon catching fish.

The art and joy of fly-fishing

With spinning sweeping the country, fly-fishing continued to endure in some corners and, for some unknown reason, it was generally clouded in an aura of mystery that defied penetration. Haig-Brown took a poke at writers who believed in the mystical approach, while trying to define the various levels of competency. This is from *A River Never Sleeps*.

Ted Trueblood casts in the Nez Perce River —Courtesy *Field and Stream*

Bing Crosby makes a catch. (At right) An angler plays a trout.
—Photos courtesy *Field and Stream*

Many writers make fly-fishing seem a very difficult and complicated art. Fly-fishing is an art, certainly, which means that it is infinitely flexible in scope; a master of the art attains skill and beauty in performance, subtlety and wisdom of conception, that are both difficult and complicated. But a reasonable proficiency is enough to give the strongest measures of pleasure and satisfaction, and a reasonable proficiency is not in the least hard to attain.

A reasonably proficient fly-fisherman inevitably wants to improve and almost as inevitably does improve as time goes on. He probably does not become a master of the art, but he probably does become a good fisherman. I often wonder about the masters anyway, whether or not they really exist outside books. In a book it is very easy to seem like a master if one writes chiefly of the days that worked out right and the casts that caught fish, and one is likely to do so because the other days and other casts are not generally so interesting. But I have known and watched quite a few really good fly-fishermen, one or two of whom probably are as good as the masters, and I never yet saw one that couldn't get himself into some fancy troubles on occasion.

Writers began to combine factual information with the aesthetic pleasures derived from fishing, attempting to urge the reader to relive the great moments through the pages of books or magazines. The next passage by Dan Holland from *The Trout Fisherman's Bible* illustrates that approach.

There's a time of day close to the heart of every man who has floated a fly. It's the time of day when the deer leaves his bed and the rabbit his form. It's the time when all is calm, and the cool mists begin to rise; and when the crickets and katydids commence to tune their fiddles, and the bull bats zoom and roar in their power dives. In short, it's the time when the May flies dance. Certainly there are many people who enjoy this time of day, no matter where they are, but I doubt if anyone gets so much out of it as the trout fisherman along his favorite stream. This is the time when all the trout go on a feeding spree; when there is so much to see and hear that less fortunate people know nothing about.

Possible the most wonderful of all for the evening fisherman is the dance of the May flies. This is the time of action; for when a heavy hatch is on, all the fish in the stream gorge themselves on the rising nymphs, the floating duns, the egg-laying spinners, and the spent flies whose brief moment is ended. The Latin name for May flies is EPHEMERIDA which stems from the same root as our word EPHEMERAL, meaning short-lived. May flies may crawl about in the seclusion of mud, moss, or tiny caverns among the rocks and gravel of a stream bottom for as long as two years, but as winged insects they enjoy only a short spell of glory, sometimes but a few hours and at the most a couple of days. Toward evening thousands of nymphs of the same species, as if by some mysterious signal, abandon their secret ways in the shadowy depths and rise carelessly to the surface, oblivious to danger.

Which one will they hit?

—Photos by Dan Holland

Mayflies in nymph and adult stages

Joe Brooks, famous angler, casting in the rain —Pennsylvania Fish Commission

Each floats momentarily while the nymph case splits down the back, then steps out of his coarse shell as a delicate and graceful May fly, complete with gossamer wings, gently curving body, and long sweeping tails. After a short ride while the wings dry, these dull-colored duns fly ashore and rest again until they shed once more. This time they emerge bright and shiny and are known as spinners. The male spinners gather in a swarm over the water, each species with its own peculiar form of flight. In a typical May fly dance, the male spinners fly directly up in the air for twenty or thirty feet, then drop back down again tail first, thousands of them making up a vast cloud of insects. The females fly out from shore to join the males; then, with their heavy egg sacs, descend to the surface to spawn. Soon they drop to the water spent, with wings outspread, and it's all over.

Taking tarpon on fly

Some outdoor scribes not only reported on advanced techniques, but they pioneered the methods themselves. The late Joe Brooks is perhaps the best known of these specialists and his exploits prompted others to

313

Stu Apte and his tarpon,
100 pounds plus —Bernice Apte photo

Lefty Krah hefts a fly-caught tarpon. —Frank Woolner photo

take up the rod, the typewriter, or both. The flyrod was his first love and he took it into salt water with determination, proving that bonefish could be taken along with many other species. In the process, he improved the techniques for flyrodding tarpon and held that world record on fly as well as several others.

Mysterious as is their beginning, there is no guess as to the willingness of a tarpon to take a fly, nor as to his ability as a fighter. He is a great fish on any tackle and reaches his peak when hooked on fly-fishing gear. Fly fishing for tarpon is rough and rugged and exciting. No other fish gives you quite the same thrill or puts up a better battle.

The fight of the big tarpon is spectacular to the NTH degree — due mostly, of course, to his great leaping ability. But because of the flashiness of his leaps, enough has not been said about the fight he makes beneath the surface. The aerial acrobatics are nervewracking enough, I'll grant you, but when a 50-pound tarpon really gets into a fight, he is at his best down below. When such a tarpon takes off on a long run and you feel his tremendous power, you begin to realize the grueling battle ahead. Against a fly rod he is capable of runs ranging from 400 to 800 feet, and when a fish takes off like that, there is nothing to do but crank up the motor and go after him. You can save what line is left that way, and even recover a little, but what then? When he decides to go again, he will strip your reel — right now!

When he begins to tire, he will come to the top and roll. Those rolls are made in order to restore the fading supply of air and experienced guides claim that every time a tarpon rolls and gets a fresh supply, he is good for fifteen minutes more. And it does seem to work that way, as you can feel the renewed power every time he grabs some ozone. Fighting a fish like that is plenty tiring and before you are through, your arms and legs feel ready to fall off.

Strictly speaking, of course, tarpon from 50 to 150 pounds are not fly-rod fish. But there is a lot of fun in hooking such monsters even though you don't expect to or intend to land them. (Big tarpon can be landed, as witness Frankee Albright's 48½-pounder and Lee Cuddy's great fly-rod catch of a 63-pound silver king.)

Joe Brooks lands a giant permit. —Joe Brooks photo

Harlan Major recognized that the angling public craved knowledge and did not always want to wade through pages of description to glean a few grains of how-to information. Because he was a technician and knew his subject, he could present the facts in a clear and concise manner. This same approach is commonplace today. The following selection is from Major's *Salt Water Fishing Tackle.*

On lures and replicas

A mechanical contrivance made in human form and dressed like a man does not look like a human being to us at close sight. If we were to take a young bird out of a nest and replace it with a stuffed replica, the old ones would see the difference and immediately throw it out or desert the nest. Likewise a mare would show no interest toward a hobbyhorse, even though it were expertly formed and painted. On the other hand, either the mechanical man or the stuffed bird might fool the horse. Each kind knows its own, once it gets close to it, and it is my belief that when we fish with what to us is a perfect replica of live bait we are the only ones being fooled. The deception may be there when the fish is at a distance and may draw him up to a close range, but from there on other factors must be brought into play or there will be no strike.

Bait manufacturers have done their utmost to imitate live bait. The glistening belly and the dark back are both accurately tinted. On many of them scales are shown and glass eyes are in their proper places. All this is fine and under some conditions forms an important function, but Lynn Bogue Hunt or Wilfred Bronson, good as they are, could not paint a dummy bait that would fool a fish at close range unless some other element were brought into play.

Large mouth bass on a fly by Tom Rost
—Photo courtesy Field and Stream

The lure of a spoon by Tom Rost
—Photo courtesy Field and Stream

A bass for the table
—George E. Dolnack, Jr. photo courtesy Pennsylvania Fish Commission

To do some guessing about what makes a fish strike an artificial lure we must consider the fact that fish have moods and under each one will react differently. The list of those conditions can be applied to man or fish, and the more we reflect on the fact that all life, including fish, is influenced by personal affections and situations, the quicker we shall improve our guessing about what bait to use. Among other influences, fish are motivated by hunger, temper and playfulness, with a certain amount of excitement interwoven in all three.

Supply and demand are important factors which must be borne in mind when choosing a bait for feeding fish. For example, if a large school of fish is working a small school of bait, the insufficient supply of food leaves no time for choosiness, and each fish must replace caution with speed before other fish satisfy their appetite and he finishes hungry. In a situation like this, almost any mild-actioned bait from a feather jig to last year's necktie fastened to a hook will produce results. The colors should approximate those of the live bait on which the fish are feeding.

If the above conditions are reversed and the school of fish is small and that of the bait is large, the fisherman will need all his skill to tempt any fish. The most important thing to consider is matching the length of the lure to the length of the natural bait being worked. If they happen to be eating six-inch sardines, give them a lure of the same length, not one of five or seven inches. This is important. Again the color should resemble that of the natural bait. This time there is no cause for haste on the part of the fish, however, and he will detect the subterfuge unless he is a little reckless. The fact that most fish are lazy when feeding and go after the easiest victim also creates possibilities. General excitement on the part of the fish can be induced by a bait swimming under difficulties—a cripple—which can be simulated by a bait with moderate action. It should dart from side to side rather than perform a wild dance of dives and jumps.

317

The fisherman as conservationist

It should be reemphasized that the outdoor writer and his reader have been the backbone of the conservation movement in America for more than a century. Every outdoor writer can take pride in the fact that his fraternity has been in the front lines to preserve our heritage and resources and the work continues. A fish is much too valuable a resource to use only once and Lee Wulff has long advocated the release of great gamefish. This excerpt is from his book *The Atlantic Salmon.*

The importance to anglers is the ability to catch and release a salmon, unharmed. In the early thirties, to release a salmon was considered heresy by both guides and anglers alike. Those were the days when Newfoundland had no limit on the number of salmon an angler might take, and when parties fishing the Big Falls of the Upper Humber returned at the end of a week's trip with three to four hundred fish. The general belief was that in order to bring a salmon to shore, he had to be played to utter exhaustion and would not recover. Since the great majority of fish were gaffed, it is obvious few had the chance to try.

Guides in general felt the played out fish would not live after capture and were certain that, if returned to the water, they would never take a fly again. They were wrong on both

Lee Wulff with bonefish taken on a fly —Lee Wulff photo

John Atherton's painting of Atlantic salmon, Fortune, *1956 (At left) Atlantic salmon chromolithograph, circa 1890 by Kilbourne*
—Both paintings courtesy Gene Anderegg

accounts. They were certain of one thing, that salmon were good eating and they (the guides) could use any the sportsman did not.

In convincing guides and reassuring myself that salmon could be played out and released and would still live, I often carried fish I had captured uninjured, either by means of the tailer or by hand, to pockets of water left high and dry by the falling of the rivers. When we returned to the pool a day or two later, we would find the fish fresh and lively in spite of his small enclosure and warmer-than-stream-temperature water.

The question of returning salmon to the water brings up the usual practice of releasing grilse or small salmon to "grow up" and keeping the big ones. It is striking how notions so commonly held can be so fallacious. It is somewhat like the common fallacy of thinking a buck deer has horns as a weapon to protect the fawns and does. His horns are growing and tender and useless from June to September when the fawns need protection most. From September to November he uses them to fight other bucks for a sexual advantage. Shortly after the rut, they fall off, and he is defenseless as a doe until September comes around again. Nature gave the doe hooves as sharp as a buck's, and those are her weapons, as they must be his, during the periods when the fawns are small and need the most protection.

Grilse rarely "grow up" to be very large salmon. There is every reason to believe that if a grilse spawns, his progeny will inherit his tendency to return to the river as a small fish. Whereas, by keeping the grilse, which have a lower commercial value in the market but which any sportsman should find equal to the large salmon for eating, and releasing the big salmon, the angler is putting back fish which could give to their spawn their own tendency of staying long at sea and returning as large fish, and which contain more spawn or milt per individual returned.

It would seem that keeping the big fish is a matter of wanting to show them off, and returning the runty salmon instead is a matter of ignorance of the salmon cycle, a situation which we can hope will be corrected in the interest of using the right breeding stock to best build up the fishing. The commercial view of limiting net mesh to "larger than a certain" size has similarly been worked out to let the commercial fishermen take the big, valuable fish and return the less marketable runts. In a thirty-year span of the records of one buyer of salmon in St. Johns, the average salmon's size had been cut more than half, and the quality of the commercial fishery, as well as the angling, dropped with it.

A high flying salmon —Lee Wulff photo

319

The warm water fisherman

In much of the literature, the bass fisherman and those who pursue species other than trout or salmon once found less reading material available. Much of that has changed now and one of the first to write for the fresh water angler who preferred warm water species was Homer Circle. Using a down home approach, Uncle Homer (as he is affectionately known) combined good writing with a folksy touch to make the reader smile while he learned. This selection is from his *The Art of Plug Fishing*.

Down Florida way, where they fish twelve months of the year and therefore are much smarter fishermen than Yankees, simply because they do about twice as much of it, there is an aged character wise in the ways of fish.

Tourists who see him go into one of his "seizures" for the first time row their boats way out around him, feeling certain the old fellow has blown a gasket. And you'd go along with their thinking the first time you saw him cut loose.

When a fisherman suddenly stands up in his boat, grabs a twenty-foot cane pole, and begins belaboring the bejabbers out of the water all around his boat until it fairly foams, it's only logical to assume things aren't exactly normal. But this old sage is a crappie fisherman and, knowing how this fish travels in large schools, he assumes if he is catching no crappies then "they are where he ain't." So he gets out his "splatterpole" and proceeds to splash up a terrific commotion.

The purpose of all this tomfoolery is to make a noise like a large school of crappies feeding on the surface. If you've ever seen a hatch come on a lake and watched the crappies go crazy churning the surface, you know the type of noise the old man is trying to create.

After the noise-making, this fisherman sits down, baits up his two cane poles, tosses them out, and settles back to watch his bobbers. He knows that chances are a school of crappies heard this commotion and, thinking it's another school of crappies feeding, they'll want some too and will move over toward his bobbers.

Homer Circle, fisherman-writer
—Photo courtesy Homer Circle

A catch of crappies —Homer Circle photo

320

Quail Cover

(On preceding page)
Redbud and Tulip Poplar—
in Great Smoky Mountain National Park

Road Runner
by Arthur Singer
—Courtesy the Artist

Woodchuck by Ned Smith

—PHOTOGRAPH BY ERWIN A. BAUER

Western Trout Fishing

—From a painting by Guy Coheleach/courtesy Guy Coheleach and Regency House

Fox Den

—Photograph by Erwin A. Bauer

First Snowfall

Man's Effect on the Environment

They do just that, and when they arrive in the vicinity and find nothing more than two lively minnows swimming around, they promptly eat these. Down go the old man's bobbers, and he is in business. It doesn't work every time. No fishing trick does. But it works often enough so that the old man never goes hungry for crappies.

Like the two ice fishermen who chopped two large holes about fifty yards apart, tied a line to a cane pole, threaded it through a series of smaller holes cut between the big holes, and finally got it running under the ice between the two larger holes. To either end of this line each tied his own casting line. At one end, where this line joined his own, one fisherman tied a six-foot dropper line with a floating plug on the end and a sinker three feet from the plug. The sinker would go to the bottom, the plug floating above it about three feet off the bottom.

Thus, rigged up, they would take turns reeling in the plug. When Joe was reeling, Pete would simply let his reel run freely until the plug reached Joe. Joe would nod his head, and Pete would start reeling while Joe payed out line. There was just one rule. Whoever was reeling when a pike or walleye struck the plug got to play the fish. The other guy had to stay out of the act!

It looked odd to see these two characters sitting there on the ice, cranking a plug back and forth. But they were the only guys taking fish on a plug in the dead of winter, under the ice!

In fishing, as in any other science or art, there is often just a hairline dividing the genius from the crackpot. This hairline is the screwball fisherman. I don't know about you, but I hope I never get too old to try an unusual gimmick. The average fisherman might look down his nose at such antics. You can take the average fisherman in your boat. But I'll take the screwball in mine and match stringers with you any day.

Until recently, the world ignored its oceans and the creatures that lived in it. Outdoor writers have worked tirelessly to direct the public's attention to the frailty of our oceans and other eco-systems. Even the great seas of the globe are not endless and bottomless wells with a supply that will never be exhausted. Frank Woolner has thought about these things and he wrote about them in his book *Modern Salt Water Sport Fishing.*

Not many years ago, I stood with a group of friends on the soft sand of a Cape Cod ocean beach while one of our first space satellites slid across a deep, blue-black zenith. It moved slowly, a miniature spark of fire, like a lazy cruiser threading a buoyage of stars.

Circle shows off two Florida bass.
—Photo courtesy Homer Circle

321

Frank Woolner and five striped bass from Cape Cod —Photo courtesy George Reiger

(At left) Three bass taken from the surf
—Frank Woolner photo

(Below) Surf casters work the Long
Island waters. —Frank Woolner photo, courtesy
The Salt Water Sportsman

A record bass —Frank Woolner photo

Thoughtfully, we went back to our fishing, casting big surface plugs out into the dark Atlantic, seeking the cat-eyed striped bass that were prowling this rim of sea. Quite suddenly the earth was made smaller while the waves still rolled as though there were no lands beyond the hissing ground swells.

I know better. To the left, had I glasses of sufficient power, it might have been possible to see the rising ground of Plymouth where the Pilgrims settled and starved and prayed and helped to build a nation. To the right? Three thousand miles of tumultuous ocean before Portugal's ancient seaports chinked the darkness with incandescent light. The sea's a very big thing.

Speeding in from outer space, our modern astronauts see a globe that grows steadily larger as their hurtling capsule devours the miles. It is a marbled sphere, glowing with faint blues and whites and irregular, scattered deeper tones, the shadowy, almost postscript shapes of land masses.

Blue predominates, for it is the color of the sea, and the sea covers almost three-quarters of our planet. Approximately 29.2 percent of the earth's surface rises above Homer's "wine dark and unvintageable ocean," so—whether we like it or not—we are all sea people. Evolutionists tell us that life originated in warm brine, and perhaps we are destined to go back to that medium in an undetermined future. Certainly the inscrutable ocean draws humankind. Men from the hinterlands annually rush to coastal resorts, hurry to the great beaches, and peer into an illimitable horizon. By God, it's the ocean! They stand there and gaze, enraptured, take pictures of themselves and their families with the sea as background. Herman Melville spoke of this in MOBY-DICK, but you can see it enacted daily on any seashore, anywhere in the world.

Everyone knows that there are seven seas—and that is nonsense! There is a world ocean; it girdles and encompasses our globe; it shapes the continents and chews away or builds headlands as the surging currents and the tides and the winds pursue their inexorable courses. There are tornadic rivers in the sea, and continent-sized lakes so generally calm that they have imprisoned ancient mariners for weary months. There are quiet bays and landlocked harbors, vast flats and savage reefs. There are murderous tidal rips and benign coves and cold upwellings. The running tides sweep into estuaries and pulse through mangrove-bordered tidal creeks where the fiddler crabs duck into foxholes under rank marsh grasses. Nowhere is life more abundant, nowhere so diverse. We probe the outermost planets, but one of our last frontiers remains the enigmatic world ocean.

Al Reinfelder and a Virginia striper
—Photo courtesy George Reiger

The seas are full of fishes, and until such time as we manage to destroy their nursery grounds or harry them into extinction by ill-advised commercial exploitation, they will remain a burgeoning renewable resource. Like the marbled globe seen by a returning astronaut, our world is small, no longer large enough to absorb all-out assault. We must practice conservation and management, else surely we will die.

This book is devoted to modern angling from a sportsman's viewpoint, but I have the greatest respect for commercial fishermen. These farmers of the sea are concerned; they employ erudite marine biologists and oceanographers to seek the truth. They desire a healthy renewable resource, a harvest well planned to ensure further wealth. Whether American, Russian, British, Japanese, Portuguese, or any of the other great sea peoples, these reapers of the ocean's largesse are fully aware of the difficulties involved. Nobody plans suicide.

I note this at the very outset, for there is a certain small contingent of ill-advised sport fishermen who seek every opportunity to harpoon the commercial operator. Too often emotion overcomes reason and the angler blames a lack of fish on professionals who—as often as not—do not even seek the species that seems in short supply. There are, it must be admitted, occasional instances of transgression, opportunism, and unscrupulous exploitation—such as unlimited longlining—but these are exceptions to prove a rule. Because their fortunes depend upon it, a majority of commercial fishermen practice good management.

The fishing writer continues to stay abreast, if not ahead, of his time, expanding his coverage to include conservation of resources. Writing is an individual endeavor and who is to say what is right or what is wrong, what pleases or what disturbs. Literature must first stand the test of time. Others, years from now, may attempt to sit in judgement

A fish story —Frank Woolner photo

A. J. McClane in an upstate New York stream —George Reiger photo

of what we pen today. The important point, however, is that fishing writing continues to focus attention on tackle, techniques, and the pleasures of man's greatest sport.

The pleasure of angling is a complex blend of sights, sounds and at times mysticism. More writers have tried to capture this ethereal "thing" than any other outdoor phenomenon. Few have succeeded in doing so well as A. J. McClane in the introduction of *The Practical Fly Fisherman.*

It was the half-dark hour when nymphal garbs are shucked and delicate wings long dried in the sun pulsate in their first feeble movement. The river had given life to the plankton, and the plankton gave life to the nymph, and the dull, crisp shell of the nymph gave birth to the mayfly. She stepped lightly from the pondwort to feel the first strong flutter in her thinly veined wings; others came from the club moss, the fern, the woodbine, and the wild grape, all bearing a queer pattern of hallmarks—like fine etchings on their transparent wings. A gentle breeze blowing clean from the new mown hay brought heavy bodied land people tumbling through the air—the ants, the beetles, and the dark brown crickets. The clumsy caddis fly hung under his mottled roof-like wings, stumbling among the dancers with weighted feet.

The angler stood motionless in the river watching the mayflies whirl on a thin film of surface and, slowly at first, the trout appeared—a few scattered rises here and there. But soon, like dozens of slender fingers poised above the gravel, they gave the water life. This was the moment he had been waiting for; a great heavy-mouthed trout came out of hiding

325

and drifted slowly to the center of the pool. His hand trembled slightly as the silk line rolled backward and forward. At the last turn forward he held his breath. The line pulled out straight and dropped softly to the river.

From somewhere deep in the chara weed the trout could see a wavering, blurred image shifting on the surface; through lidless eyes it examined pinpoints of light made by the hackles — the same delicate impressions made by the legs of a mayfly. The fish slipped upward in a confident turn and sucked the fly under. In that instant the angler's wrist snapped backward and the fine wire barb held like a serpent's tooth. There was very little he could measure beyond the end of his rod tip — the length he had cast, perhaps — but not this first wild rush that quickened the imagination, the strong leap against dark willows when his eyes strained and his hand tightened, and the deep throbbing of the rod, pulsing with each twist of a heavy body. The trout bored down to the gravel to worry the fly, ripping bright yellow line from the angler's fingers. Suddenly the trout bolted away with the current and then up — up into the air, turning end over end. The play was over.

Lifting the great fish from the water, the angler held his net at arm's length. Did he see a trout, or all trout — the tired ones, the clowns, the acrobats, tight-skinned fish bursting

A. J. McClane displays rainbow from a western stream (left) and fishes a Catskill stream (below) —George Reiger photos

with ova, slack-skinned fish dulled by winter currents, the hard-muscled ones who broke to freedom? Did he see a trout — an emotionless creature so removed in the chain of evolution that it carried the marks of age on its scales? Or did he see flaming gold and burnished silver, the deeper yellow of dust-coated fins, and the crimson spots — brilliant blood jewels of time, conceived in the womb of the river? For a moment he had halted life, to hold it in his net and wonder at its truth. A trout is not a snow covered mountain peak standing like a giant on the land for all to see. A mountain is a fact — a trout is a moment of beauty known only to men who seek them.

In his youth the angler had looked upon the face of the river and it revealed nothing; it was a blanket of glare without depth or meaning. Boy-like, he probed the surface with inquisitive casts, hour after hour, sometimes in a gray mist of wetness when black twigs spilled droplets on the earth. Sometimes under the intense blue of a summer sky when bleached rocks lay bare, sometimes he probed when red-brown leaves spiraled down and floated in heavy mats on the water. The boy cast to the boulders and searched the rapids, and the maiden fish and the kelt passed him by. He followed the shore and watched the currents, as millions had before him; the length of the river was out of the compass of his time, but her depth was the soul of all men born to angling.

And then one day he killed a trout, which he carefully washed clean and wrapped in ferns to bring to his father. The older man saw only a silent, glassy-eyed creature, so the boy scrubbed it all the harder, running cold water over the skin while telling of the flaming gold and burnished silver — but his treasures never came back. His father, wise in the ways of a fly-fisher, knew that the color was simply a pigment, a trick played by the chromatophores, and that his son saw a fragment of time which belonged to him alone. Perhaps this was what the angler remembered as he lowered the net and shook his trout free.

For two thousand years men have speculated on the ways of trout and their anglers so when you begin the sport of fly-fishing it is important to know that there is much more here than meets the eye. To wear the clothing of an angler is not necessarily to be one, and the mere catching of fish is no recommendation to Walton's brotherhood of honest men. But this book is hardly a philosophy; I want to tell you something about fishing with artificial flies — and if in the course of it you discover that fly-fishing is as much a way of living as it is a method of angling, then so much the better.

A. J. takes a rainbow (above) and a tiger trout (below). McClane experimented with new breeds of trout. —George Reiger photos

327

Ernest Hemingway, writer, sportsman

Ernest Hemingway's first bluefin
—Courtesy *Field and Stream*

Ernest Hemingway is considered by some to be America's finest writer. He knew and wrote about the outdoor scene with a flair that will probably never be matched. It is distressingly painful to the editors of this book to be compelled to omit the passages chosen by associate editor Bob Bell. Legal entanglements prevent us from including them. We can only encourage the interested reader to search out the mentioned works and read or reread them at his leisure. For us to totally ignore Hemingway would be an unforgivable mistake.

It was 1936, and Marjorie Rawlings, trying to understand Hemingway and his sporting friends, concluded: "They are the only people who would be pleased by the things in his work that distress all the rest of us."

That's a sad conclusion to be reached by an intelligent person; pathetic, really, for it shows Mrs. Rawlings' understanding of a large portion of our population was miniscule.

Hemingway explained to her that he had fished and hunted all his life and would continue to do so. "Writing," he said, "was for him a soul-searing process . . . When it went well, nothing could match it for reward and enjoyment. When it did not, unless he wished to go crazy, he had no recourse but to take up the instruments of his second trade — the guns, the rods . . . Nothing but writing could give him as much genuine pleasure as killing a bear, a buffalo, a kudu, a black-maned lion, or fighting to its death a huge and lordly marlin, a giant tuna . . ."

No one denies Hemingway's place in literature. And no one who has read his work, from his first, Michigan-based short stories on through his posthumously-published *Islands in the Stream,* can deny the importance the outdoors played in his life. Hemingway was, for the most part, writing fiction, but his knowledge of the woods and streams and fish and animals was obvious in almost everything he wrote. It would be easy to pick out examples. Many have special meaning for outdoorsmen.

Searching for tuna —Courtesy *Field and Stream*

A big one whitens the water. —Courtesy *Field and Stream*

The earliest, dating from 1924, is based on a fishing trip to the Upper Peninsula's Fox River, which Hemingway, with his gift for names, rechristened "Big Two-Hearted River." The camp-making scene is close to perfect on its own objective terms, as complete and unique as a circle. But even then Hemingway's real meanings were "written in the white spaces between the lines," and this seemingly simple camping/fishing story was actually one of suppressed terror as Nick Adams, young wounded veteran of the Italian front, fights alone to regain his physical and mental faculties.

Nick Adams does not win his fight by the river, there's too much fear in him yet, but neither does he lose it. A story that seemed to have the simple perfection of a circle takes on the complex perfection of a sphere. Few have carried outdoor writing to such heights — but then few if any besides Hemingway have used such backgrounds to whittle their way to the Pulitzer and Nobel prizes for literature.

Hemingway's prizes were a long time coming. In 1940, no Pulitzer award for fiction was given, despite the fact that the judges unanimously selected *For Whom the Bell Tolls,* his story of a guerrilla band fighting in the mountains of Spain, as that year's best novel by an American. Not until 1953, after the publication of *The Old Man and the Sea,* did Hemingway receive a Pulitzer; it was followed two years later by the Nobel Prize.

Deep sea fishing expertise continues its importance in *To Have and Have Not,* a vital turn in the plot coming out of the early fishing sequences.

When Johnson gyps Harry Morgan out of his pay for this fishing trip, Morgan becomes a modern-day freebooter and, so typical of Hemingway characters, winds up dead. A bit melodramatic from the viewpoint of outdoor writing, perhaps, but Hemingway's stories are fiction even if based on fact, and he used his knowledge in this area primarily to provide believable settings for his dramatic purposes.

One book, *Green Hills of Africa,* was an attempt to write a true account of a hunting trip, his first safari. Using the technique of fiction rather than a simple reportorial style, he achieved his goal. Rarely has a hunting story hewed so close to the truth as this one—or made so many readers so uncomfortable. It shows the competitiveness and meanness of a self-driven hunter as well as the camaraderie—more than that, the genuine affection, as for a brother-in-arms—that exists between hunters. Seldom has a writer had the nerve, or perhaps the ability, to tell everything as it really happened on a big hunting trip.

Perhaps the most notable effect of this book was not on other writers but on other hunters. *Green Hills of Africa* created the cult of the kudu. Hunters had always been overawed by the thought of lion, buffalo or elephant in their gunsights, but not until they read Hemingway's account of his hunt for this big spiral-horned antelope did they realize the kudu was one of the world's great trophies. Now, more than four decades later, this quiet craze still carries on. For those affected hunters, many of whom were infected third-, fourth- or fifth-hand, the climax of the hunt is what started it all.

And eventually, for everything and everyone, the hunter as well as the hunted, it has to end. Death is the subject Hemingway studied all his life and wrote about constantly. In a few short paragraphs in *Across the River and Into the Trees,* he said it all.

Hemingway's apparent preoccupation with death seemed morbid to some who read him during his zenith. Perhaps it seems even more so today. Considering the larger dimensions that must be used for measuring such writers, a study of Hemingway's outdoor prose indicates that this was no idle fascination with dying. It was the acceptance of a basic fact that eludes many human beings. Since we must all eventually give up this world, man and beast alike, we may as well make the most of our departure.

Death at the end of the hunt
—Pete Czura photo

State conservation magazines fought to save game. As early as 1928 deer were being trucked to new feeding grounds in Arkansas.

—Arkansas Fish and Game Commission photos

The development of state magazines

A phenomenon of post-WW II outdoor communications has been the development of what George Feltner calls "state conservation agency magazines." Feltner, retired as an editor in the Colorado wildlife agency but free-lancing and editing *Balance Wheel,* the inhouse publication of U. S. State and Canadian Provincial conservation publicists, has taken a long look at these periodicals; there are forty of them in the States, most issued monthly, some bimonthly.

They are "comparative newcomers in the outdoor publication field," he wrote, that obviously "fill a local need for both outdoorsmen and agencies. From fumbling beginnings, they now rank with the best outdoor magazines in quality of writing, editing, layout and illustration," although the articles have an interpretive slant geared more toward education than entertainment.

And they have found an audience: "In 1974, the total circulation of state wildlife and forestry magazines was 2.4 million. With some surveys reporting as many as five readers per copy, these magazines reach an impressive audience." They also were and are a testing ground for a goodly number of writers and administrators who first spread their editorial wings on the staffs of these publications. They have sometimes led checkered careers, at the whims of budgeteers and conservation directors, but the best of them generally have been around for a long time now. The beginnings were more than fifty years ago in the Mid-South, Feltner found, and the first one apparently was in Arkansas. The veteran Coloradoan writes it thus:

Although many states preceded Arkansas with well-organized game and fish departments, that state was the first to issue a conservation magazine, with its avowed purpose to educate die-hard hunters away from their "God-given" right to hunt where they pleased. In the summer of 1924, hunting license holders in the state received their first copies of *Arkansas Deer.* Its editor, Guy Amsler, put the slogan "Education Means Conservation" on the frontispiece so it couldn't be missed. He also appealed for a better name for the magazine. The second and subsequent issues were titled *Arkansas Conservationist.*

With no examples to follow, cornball jokes mingled with impact articles, and photos of hunting dogs outnumbered other illustrations. The lead article of the first issue promised "more game, better laws and finer dogs." But when funds were needed to cover part of the cost of a fish hatchery, the great experiment was killed in March, 1931, to be revived spasmodically over the years through 1975's attractive publication.

Just to the north, Missouri began its own periodical experiment a year later, in 1925, with the first edition of *Missouri Game and Fish News*. The pioneer editor was Keith McCanse, an ardent practitioner of public relations, and also the first wildlife agency magazine man to move into a more lucrative field. Radio broadcasting was in its infancy and had a place for him; he thrived there, and was still active in his eighties. The magazine survived McCanse's departure; Townsend Godsey kept it alive until fired in a political shift in the Thirties. Godsey, still a widely-known photographer, has just retired from the School of the Ozarks in Southwest Missouri after teaching at Stephens College in Columbia, the University of Oklahoma and Missouri's Central State University.

With a 1936 constitutional revision creating a non-partisan Conservation Commission, the magazine revived as *The Missouri Conservationist* under the editorship of Charles Callison, now executive vice-president of the National Audubon Society. Dan Saults became editor in 1947. His crusty editorials were widely quoted in other publications and he was given an unprecedented boost into a director's chair, later moving to Washington with the Bureau of Land Management and the Fish and Wildlife Service.

It probably is no coincidence that the three editors of this book, James Bashline, George Harrison and Saults, are all graduates of state magazines. Bashline was editor of Pennsylvania's *Game News;* so was Harrison, who also served as feature editor of *Virginia Wildlife,* There are many more names on the list of alumni.

Missouri has had a magazine almost continuously for fifty years, and present editor Jim Keefe's opinion is quotable on the subject; he has spent the quarter-century of his professional life in information work with the Missouri department and has been chief of its Information section since 1958.

"I think our *Conservationist* has won a great deal of support to our department and its program," he wrote. "It is the single most visible thing the department does, highly acceptable and welcome. We have tried to make the magazine professional and attractive; the image rubs off on the agency. I'm not kidding myself. No magazine can long make a lousy program look good; there has to be a good department. But I firmly believe the publication is at least as important as any other single program we have.

"There was a time in the late 50s when we thought of downgrading the published word for the magic of television. No one seriously considers that today. We find there is a place for the magazine that TV can't touch. It has permanence and repetitiveness; a reader can turn to it again and again for consultation; it can be a permanent file for reference in personal collections or public libraries. I am sold on the printed word."

Those Keefe observations blend with the views of sportsmen I've listened to during my 16 years as assistant of *Colorado Outdoors.* A surprising number of them had well preserved collections of a variety of wildlife agency magazines, and not just those of their home state. And these are the people who keep the editors' and writers' minds sharp. The readers are quick to detect discrepancies. Contacting hunters in my job, I was cornered frequently by one who questioned something in our articles.

"Point that gun another way. That buzzard's been watching me for ten minutes!"
—*Drawn by Ennis Rogers for the Missouri Conservation Commission.*

333

In my experience, working on a conservation magazine was much more challenging and, as a rule, more interesting than newspaper reporting. These state periodicals challenge writers, editors and photographers; they attract good ones and they lose good ones.

The Colorado magazine ranks as an early publication, too. *Colorado Conservation Comments,* predecessor to the present *Colorado Outdoors,* came into being in 1938—and the great Arthur H. Carhart played a part in its founding. Art, of course, went on to be a famous land-use planner, author of 24 books, conservation consultant and winner of many awards, primarily OWAA's Jade of Chiefs and the Izaak Walton League's Founders' Award.

Eastern magazines have not usually ranked as highly in home influence as those in more western states, with some important exceptions such as *Game News* or *Pennsylvania Angler* in Penn's commonwealth or Virginia's *Wildlife,* famed for its covers. *Massachusetts Wildlife Magazine* has been editorially strong for several years now, under Bryant "Red" Chaplin, presently publisher of *Campfire Chatter,* and current editor Ted Williams, who wrote in February, 1975, that:

"America's perception of nature is evolving. If hunters and wildlife managers evolve with it, they can be the conservation leaders of tomorrow as they have been the conservation leaders of yesterday. If they do not evolve, they will simply become the fossilized relics of a past epoch —the trilobites of early environmentalism."

Part of that evolvement, perhaps most of it, is the responsibility of state wildlife magazines dealing directly with local hunters, fishermen, land owners—and professional game managers.

New York's *Conservationist* was once probably the most attractive and best written of all the state journals. Clayton Seagers, who built that magazine to its peak, used to ponder his relatively low circulation when measured against the population potential, and concluded that despite his subscription drives he had too few New Yorkers who felt a strong attraction to the outdoors.

There are other good Eastern state magazines which have been consistently well done, but in general these publications have never had the strong public effect and heavy circulations of some Midwest and Moun-

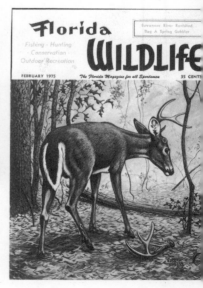

tain states, or states of the midsouth like Kentucky. But regional generalities don't work out, either; there are always too many exceptions. And too many starts that stop, too many magazines that glitter, glow and fade.

The best track records are in those states that have had a tradition of conservation and of sound wildlife management. Perhaps the better magazines set up the more informed citizenry and thus prophesied their own continuation. And perhaps not. Hen or egg?

In truth, these periodicals vary widely even among the old regulars. *Wisconsin Conservation Bulletin* is good, gray and scholary; *The Minnesota Volunteer* is earnest and frankly educational; *Florida Wildlife* is geared inevitably to tourism as is, less inevitably, *NEBRASKAland,* though otherwise the two publications are little alike. Some bulletins are pocketsize, others go at 8½ by 11 inches. Some are famed for their covers, some are flashy and colorful, a few are eight-page folders but most are printed in good (and expensive) taste.

But one characteristic they all have in common: local pride by both the agency and the readers in their wild resources. *Wyoming Wildlife* will not express it in the same fashion as *Michigan Natural Resources,* but the idea will be there.

About ten years ago, a grizzled old Iowa hunter told me as he thumbed a copy of *Colorado Outdoors* that "we didn't have anything like this when I was a kid." And then he added: "I'll bet you don't know the Tin Lizzies helped start these magazines." Then he explained what that attention getter meant.

"Man had to walk to hunting spots, or take the old gray mare. It took work and time; not many of us hunted. Lots of people lazy then, like now. Then came the Tin Lizzies, and later cars, so people swarmed into hunting places. Now you got to educate 'em, what with too many people going out too often and too easy."

It was a simple explanation of the state outdoor magazines. And a sound one.

At their best, these publications are effective, interesting to write and edit, and influential. Why do so many good men leave them? Roger Latham, once of the Pennsylvania Game Commission, now out-

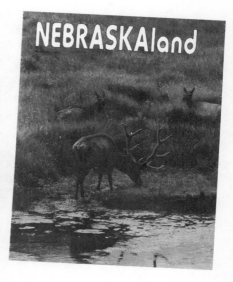

335

door editor of the *Pittsburgh Press;* or Ron Schara of the *Minneapolis Tribune,* who was editor of South Dakota's *Conservation Digest?* Or prolific freelancer Irwin ("Joe") Bauer, once of Ohio's Department of Natural Resources?

Glenn Titus, outdoor editor of the *Daily Oklahoman,* aired *his* reasons for leaving state jobs, after working with South Dakota's Department of Game, Fish and Parks and Oklahoma's Department of Wildlife Conservation. Glenn was primarily a movie maker and administrator, who usually hired the best writers he could afford, but he wasn't a very political animal and the ebbs and flows of elective processes bugged him. So did shoddy newspaper reporting on wildlife. When a managing editor to whom he was complaining suggested he do the reporting himself, both on wildlife management and pork barrel politics involving fish and game, Titus took him up on it.

"My background in conservation has given me the ability to spot pseudobiologists who are blowing smoke at me . . . it also gives me acceptance by professionals," he says. And "I like the freedom of newspaper work, and being able to call things as I see them."

How well does that fit others who have departed? Not too well, probably, in many cases. State pay is low, usually, and ambition is often strong — for administrative jobs, for more power to make decisions, for higher income. Politics-plagued wildlife agencies can be harassing, and of course many creative editors or writers are restless by nature.

Whatever the reasons, you've got people like Tim Renken, outdoor editor of the St. Louis *Post-Dispatch,* once part of the Nebraska staff (his mother, Aleda, retired from the Information Office of the Missouri department a few years ago and wrote a couple of published books). Or Keith Hay, now conservation director with the American Petroleum Institute in Washington, D. C., once assistant editor of Colorado's magazine. Or Grits Gresham, freelancer, author and TV documentarian, who was a state writer/editor for Arizona and Louisiana. And Will Johns, who went from Pennsylvania Game to the National Wildlife Federation — and then back to information director of the Pennsylvania Fish Commission. And lots mo'.

But the state conservation magazines are far more than a training ground; for a good many years now, they have been presenting good writing, tough editing, fine photography and sound education in America's outdoor needs. They are, collectively, a major reason why wildlife in the United States is still well-handled and habitat has not been more rapidly destroyed.

Outdoor writers who really *know* the outdoors (and some who don't) have been trying with limited success to explain man's place in the environment for several hundred years. It will be obvious to even the most casual reader that many philosophies from people who do know the outdoors are represented in this book. The dedicated trophy hunters whose words appear here are no less meaningful than those of the avowed protectionist who deplores the taking of any form of life.

John Madson does not make a case for either but here, from *Stories From Under the Sky* he clearly states his personal relationship with nature.

Among modern Americans there are two sharply divergent views of nature. At one pole is Thoreau, who declaims: "In wilderness is the preservation of the world." At the other is Helen Bell who, learning that a friend plans a walk in the country, quips: "Well, kick a tree for me."

My own view lies somewhere north of the equator. I incline strongly to the Thoreaus, but only to a point. For if I am outraged by sophisticates and their witty rejections of the natural world, I'm irked by the "Oh-the-wonder-of-it-all" school that includes most assistant scoutmasters, garden club

Ansel Adams caught the majestic stillness of the northern California redwoods in this photograph. —Courtesy Sierra Club, San Francisco

Canada goose and gosling
—Don Wooldridge photo,
Missouri Department of Conservation

ladies, poets at picnics, and the presumptuous asses who clutter perfectly good mountaintops with neon crosses.

From the leftist pole, I could never view nature with frivolity. She has chilled me too many times, baked me too often, and thrown her assorted rocks, lightnings and poison stings at me for too long to permit disrespect. Fear engenders respect, and I have spent enough time alone with nature to fear her and to accept my subordinate position.

There are a few who regard nature as a force in bondage, driven to its knees by an advanced human technology that has overcome the elemental obstacles of air, earth, fire and water. But man has shackled nothing but himself. The mischievous, ingenious imp has turned a few simple natural functions to his own ends and, as often as not, even these functions retaliate by killing or sickening him. He has sacrificed some of his most valuable animal gifts in his climb to dominance, yet remains subject to the biological checks which have always existed. Man may synthesize microclimates in which to polish his arts, but he remains forever subject to the great controls—disease, starvation, and interspecific and intraspecific strife—that dominate all biota.

From the liberal pole, I cannot regard nature with reverence in the accepted definition, and I'm puzzled by suburban transcendentalists who must rationalize a Sunday morning picnic as worship in the Great Green Church. The simple act of taking to the woods, on Sunday or otherwise, is testimony enough and needs no bowed head or bent knee to sanctify it. In any case, the infusion of wild nature into tame religion smacks of hypocrisy, for no western religion today actively defends or apparently understands what some ecclesiastics blandly call "God's Wild Wonders."

Nor can I regard nature with any particular affection, nor understand clubwomen who gush: "I simply adore Mother Nature!"

Adoration is as alien to wild nature as blasphemy. Nature transcends love, goodness, malevolence or evil. It is simple a primordial force—shining, aloof and brooding, a vast sweep of power too awful to be imbued with human emotions, virtues or mischiefs. It is as presumptuous to adore nature as it is to kick a redwood.

At one pole, the poets and the Spartan Scoutmaster of Walden Pond. At the other, the darling of the Back Bay parlors and her bright, synthetic retinue.

And somewhere in between, several million of us awed, abashed savages who wonder at lightning and the flight of the crane, and who walk in the open world because we are not content to walk elsewhere, and because it is the only real home—however mystic and terrifying—that we shall ever know.

A Glacier Park ground squirrel
—Henry E. Bradshaw photo

A whooping crane protects his territory. —Luther Goldman photo

Outdoor wet-plate photography of the 1870s was an arduous art.
—Courtesy Eastman Kodak Company

F. Wallace Taber of the world and Dallas is too young to have pioneered outdoor photography but old enough to have been the first student using a scholastic grants program set up by OWAA three decades ago—a program, incidentally, to which the proceeds from this book will go. A spiritual descendant of the magic-lantern travelogues he mentions here, he is an intellectual scion of the nineteenth century commentators, a man of many parts.

Wally has been filming wildlife all over this earth, and lecturing on those films, since the 1950s. A degree and constant study in game management backs up his career in newspapers, radio and television. Anthropology and archeology are his hobbies. He carries a movie camera in the automatic way that other people carry watches.

His first love is filming but he does not think the art began with Wally Taber. Here, in concise phrasing he outlines the century-old history of photography, particularly wildlife filming, carefully not telling you as much as you might want to know about the subject:

Outdoor photography comes of age

The impact of photography on the ascent of man can be favorably compared with development of the arch, invention of the wheel and discovery of gunpowder. This volume's mechanical basis of production is photographical. Photography has advanced mass education, developed the world's greatest entertainment media and provided proof of world existence for all mankind. And photography has allowed us to bring the out-of-doors indoors.

The still-picture is at least father, if not also mother, of cinema. And as frequently happens, theory preceded fact. It was Peter Mark Roget (of *Thesaurus* fame) who in 1824 announced his theory of "The Persistence of Vision with Regard to Moving Objects" that set the stage for rapid progressions toward photography and projection.

Almost immediately, scientists throughout Europe began the test. Their devices—whirling discs, twirling coins, booklets of pictures flipped with the thumb—established the basic truth of Roger's conten-

A wet-plate photographer's pack
—Courtesy Eastman Kodak Company

340

tion that an image is retained for a fraction of a second longer than it actually appears.

On this peculiarity rests the motion-picture industry. Essentially, cinema is a series of still pictures printed on a long ribbon of film. Each picture is projected on a screen, then removed in a flash and another picture substituted. Whether run at 16 frames per second, as in silent film, or at 24 frames per second as required for sound, enough phases of action appear on the screen for the eye to bridge between one picture and the next, creating the illusion of uninterrupted motion.

Even as scientists were passing Roget's theory into law, developments of the still-picture were creating the art of photography. In 1839 French scientist Louis Jacques Mande Daguerre was granted 6,000 francs annually by his government for revealing to the world a process which produced a picture on the face of a copper plate. That same year, Samuel B. Morse, inventor of telegraph and first American to learn from Daguerre, took the world's first Daguerreotype photograph. Only one year later, Alexander S. Wolcott patented the first American camera and opened the first portrait studio.

Morse taught photographic process to Mathew B. Brady who, in 1844, opened his own gallery in the heart of Times Square; one of his apprentices was one Timothy H. O'Sullivan, fresh from the rotting potatoes of Ireland.

By 1852, Daguerreotype was dying and paper-photography had begun. There followed "Ambrotypes," replaced by "Tintypes" which were strong enough to be sent through the mails. But paper photography persisted and tintypes also disappeared.

All this historical briefing introduces the amazing era of outdoor photography. A "new educational device" called the stereoscope appeared in Europe in 1860 and did much to advance outdoor photography, especially when Oliver Wendell Holmes developed a better stereo than the cumbersome European boxes.

A long, slow process —Courtesy Eastman Kodak Company

He may have looked like a prospector or a cowpoke, but he was one of the West's earliest artist-photographers. William Henry Jackson in front of his wet-plate tent (far left) and with his horse.
—Courtesy National Park Service

While Timothy O'Sullivan was learning his trade in New York, a budding outdoor photographer named William Henry Jackson was serving apprenticeship to one F. Styles in Burlington, Vermont. O'Sullivan and Jackson pioneered outdoor photography. Best known is Jackson but during the 1860s and 70s, O'Sullivan's photo work on the western frontier was amazing. His monumental photo coverage from Death Valley to Virginia City illustrates early U. S. geographical surveys. He accompanied Commander Selfridge on his Darien jungle expedition in 1870 to Panama. Lugging a mammoth 20 x 24 camera, O'Sullivan had to make his own wet plates in the field and immediately expose and develop them, using an ambulance drawn by mules as a portable darkroom. Unlike Jackson, who lived to be 100, O'Sullivan died from tuberculosis at 42.

F. Jay Hayes, western photographer

In 1877, F. Jay Hayes put on a one-man photographic exhibit at the Minnesota State Fair. Maps in those days indicated most of the west as "Great American Desert." Hayes' exhibit showed that here was a vast wonderland for visitors, even settlers. He did such a promotional job that the Northern Pacific Railroad appointed him its official photographer.

For years before the first wheel turned on that railway, Hayes was tramping or riding over prairies and through forests, picking his way "through the debris in canyons, everywhere taking sittings from mother nature." Then, in 1885, the Hayes Palace Studio was put into operation: a Pullman car became a rolling studio. A year earlier he had built a studio in Yellowstone National Park; it lasted until 1929! The rolling studio not only documented many landscapes for the Northern Pacific with a 20 × 24 camera, it was perfectly adapted to the needs of the time. When the Northern Pacific started operations across Dakota and Montana, many passengers carried rifles or shotguns and had only to go a

(Continued on page 346)

342

Jackson shot these photos in Yellowstone National Park in 1871-72. Lower Falls of the Yellowstone River (top). Bull elk in the velvet (above). Formations on Mammoth Hot Springs terraces (left).

—Courtesy National Park Service

343

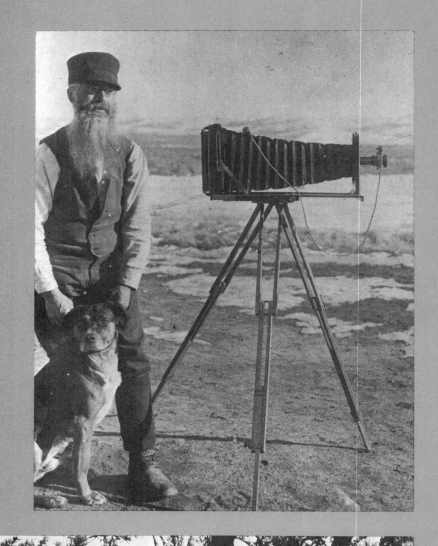

A. G. WALLIHANS:
Pioneer Wildlife Photographers

Though we cannot be sure, it is possible that America's first wildlife photographers were the A. G. Wallihans, a husband and wife team from Colorado working in the 1890s.

Anyone who has tried to photograph big game animals in their natural haunts using modern-day camera equipment and film can appreciate the work of the Wallihans who had only primitive equipment. Imagine dragging those heavy tripods, huge view cameras and large format film plates across the kind of terrain inhabited by elk, bear, cougars and deer!

Having been raised as a wildlife photographer on a 4x5 Speed Graphic myself, I know the problems the Wallihans had taking a photograph of a moving bear, for example. Just finding the bear was a major problem, but to be able to track it, set up and focus with a dark cloth, insert the 8x10 film plate and shoot the photograph while the bear was still in focus was a miracle. The speed of their film had to be around 10, compared to our high speed black and white films of today with ASA speeds of 125 or 400. And they probably had no flash. It was hard enough to get the camera and tripod through the woods, let alone flash powder equipment.

But the Wallihans were successful and attracted the attention of Theodore Roosevelt who wrote the introductions to their two books: Hoof, Claws and Antlers of the Rocky Mountains *(1894) and* Camera Shots at Big Game *(1904).*

—Photos courtesy Denver Public L.

344

In their first book Roosevelt wrote:

"Knowing as I do by long experience the extreme difficulty of getting so much as a shot with the rifle at either wolf or cougar, I cannot express my astonishment at seeing these remarkable and characteristic photographs of both. The cougar in the tree has a special and peculiar value, showing as it does the way the beast stands. . . . So it is with the bull elk standing in the snow among the sage brush, with the head of the black-tail doe swimming through the icy water, and with the bands of cow elk and of antelope. . . ."

The tone of the second introduction indicated that the conscious of Theodore Roosevelt had turned to one of concern for our vanishing resources. Perhaps it was through his contacts with people like the A. G. Wallihans that Theodore Roosevelt rose to the stature of our first truly great conservationist.—George H. Harrison

ern History Department

345

(Continued from page 342)

Eastman Kodak Camera Number One, 1888 —Courtesy Eastman Kodak Company

GEORGE EASTMAN, AS AN AMATEUR, RIGGED UP HIS FIRST PORTABLE PHOTOGRAPHIC OUTFIT WHILE WORKING IN A BANK IN ROCHESTER, N.Y.

—Courtesy Eastman Kodak Company

short distance from their cars to shoot pronghorn, grouse or prairie chicken. The engineer blew his whistle when it was time to move on. So the earliest photographs of hunters with their enormous bags were made by Hayes. Even European royalty who came out to hunt sought Hayes to document their gross bags of game.

A "rich strike" hardly had been made in the Montana or Idaho mountains before Hayes appeared with his cameras. He was in Yellowstone in 1888 to record the only photo ever made of Excelsior Geyser, world's greatest, in eruption. It has not erupted since!

Essentially, Hayes was a journalist, with a lens, forerunner of the modern news photographer. With his 5 × 8 wet-plate stereo-camera, he completed a 3,000-mile trip, the length of the Missouri River. When the United States purchased Alaska from the Tsar at two cents an acre, his stereo and 8 × 10 cameras covered the event. There, in 1879, he met celebrated naturalist John Muir.

But not everyone could travel except with the stereoptican slides of Hayes and Jackson and O'Sullivan. The stereoscope substituted for mobility and became as much a part of the home as the family Bible.

And now came celebrated lecturers armed with hand-colored lantern slides, bringing the world to everyone's door. Hayes made slides and hand-tinted them for such traveling lecturers as John L. Stoddard and Burton Holmes.

In 1888, George Eastman marketed his Kodak camera (you push the button, we do all the rest) and photography came within the reach of the masses. The following year, as John Muir recorded it, "the steamer *Queen* brought 230 passenger-tourists to Alaska, some carried Kodaks."

Movies are born

The same year, Thomas A. Edison had produced his phonograph. He had earlier seen the work of Edward Muggeridge, who used a battery of 24 cameras in sequence to photograph Leland Stanford's race horse in

346

motion. The idea of combining moving pictures with sound seems to have been in Edison's mind before his phonograph was offered the public. But, when he failed to achieve that combination, he turned his experiments over to William Kennedy Laurie Dickson, together with a new film-base developed by George Eastman—thin strips of clear, supple celluloid coated with photographic emulsion.

The following year, Eastman virtually put an end to one brief era while launching another of greater impact: he developed a film for "roller" photography, climaxing 75 years of striving toward motion-picture photography. And Edison promptly produced the Kinetoscope. That remarkable machine made its first public showing in 1894 and for five mad years, profitably occupied the Kinetoscope Parlor at 1155 Broadway, New York City. Using a continuous loop of about 50 feet of film, the Kinetoscope commanded a penny-in-the-slot.

Within two years, the Kinetoscope was married with the Magic Lantern, that projection tool for lecturers. Now a screen could entertain whole audiences rather than the one-at-a-time pace of penny peepshows. Parlors sprouted like mushrooms, all over the United States and Europe. The era of film-in-theatres had begun.

Edison was so engrossed in lucrative Kinetoscope business that he overlooked an invention by his talented assistant Dickson. For Dickson not only had married sound to film to produce the world's first "talkies," he had developed the sprocket-hole system which to this day guides and propels film through the camera and projector. But nothing came of all this right then.

For the next few years, minute-length shorts flooded the market to

The first Brownie, 1900,
cost—one dollar
—Courtesy Eastman Kodak Company

An illustration promoting an early Kodak camera

347

demonstrate the marvelous invention with marching soldiers, dancing girls, men felling trees, prize fights, Annie Oakley shooting clay balls.

In 1900, George Melies, French magician, combined his magic with pantomimed stories to provide the world's first narrative film. *The Great Train Robbery* of Edison's cameraman, Edwin S. Porter, often is heralded as the first narrative film, but Melies' *A Trip To The Moon* was first.

By 1905, movie theatres were springing up in all large cities, while the demand for stereoscopic stills for twin-lensed, hand-held parlor viewers seemed insatiable. Photos by Hayes, Jackson, O'Sullivan and dozens of others were providing stereoscopic slides.

Probably Edison's cameraman Porter was the forerunner of outdoor movie photographers. In *The Great Train Robbery* he revealed the function of the "cut" in telling a story on the screen; he developed the first parallel action, he used drop-back in time and leap-frogs ahead. This little 8-minute Western provided the key to film editing, the joining together of bits of film shot in different places and at different times to form a unified narrative.

The success of this film inspired others to explore implications of editing to juggle time and space. They increased the number of scenes in their little dramas. Their cameras were no longer confined to the studio; scenes taken on location were combined with shots staged against painted sets. And as these little stories began to reach the screen, the movies became the poor man's theatre. The demand was tremendous.

So Carl Akeley, returned from his first African expedition with Daniel Giraud Elliot in 1896, was fired with ambition not only to go on safari again, but armed with a camera. Akeley saw photography as a mass educational medium and a guide to making taxidermy an exacting science. He sensed the value of photographic documentations to fortify sketches, measurements and memory. When he moved to the American Museum of Natural History in New York, where 17 years of his life went into the Akeley African Hall, he also launched his photography.

It was in 1910, in Kenya Colony, that Akeley brought together a band of Nandi tribesmen for a lion hunt. When they pursued the lion with spears and held him at bay, Akeley secured the first motion pictures of this historic contest between naked savages and the king of beasts. Cameras of that vintage, however, were not intended for his requirements, so Akeley improved on them, seeking a camera that would follow swift action at both close and long range.

From newsreels to melodrama

The motion picture brought drama within walking distance of America. At the peak — 1913 to 1916 — 28,000 motion-picture theatres dotted the U.S.

Pathé News Weekly was stimulated in 1912 when a hand-cranked, light-weight camera holding a 400-foot roll of film hit the market. That same year, a young news photographer named Arthur Miller came

Film perforating room

(At right) Early film printer,
circa late 1910s

EARLY
BELL AND HOWELL
FILM
EQUIPMENT

(At left) Early 35mm
professional projector

Original Bell & Howell
professional 35mm wooden
case camera, manufactured
about 1909

(Below) Largest group of cameras ever assembled by a
Hollywood studio (as of the early 1920s) to film one movie sequence
...a forest fire for "Hearts Aflame."

to Detroit where he covered ice-boat racing on Lake St. Clair around Belle Isle and Grosse Pointe, and learned to fake an inoperative crank whenever publicity-seekers insisted on being filmed. Miller moved from newsreel to shoot the *Perils of Pauline,* a Pathé serial. Such serials were the rage of screens for years to come.

In 1914, Bell & Howell came out with their first 35mm movie camera, lightweight and with all shafts turning in ball bearings. Feed and take-up reels were made from a single casting with light-proof grooves. More importantly, for Akeley's ilk, it handled four interchangeable lenses, which speeded up camera work immeasurably.

In 1926, a revolutionary change came upon the scene with electronic sound recording and reproduction, a by-product of telephone and radio. The Esperanto of pantomime no longer was an asset. In the next three years, the industry was completely made over once again; the era of the *"Talkies"* was upon us. So through 80 years of trial and error, the novelty of 1895 had been transformed into the new art of the 20th century, the form that feeds an insatiable maw of theatres and television stations around the world.

Possibly the most successful outdoor movie photographer was Robert J. Flaherty, a mining engineer who in 1921 saw his first 70,000 feet of film go up in flames. Sensing he needed more knowledge anyway, Flaherty moved to Rochester where he spent several weeks working under George Eastman to learn developing and printing. From his first experience, he realized the importance of "rushes" to allow immediate re-shooting if necessary. On-the-spot development was particularly necessary for Flaherty, for he had selected as his subject the far-north Eskimos. He battled, and solved, many Arctic photo problems. His finished product was the world's first outdoor documentary, still widely acclaimed for its perfection. He was the initiator of the naturalist tradition in cinema and is still high priest of spontaneities.

That first film, *Nanook of The North,* the year-long survival of an Eskimo family, is a masterpiece of creativity. He followed with *Moana,* the life of the Polynesians, and then half a dozen others, all acclaimed for originality and intimacy. Seeing with the eye of a poet, Flaherty set high standards for the outdoor documentaries that followed.

While Flaherty filmed in the Arctic, Akeley returned to his beloved Africa. Using improved cameras among the Kivu volcanoes of the Belgian Congo, he filmed the first motion pictures ever made of wild gorillas. On the opposite side of the continent, Martin and Osa Johnson were experiencing their first African safari. In 1906 Martin had accompanied Jack London around the world in a 45-foot boat. With earnings from his films made with London, Johnson married Osa and took her on a South Seas expedition. His equipment consisted of a second-hand rifle and hand-cranked Universal 35mm camera.

On a subsequent trip to the New Hebrides, the Johnsons, better equipped, made the first films ever of cannibals. Even so, they had to fortify their funds in Australia with a lecture tour. Johnson showed his

Anyone can be a wildlife photographer today.
—Leonard Lee Rue III photo

350

films and narrated while, between reels, Osa danced the hula and played her ukelele. When they had accumulated $5,000, they resumed their filming. In 1923, the Johnsons went to Africa on a fully first-class safari financed by Eastman and sanctioned by the American Museum of Natural History.

For equipment, the Johnsons assembled a battery that previously had not been available for scientific photography: twenty cameras in all, ten for motion pictures and ten for stills. To achieve a series from which scientists might study animal motion, two cameras were mounted together, allowing two films to be exposed simultaneously, one shot at the usual 16 f.p.s. while the other was timed at 64 f.p.s. They even boasted a series of cameras operated by remote control. During the four years they resided at Lake Paradise in Kenya, the Johnsons shot nearly a quarter million feet of film!

A smaller film at 16mm came on the market in 1923, intended to cut the rising costs of 35mm photography and to be somewhat safer and far more portable, but it was very slow in catching on. Industry and business, eager to cut expenses, did adopt the 16mm film, however, and its use grew.

Meanwhile, in Africa, Eastman joined Johnson. Akeley also arrived in Nairobi and they joined Johnson. With cameras and cameramen vastly improved, ten days of filming by this crew produced startling results never equaled. Afterwards Akeley journeyed to his beloved Congo where he died and was buried on the slopes of the Ruwenzori Mountains.

During the 1930s Depression, industry initiated an era of "free" films with a few educational films sprinkled in. Before World War II, the total number of general interest 16mm films totaled 500 titles. In the first seven years after World War II, 25,000 were produced! In 1941, Detroit had 16 projectors in its high schools; in 1946 alone, it purchased 300! When introduced to classrooms, the first projector salesman boasted there were 20,000 feet of film that could be shown on the 16mm machine. Today, almost 4,000,000 feet are produced a year with an annual output of some 5,000 titles.

Walt Disney, who was convinced that animated cartoons had a place in the theatre, gave outdoor photography its greatest modern injection. When his cartoons were peaking in popularity in the 1950s, he launched into a series of true-life films involving natural history. As a personal footnote to the century of photo history: on my second African safari, in 1953, I met Al and Alma Malotte, newly arrived for a year in Africa to shoot footage from which Disney edited his film *African Lion*. By then, a dozen wildlife photographers were shooting and selling footage to Disney at the unheard-of price of $5 per foot!

On that same safari, I camped at Lake Paradise beside the decaying ruins of the Johnson enclave where I thought of Akeley, of Eastman, of O'Sullivan and Jackson. More than twenty years later, there are too many cameramen working to name them all—but I hope some of them will think of me in 1996.

Marlin Perkins saves a buffalo cub from a forest fire near the National Bison Range at Missoula, Montana.
—Don Meier Productions Photo

351

Outdoor columns in newspapers date back at least to 1839, when Matt Field handled that beat on the New Orleans *Picayune:* but as in other fields the numbers have expanded greatly since World War II. At least 1,000 United States newspapers carry weekly, twice-weekly or daily reports about hunting, fishing or other ventures under open skies. These columns range from jotting by mail carriers for village weeklies (sometimes very good) to the metropolitan press where full-time outdoor writers work week-long at their material with the aid of photographers and expense accounts. But all are written for *now:* the moment of reading; for today, not for posterity.

Homer Circle, who has done books, television, magazine writing and editing, press columns and public relations, studied hundreds of outdoor columns by dozens of press scribes. From his recommendations, these samplings of six outdoor newspaper men have been chosen as representative of the modern species.

Great Outdoors

By Roger Latham
Outdoors Editor

The first is Roger Latham, a Ph.D. who left a top executive job with the Pennsylvania Game Commission in 1957 to write for the *Pittsburgh Press.* His views are studied by the scientific community as well as his public. He left research and took up writing because, in his words:

"My columns are designed to sell conservation, and to inform people about wildlife programs that have significance for them. They are planned so readers will better understand the out-of-doors, will want to protect these things that bring them pleasure, and will have more fun in their activities . . . while returning home safely. And my writing is designed to get youngsters started right, so they will learn to be true sportsmen and sportswomen."

This selection is from an article that appeared in the *Press* of March 25, 1973, illustrating his thesis that appreciation requires a touch of science and a touch of the poet.

The born naturalist

"The born naturalist is one of the luckiest men in the world. Winter or summer, rain or shine, walking or riding, his pleasures are near at hand. The great book of nature is open before him, and he has only to turn its leaves."

John Burroughs said that in his book Under the Maples,

and he is so right. The only point where I would amend is where he says "born" naturalist. I believe the "made" naturalist is just as lucky and enjoys nature as much.

A naturalist might be defined as one who finds fascination in nature. Yet his fascination goes beyond an emotional response to things which please the senses . . . he may be enraptured by a sunset, by the view from a mountain, by fall foliage or the color patterns of a bird or flower, but these are not the really significant things in his natural world.

He will watch the fox pounce upon a meadow mouse, the snipe winnow over the sky, the osprey dive for its prey, or the trout rise to pluck a mayfly off the surface; but his mind sees beyond the mere action of the moment.

He will hear the sounds of day and night, for he is attuned to nature. He hears spring peepers in the marsh, the trill of a toad as it calls to a mate, the drumming of a ruffed grouse and the melody of a warbler. His ears record more subtle things, too: the whisper of waterfowl wings, the gentle flutter of aspen, the wind song of plovers.

If he is a "graduate" naturalist, with thousands of hours of watching, listening and studying, he is not content with commonplace observations. His curiosity, a thirst for knowledge, make him seek answers to two questions: What and Why. He must know what animal makes the sound, what plant produced the odor, what the sparrow hawk captured when it plunged into the grass near its perch on the telephone pole.

He wants to be intimate with everything he sees or hears at any season. When he walks in the woods he does not see through and beyond, like a city man walking a busy downtown street among strangers. Instead, he is like the old-time resident of a small town, who strolls down Main Street and expects to know everyone he passes.

Dan Klepper serves the *San Antonio Express* and he has been writing about fields and streams for more than two decades, mostly in Texas. He says: "The newspaper outdoor writer's job is complex. His readers consist of little old ladies (with and without tennis shoes), teens, preteens, beginners in outdoor sports and old hands who know far more than the writer does. I do not pretend to be an expert in any field, but I try to write so that the inexperienced can understand. Entertaining and instructing: the important aspects of outdoor writing."

His column in the March 1, 1970, issue of the *Express/News* may not have entertained San Antonio's city fathers, but it certainly instructed them.

San Antonio's River Walk

San Antonio's most famous River Walk is one of this city's foremost tourist attractions. Most visitors consider a shady stroll along the scenic river as enchanting as a tour of the historic Alamo and our ancient missions.

But, oh, what the tourists don't see . . . or usually don't see. One never knows when those aquatic inhabitants of the river, the fish, will turn their white bellies toward the surface and kick the bucket before our very eyes.

You see, the San Antonio River is polluted.

Sure, it's a pretty little stream as it meanders through the downtown section of the city. But it's still polluted. It's so filled with pollutants — not to mention cans, bottles, old tires and other trash — that it is nothing more than an open sewer to the sea!

Most — but not all — of the filth and lethal material carried in the water will be found downstream where the tourists won't see it, where most residents of this city won't see it. In fact, no one can see many of the pollutants with the naked eye.

The foaming detergents, the lumps of raw sewage, the scum of floating oil . . . these things we can see.

Unless we make laboratory tests, however, we cannot see the insecticides, the ammonia, the chlorides, the . . . well . . . just pick a chemical. Chances are it will be found in our beautiful, beautiful river.

Those chemicals can be extremely destructive. All of them aren't there all of the time, of course. The condition of the water changes from week to week and from day to day. It might be filled with fish one minute, then something goes wrong somewhere along the river bank.

A pump breaks, a valve is left open or a pipeline becomes overloaded and . . . oops! There's only one alternative: Dump it in the river!

The damage might not be noticed right away. The point of entry of a chemical might not be traced. But downstream . . . maybe miles away . . . the fish start dying, and the river starts stinking.

Did you know that 40 years ago the river had clean water, all the way to the coast? Heavy pumping of underground water dried up many of the springs that fed the river, then we started dumping our crud into what little was left.

Now we have to keep flushing our toilets so that we still can call our uncovered sewer line a river, otherwise there would not be enough water to create a downstream flow.

Lou Klewer is the dean of working outdoor editors in newspaperdom; he has been writing "Outdoors with Lou Klewer" in the *Toledo Blade* for more than fifty years. And all things that take place beyond the roofs and the lights are his province. "My writing is diverse," he says, "not merely hunting and fishing. It covers everything outdoors: angling, archery or astronomy; camping, canoeing and conservation."

Perhaps that is why Klewer's column holds the record for longevity. The following sample is datelined December 2, 1973.

December

This is the opening of the Long Night Moon of the Indians, that month of the year when there is more darkness than light, when the sun is hidden much of the time by clouds, snow, rain, or by the curvature of the earth. It is not until the month is more than half over before the hours of daylight start growing longer.

December is the first real month of winter, and even then, in this latitude, it can have its warm snow and ice-melting days. November, which frequently brings in many indications of winter, had few of those days this year, for the month was delightfully warm; those cold days of the late duck season were missing—and so was most of the good duck hunting.

Regardless of the weather, December is an excellent month to be outdoors. There is much for the nature lover to see, and many more things are noticeable than were before the frost hit the vegetation and the trees abandoned their leaves. As Thoreau said more than 100 years ago, "Another bright winter's day to see what birds' nests are made of."

One can find a variety of nests in the hedges—those of robins, blue jays, brown thrashers, song sparrows, chippies, hummingbirds, warblers and others—and still more in nearby trees, some being quite a surprise.

Bird nests are interesting, for each species makes a different kind of nest and usually of different materials. The nests of robins are probably the best known of all, with their mud-lined interiors. Barn swallow's nests, found in old barns, on cliffs and even in hollow trees, are made of mud and grass and lined with feathers.

Wren nests are collections of twigs, lined with small grasses and hairs; those of hummingbirds—so small that a quarter would make a cover—are made of mosses, lichens, fern wool and red oak leaf down. They also look so much like a knot on a branch they are not easy to find.

But December is a month for the sportsmen, too. It is a time for the hunter with his beagles after rabbits. Coon hunters will still be pursuing raccoon and opossum; mink and muskrat trappers will be abroad getting their furs for a market that is expected to be very good this winter. Fox trappers are out but fox hunters are awaiting a tracking snow and some cold weather before they start. The heavy plowing that has been going on all fall leaves few pastures, weed fields or old corn fields to roam; most of these have been turned under. Now a hunter might spot a red fox lying out in the middle of a plowed field, nearly hidden in a blind furrow where it can see in any direction and will be almost impossible to surprise.

HEADWATERS 'N TAILFEATHERS By Bob Steber

Bob Steber has been crusading as outdoor editor of the Nashville *Tennessean* for over 30 years, during which time he alternately entertained, educated, challenged and amused his followers. From the gentle pat for kids to the straight-arm for despoilers, he writes on this philosophy.

"You've got to hit 'em hard and nasty, bringing public opinion to bear on environmental pollution problems. If you can make readers see what's happening, they'll lend a chorus of protest that usually causes environmental polluters to back off, or even cancel plans they thought they could get by with because no one was looking. Saving a lake, stream or land for the future is the most important work an outdoor editor can do."

Serving on a state capital newspaper has made Bob Steber a political observer, and much of his writing attempts to influence legislation.

356

From the April 27, 1975, edition of *The Tennessean* here is factual reporting plus some plain name-calling.

Wildlife and fisheries programs in Tennessee

It'll be Tuesday at the earliest before Tennessee's outdoorsmen get to know just how much revenue will be given the Wildlife Resources Agency to spend on vitally needed wildlife and fisheries programs.

That's when the license-increase bill is scheduled to go to Gentry Crowell's calendar committee to be given its number for debate on the floor of the House.

Now that the wildlife committee has succeeded in beating the combination license figure down to $7.25 from the agreed-upon $7.50 in the bill's first go-around before Bill Watson's committee, outdoorsmen hope Camden's Rep. Frank Lashlee and his cohorts will be satisfied.

But that's not all the mischief they managed in committee. Lashlee and Company succeeded in giving another two years of free license time to teen-agers, raising the requirements to 18 from the 16 years it's been since even before the Game and Fish Commission was created back in 1949.

By the time he's 16, a properly brought up youngster wants to feel he's paying his way in enjoyment of the Great Outdoors. At 18, a boy's a man, permitted to vote and to have his say in who'll represent him in government.

It's doubtful if he appreciates the free fisherman ride Lashlee's committee has bestowed. It was estimated that the action by the subcommittee cost the Agency an additional major reduction in the estimated figure of $1.9 million to be realized from a $7.25 combination license.

Hopefully, in the calendar committee, or on the floor of the House itself, some courageous representative will see fit to restore the status quo of the teen-agers, make them nondependent on legislative largesse to go fishing with Dad. It'll mean more that way!

Tom Opre is outdoor editor of the Detroit *Free Press* where he ambles over a broad range of topics. Many of his followers are so far removed from wilderness that their only contact is via vicarious trips with him. Opre says "An outdoor page should inform and entertain. Outdoor sports are escapes from the strident world in which we live. The fun, the appreciation of things natural should be reflected in the outdoor column."

But he sermonizes, too, as in the *Free Press* on September 14, 1972. This column illustrated that hoodlums exist in rural areas as well as city streets.

Hoodlums in rural areas

Last Sunday, Michigan lost a conservation officer, killed by would-be poachers if reports are accurate. It was the first such death since the 1930s when another Upper Peninsula game warden was shot . . . Gerald Welling, a 32-year veteran of the Department of Natural Resources, was run over. The weapon was a pickup truck carrying a snowplow apparatus on the front.

"He never had a chance," said Prosecutor Ed Soronen. Two men were arrested by state police and arraigned on first-degree murder charges in Circuit Court.

Both had known Welling. One was a neighbor. The other, allegedly the driver, had been arrested twice previously by Welling for poaching. Prosecutor Soronen described him as a "hothead" and a "professional poacher."

"It's just tragic," declared Soronen. "Welling was probably the hardest working conservation officer I've ever come in contact with. I've never met anyone quite like him."

Innocence or guilt will be determined by a court and jury, of course. But it's my opinion that blame for this kind of tragic outcome—a human death to protect a wild animal—goes far beyond this one courtroom, these two men charged with murder. . . . Its roots reach deep into the moral fiber of many northern Michigan residents, deep into their general disrespect and distrust of the Department of Natural Resources.

The attitude is . . . fostered by judges who refuse to uphold game and fish laws, by prosecutors who won't act, by teachers who degrade professional management in schools, by politicians who openly encourage flaunting of game and fish laws. It's even fostered by fathers, men convincing their young sons that the DNR is wrong and stupid. Ignore the game laws, they say.

Gerald Welling never believed that. And he paid for his convictions with his life.

One hears a lot of talk in upstate small towns about big-city lawlessness. They're proud of not being saddled with these problems.

What hypocrisy! Laws are not made—even simple game and fish codes—for just some of the people. They're made for all of us. And when you blandly encourage anyone, especially a kid, to disregard one law, he can likely find excuses to disregard others.

By JACK PARRY

Sportsmen's Den

OUTDOOR EDITOR

Jack Parry, outdoor editor of the Gary, Indiana *Post-Tribune,* is an outdoorsman who has covered three continents to bring his readers information. He's a private pilot, hosts a TV outdoor show and has contributed dozens of stories to America's top outdoor monthlies. On newspapering he says:

"The successful outdoor column should be credible and informative, as well as entertaining. By trying to put himself in the place of his readers, the columnist develops a rapport with them The writer must be willing to fight for their rights; often he is their only spokesman against governmental and industrial abuses."

This offering by Parry from the *Post-Tribune* has the facts, but the short story approach hangs them on to the reader's attention.

A boat in distress

It's Labor Day and you are operating the Park Department-Police Patrol Boat. Most folks are off for the holiday, but you're a cop and it's just another day. The wind during the night had swung to the north and Lake Michigan has turned into a churning nightmare. Waves seven feet high crash against the sandy beach. You haven't seen any fishermen go out and feel sure everything is all right as you cruise down Burns Ditch.

Then your radio crackles: "Michigan City Coast Guard calling Gary Patrol Boat . . ."

"Go ahead, Michigan City."

"Gary, we have a boat in your area with no power, dead in the water . . . man, woman and two children on board . . . we are covered up by Mayday calls . . . can you help?"

"Affirmative, Michigan City . . . give us a heading . . ."

"Zero-two-zero off Burns Ditch . . ."

"We're leaving now."

Who would be out there on a day like this? And as you reach the narrow opening which sees the Ditch pour into the big lake, you wonder how anyone—except an ore boat—could still be afloat.

". . . A man, a woman and two children. . ." the radio had said. You watch the towering waves crash over your bow as you press out into the big lake, where you have no logical right to be in a 23-foot craft.

"A man, a woman and two children. . ." The angry seas smash over your bow, then heave it skyward as the next snarling wave waits for its chance.

Eight miles in this kind of sea? You don't get paid for this kind of duty. That's Coast Guard work . . . guys in broad-beamed cutters designed to take the worst the Atlantic or Pacific can dish out.

But do the man and woman and two kids understand that? You know how terrified they are, for you can feel that clockspring winding in your stomach. You've seen Big Mich rough, but never like this.

Your partner at the helm fights to keep the bow into a wind gusting to 30 knots. He shakes his head grimly, and keeps his eye on the next curl of dark water breaking over the bow. You're used to spray flinging off the top of white-caps, but the dark water crashing over you is something new. Scared? Hell yes.

Then you see a fiery red glow in the north . . . thank God they had a flare on board.

Their 18-foot boat couldn't have lasted much longer. As you get a line on to take it in tow you can hear the mother comforting her kids. . . . "It's going to be all right now. . . ."

Getting into the mouth of Burns Ditch with following seas is no lark; finally that is behind and you are cruising down the Ditch.

"Gotta be easier ways to make a living than this," your partner says. You nod and think of the next meeting of the Gary Park Board when somebody will get up and say . . .

"You know, I've heard that all they do on that patrol boat is fish. . . ."

—Leonard Lee Rue III Photo

INDEX